Open Access and its Practical Impact on the Work of Academic Librarians

CHANDOS
INFORMATION PROFESSIONAL SERIES

Series Editor: Ruth Rikowski
(email: Rikowskigr@aol.com)

Chandos' new series of books are aimed at the busy information professional. They have been specially commissioned to provide the reader with an authoritative view of current thinking. They are designed to provide easy-to-read and (most importantly) practical coverage of topics that are of interest to librarians and other information professionals. If you would like a full listing of current and forthcoming titles, please visit our website www.chandospublishing.com or email info@chandospublishing.com or telephone +44 (0) 1223 891358.

New authors: we are always pleased to receive ideas for new titles; if you would like to write a book for Chandos, please contact Dr Glyn Jones on email gjones@chandospublishing.com or telephone number +44 (0) 1993 848726.

Bulk orders: some organisations buy a number of copies of our books. If you are interested in doing this, we would be pleased to discuss a discount. Please contact Hannah Grace-Williams on email info@chandospublishing.com or telephone +44 (0) 1223 891358.

Open Access and its Practical Impact on the Work of Academic Librarians

Collection development, public services, and the library and information science literature

LAURA BOWERING MULLEN

Chandos Publishing

Oxford • Cambridge • New Delhi

Chandos Publishing
TBAC Business Centre
Avenue 4
Station Lane
Witney
Oxford OX28 4BN
UK
Tel: +44 (0) 1993 848726
Email: info@chandospublishing.com
www.chandospublishing.com

Chandos Publishing is an imprint of Woodhead Publishing Limited

Woodhead Publishing Limited
Abington Hall
Granta Park
Great Abington
Cambridge CB21 6AH
UK
www.woodheadpublishing.com

First published in 2010

ISBN:
978 1 84334 593 0

© L. B. Mullen, 2010

British Library Cataloguing-in-Publication Data.
A catalogue record for this book is available from the British Library.

Typeset by Domex e-Data Pvt. Ltd.
Printed in the UK and USA.

Contents

About the author

Laura Bowering Mullen is the Behavioral Sciences Librarian at the Library of Science and Medicine of Rutgers, The State University of New Jersey. She has had many years of experience as an academic science reference librarian, and is involved in collection development, faculty liaison and public services capacities. Mullen has co-authored recent articles on topics such as Google Scholar's integration into the academic library, the continued relevance of 'core lists' for collection development, and librarians' roles in assisting faculty with increasing research impact. She is presently Chair of the Association of College and Research Libraries' Education and Behavioral Sciences Section (EBSS) Psychology Committee and the ACRL EBSS Scholarly Communication Committee, as well as a member of the American Psychological Association's Library Advisory Council.

The author may be contacted at:

Laura Bowering Mullen
Library of Science and Medicine
Rutgers, The State University of New Jersey
165 Bevier Road
Piscataway
NJ 08854-8009
USA

E-mail: *lbmullen@rci.rutgers.edu*

Preface

As an academic librarian working on the front-lines of reference, collection development, liaison work and instruction for many years, I have seen firsthand the rapid transformation of almost every aspect of academic libraries. The idea for this book was generated out of a genuine curiosity about the open access movement as it relates to the everyday work of academic librarians. There has been so much discussion that seemingly permeates the library discourse, but in reality, after ten years of advocacy by many library-related groups, one has to wonder why daily academic library work has not been transformed to any great extent. Scholarly communication paradigms are changing, publishers and libraries have moved to digital environments, but budgets are straining more than ever under the continuous cost of doing business, especially due to the serials pricing models that open access was supposed to transform.

The open access conversations taking place in the library and publishing worlds seem almost peripheral to the daily work of academic librarians. Collection development, reference, instruction and librarian scholarship seem to proceed as before. Rather than changing practices, the open access movement may actually be an add-on to the work of academic librarians. Any future vision for open access would want to take into account the need for not only discussion, but transformation of actual work practices. This would allow the changes needed for the positive results of the open access movement to come to fruition, and to percolate through more layers of the library. The need for change and the tools to make it happen would finally reach the librarians on the front-lines of reference and instruction, and those who build the collections to support that work. In many cases, open access has not had much effect on many of those working in academic libraries. Open access may not change the library to the extent that was originally expected.

The impetus for change to open access may come from university or college leadership at the provost level where changes to tenure and promotion scholarship guidelines may be manifest, or from the library administration level in response to issues related to serials pricing models and dwindling budgets. It does then follow that librarians must carry out the actual work of decision-making and changing practices that is required in any move away from traditional behaviour. Librarians will make decisions on whether to move open access alternatives into daily reference, collections or instruction work. Librarians have a great deal of influence because they are on the front-lines, assisting faculty and graduate students with library research, and also affecting to some degree the information practices and competencies of undergraduates and even the public they serve. While most librarians' rhetoric is one of support for open access, it is not yet clear how extensively the practical aspects of open access have made a difference in library positions, hiring, workload, or the user experience in academic libraries. Little research has been done on how librarians are actually promoting the open access movement in their daily work with library users and faculty groups, or on actual librarian attitudes toward the promised changes offered by the open access movement.

This book is written for librarians, and students of library and information science (LIS), and all of those interested in how open access in all of its iterations may actually be affecting academic library practices, or how it is not. Are librarians convinced strong advocacy for the open access movement will create the library collections and services that the researchers say they want and need? Do librarians actually see changes to the library as a result of open access? It is a transformative time, but so much of the action is in the hands of librarians in the collective sense. With thousands of articles written on the subject of open access and scholarly communication issues, and a whole world of new publishing paradigms, it may truly be time to examine the relationships that librarians have with the scholarly information that is being produced and disseminated in new ways all over the web. This book will not attempt to regurgitate all of the information about open access or scholarly communication already available, but instead aims to provoke thought and discussion about how academic library work might begin to incorporate new paradigms of collections, services and librarian publishing behaviours. The aspects of open access that directly affect not only the work of librarians but also issues relevant to the LIS literature will be covered. The treatment in this volume is mainly of a general, informative nature, and not written for those who are already scholarly communication or open access experts. It is important to write for mainstream library audiences, and not keep the conversation at a level that is 'preaching to the choir'. Mainly, at this juncture, it may be time for academic librarians to decide to integrate open access much more fully into daily workflows and public services efforts, or risk seeing a transformative vision become just that; an idea not easily translated into practical action in the workplace, especially in difficult economic times for libraries. These days, more than ever, libraries need the relief promised by the open access movement as they grapple with difficulties of paying bills to publishers and struggle with changes at every turn. It may be time for a real discussion among librarians, with a goal of assessing their attitudes and work practices toward open access advocacy and what it could mean for individual academic libraries. This volume is an attempt to provide information to librarians seeking an update on how their profession is responding to open access in the practical sense. It is meant to inform out of a concern of a possible disconnect between rhetoric and actual practice, not to provide further advocacy or plans for activism.

The issues discussed in this book will revolve mainly around new forms of scholarship as they relate to the scholarly journal article literature, especially the issues of self-archiving and open access journals. Librarians who write for publication in the LIS literature would be assumed to be seeking out open access journals as outlets for their work as well as self-archiving their work in the repositories that exist to pull together the global literature of librarianship. It would be assumed that academic librarians and faculty teaching in library school programmes would be early adopters of self-archiving behaviour as members of the field most committed to open access as an agent of change. It is not enough for librarians and their organisations to proclaim open access as a societal value, as well as a very important library imperative without doing the hard work to make it happen in the library. It is time for all librarians to be part of the open access discussion one way or another, and reaffirm the value of librarians' work, traditional or transformative, as an integral part of the scholarly communication landscape at every institution.

Introduction

Open access in the library: implications for academic librarians

It has been stated that librarians 'embrace' open access. Vocal activism by librarians has even been credited with fuelling the earliest conversations about open access in response to changes in the formal scholarly communication systems in place for most disciplines, including library and information science (LIS). The assumption is that librarians are staunch advocates of all open access initiatives. Open access seems to have become a basic tenet of librarianship in recent years. With academic librarianship changing at lightning speed due to the constant demands of a digital world, one wonders whether librarians working in academic libraries are responding to continued open access advocacy, or whether it has instead developed as somewhat of a 'parallel universe'. Librarians may indeed wonder how they can and should be responding to repeated calls for action. Librarians working in public services in instruction and reference roles, as well as those in collection development may be affected, but there has been little research to date examining how academic librarians have responded to the open access movement in their daily work, or in their own writing for the LIS literature. As readers, editors, reviewers or publishers, librarians would seem to want to effect change within their own literature first. Following a now established outcry, one would assume the LIS journal literature would be the first to show a transition to open access models and other new forms of scholarship. It seems librarians have signed on to an open access agenda, and that the agenda should drive changes in reference, collections and the LIS literature. The movement toward integrating free scholarly material and products has certainly affected the technical services areas in many ways, most prominently in the development of institutional repositories. It would seem to follow that librarians would be the first responders to the call to populate the institutional repository, even as they exhort their teaching faculty colleagues to self-archive all scholarly work. Librarians in their various roles as writers, researchers, collection development specialists, administrators, or while working on the front-lines of reference and instruction surely must be concerned about how the open access movement, now somewhat mature, has been affecting daily workflows as well as plans for the very future of the academic library. The stakes are high, as the transformative nature of open access has the potential to affect the culture of every discipline and all of the associated research which the library has traditionally been charged with collecting, providing access to, and preserving. Reference and instruction librarians, in their roles on the front-lines, have tremendous ability to influence library user behaviour, and could potentially provide a needed impetus to the momentum of the open access movement. While there is ubiquitous talk about open access, there is often little action on the part of librarians. It is necessary to study the reasons for the lack of trickle-down as well as to discuss librarian attitudes toward open access in their own work and behaviour.

Librarians are assumed to have much to gain by the eventual success of open access to the world's scholarly literature, especially in terms of freeing libraries from the tyrannical pricing structures of commercial journals. Stevan Harnad, Professor of Cognitive Science at the University of Southampton, describes open access as the 'toll-free online access to the full text of scholarly peer-reviewed journals' (Kaser and Ojala, 2005). Peter Suber, another champion of open access, offers this definition in his blog, OA News: 'The open access movement: putting peer-reviewed scientific and scholarly literature on the internet. Making it available free of charge and free of most copyright and licensing restrictions. Removing the barriers to serious research' (Suber, 2007a). The premise is that once the refereed research literature is freed from tolls, authors will once again be the owners of their scholarly output. In the words of Kaser and Ojala (2005), the central question for all, whether librarian, scholar or publisher, seems to be the same – what will this cost me? What role does open access play in the everyday work of the academic librarian, whether it be at the reference desk, in collection development, or various areas of digital library development? How are open access initiatives, supposedly promoted by librarians, affecting the library literature?

The LIS literature is rife with articles about all iterations of open access. There are many comprehensive treatments in the literature outlining the open access movement, from its beginnings in the 1990s to the state of the art at present. Many of these articles describe the many 'roads' to open access. Whether 'green', 'gold', or other, Harnad uses colour descriptions to distinguish the many types of open access (eprints, 2007). Some notable compilations of citations on the subject include Bailey's open access bibliography (Bailey, 2005) and Peter Suber's open access timeline (Suber, 2007). Still, it may be asserted that the roots of the open access movement may be traced to the activism of librarians, and Harnad can be considered the movement's 'chief architect' (Poynder, 2004a). Harnad even calls librarians 'the heroes of the first phase of the open access movement' (Kaser and Ojala, 2005). It may follow that the eventual success of the open access movement might be in the hands of librarians, and might be dependent on their continued advocacy and activism. Librarians may still have to decide, as a group, whether to change their daily work in support of open access by promoting both self-archiving and open access journals. This promotion can take the form of increasing acquisition of open access journals and repository materials, promoting these materials in reference and instruction sessions and standards, or in choosing open access venues for the publications that they author.

A driving force behind the open access movement is the serials crisis, also referred to as the 'pricing crisis', where the price of serials has increased exponentially, while the growth in academic library budgets has lagged rather than follow suit. As library budgets continue to shrink, and fail to keep up with serial costs and inflation, it is felt that open access initiatives could provide an alternative model for relief of pressure on collections costs. This has been a common topic in the literature as collections budgets, especially those devoted to the science, technology, engineering and mathematics (STEM) literature, have been disproportionately spent on sciences and on 'big deal' full-text package purchases. The worsening global economy only compounds the urgency of this issue for academic libraries, both public and privately funded.

The LIS literature faces similar concerns, albeit on a smaller scale. In Schmidle and Via's study of a subset of LIS journals represented in the coverage lists of H.W. Wilson's 'Library Literature and Information Science', extreme differences in pricing models were found between commercially-published titles and academic/university titles. This study points out that commercial buyouts in the LIS literature have been very expensive to libraries. An example is given of Emerald Press, where the price of one LIS title rose 483 per cent between 1997 and 2002. Emerald publishes seven of the ten most expensive LIS journals in this study (Schmidle and Via, 2004). Librarians responsible for LIS literature collections must be watching these pricing trends carefully and advocating for change. At the same time, librarians must be searching for quality open access alternatives within their own corpus of literature, while making sure that researchers and readers are aware of these alternatives. Librarians could consider moves toward starting new journals for their field, retaining top editors and reviewers who see open access as a library 'value'. The academic librarian may be a main marketing agent for new quality open access peer-reviewed journals and will be able to speak with authority and credibility if actively publishing and contributing to LIS journals that fit open criteria.

Jean-Claude Guedon's article, 'In Oldenburg's long shadow: librarians, research scientists, publishers, and the control of scientific publishing', gives librarians a good overview of the history of the serials pricing crisis that is fuelling the open access movement (Guedon, 2001). After the publication of Bradford's Law in 1934, libraries began to develop core lists of periodicals in earnest, and attempts were made to buy only the titles that researchers really needed. The Institute for Scientific Information (ISI) limited its indexing to certain core journals, and an elitism among titles was introduced. These core titles became 'indispensable' and 'unavoidable', and they developed real economic possibilities. As Guedon states, 'there was gold in those there stacks after all!' (Guedon, 2001).

These days, a smaller number of large publishers control the large majority of the prestigious, core publications. Packages abound where all of the electronic journals of a publisher are bundled together in 'big deal' arrangements. Much of the academic library's budget is paid to a few large commercial publishers. University libraries cannot keep up with the inflation rate of 6–12 per cent in the price of scholarly journals, and many states are facing unprecedented budget cuts (Atkinson, 2006). Libraries are looking for ways to cut costs, retain quality of holdings, and continue their mission of provision of access to publications in demand. With demand for online access increasing, libraries look to transfer paper subscriptions to online only, thereby decreasing the number of print archival journals on shelves. The more online content a library accesses, the more the demand for it increases. The prestige of the individual library is dependent on the number and quality of subscriptions it accesses, and the institution's faculty recruitment and reputation for excellence may also be impacted. The library has often been called the 'intellectual heart of the university'. Librarians in their everyday roles are facing important decisions about their own literature, and that of all other disciplines as well. Librarians are left wondering if open access initiatives will address at least some of the pressures that are now inherent in today's collection development work. On the other hand, librarians may not have a vested interest in challenging the status quo. Librarians may enjoy the gatekeeper role, and the push for open access may change the collection development librarian's traditional roles and relationships with faculty, students, publishers, budgets and assessment offices. The movement away from traditional collection development activities might not appeal to many librarians, slowing down the movement toward pushing the parameters of library collections toward more open scholarship. Librarians may protect traditional publishing due to fear of irreversible changes to the library as we know it. The future of the library's role is not always clear.

Librarians in many subject disciplines have traditionally relied on published 'core lists' to guide their purchasing decisions, but also to assess their collections when comparing with the libraries of peer institutions. These core lists were based on a variety of factors including programme strengths, opinions of domain experts, stature of publishers, and metrics such as 'impact factor' in certain disciplines. The core lists are important for publishers as well as librarians, and top journals are worth more in subscription revenue. The concept of core lists must be re-evaluated, and needs to include assessment of open access journals as well. Thomson Reuters includes open access journals its Journal Citation Reports product, allowing study of impact factor for open access titles in some fields. Clearly, open access journals will be challenging traditional journals in core lists as this conversation finds new interest and involves new and changing metrics and methods. In terms of establishing excellence, assessment is more important to library collections than ever before, even as boundaries are blurring and everything is changing, mainly due to the digital transformation in libraries and society. Librarians may still need some new community-established guidelines to establish new core lists with new types of journals. An age-old question still matters: who will decide what core lists will represent, and which individual or organisation will compile them for each discipline? Faculty, especially junior scholars want to know what the 'top tier' journals are for their discipline and will seek out this information from librarians, who can choose to look more liberally at open access journals, or stick with traditionally published literature. In advising scholars as to publication outlets, librarians can exert opinions on open access if that is the prevailing best practice. Librarians will need to collaborate closely with departmental faculty and other committees with oversight over promotion and tenure guidelines at an institutional and disciplinary level. Journal 'core lists' may have implications for ranking as well as for collection assessment, and new forms of scholarship will need to be evaluated in similar ways to traditional journals and books.

Only larger research libraries are able to subscribe to the world's LIS literature (Morrison, 2004). Librarians need access to current LIS research studies and analyses in order to develop current and relevant collections and services. The movement of scholarly materials originating from the open web to the library's collections benefits all those who do not have access to the largest research libraries. Open access journals of quality are often welcome in the academic library's collection and may be finding their way into library collections and services. The core lists may be changing, with different paradigms forcing changes in the way librarians and others measure impact. Thomson Reuters' citation analysis products are no longer the only game in town when it comes to measuring impact. Scopus (Elsevier), some of the subject indexes, and now Google Scholar are providing competition and fuelling discussion of alternative models of citation searching and analysis. New metrics such as Eigenfactor (reported in Thomson Reuters' Journal Citation Reports), five-year impact factor trend analysis (Thomson Reuters), and the Scopus Journal Analyzer are able to assist in analysing journals for performance. Open access journals of all types are included in these newer systems if they meet established coverage criteria.

Even if they are managing successful institutional repositories, libraries must continue to buy access to their own faculty's work in traditional journals and books. Librarian authors writing for traditional journals, having signed away copyright to publishers, may also find themselves at work in the library paying invoices to buy access to their own published articles for inclusion in their institution's collections. Open access offers librarian authors as well as teaching faculty authors attractive, inexpensive alternatives that allow retention of rights. It is unclear at this point whether librarians are doing all that they can to change the system by challenging publishers' copyright transfer agreements (CTAs), or using or developing addenda to retain their rights. Librarians may not know the mechanisms that can effect change even with their own literature, such as giving publishers a licence to publish, rather than signing away copyright. Librarians may be safeguarding their own LIS journal traditions, not wanting to upset the discipline's longstanding core list of journal publications. For those seeking tenure as library faculty, there may be added pressure to preserve the stature of the traditional LIS journals, knowing the weight they have carried for tenure decision-making and the comfortable familiarity that these journals hold with the library community. Librarians may not want their literature to undergo drastic change and may not feel motivated to upset the traditions of the professional LIS literature.

Librarians are fighting back against the serials pricing crisis in many ways. For instance, the Scholarly Publishing and Academic Resources Coalition (SPARC) suggests that reintroducing competition 'requires creating or supporting journals that will compete head to head with the big, expensive journals of the large commercial publishers' (Guedon, 2001). There have been many university actions undertaken in support of open access. (Crawford, 2006). Currently there are many market forces at play, and librarians are in a unique position to be the point people in institutions trying to understand how to make sure that research needs are met. Librarians must be engaged and well read to keep up with the complex changes in scholarly communication in their own discipline, as well as in other subject areas served. Librarians working on the front-lines may be able to demystify new modes of scholarly communications for all constituents. Librarians may find that they need new knowledge and skills to translate all of the discussion on open access to actual practice with library users. Many are not sure exactly what practical information they should be providing (or why) in advocating for open access. In fact, some studies have attempted to show that librarians have trouble keeping up with all of the information coming from myriad directions in a rapidly changing digital library environment (Hardesty and Sugarman, 2007). Librarians need to have a broad knowledge of scholarly communication issues, even as these issues affect every discipline differently. It is a tall order for librarians to also be active in their advocacy for their own LIS literature, especially when they may not see clear advantages for the library or for themselves as authors.

The crisis in scholarly communications is much more pronounced in some scientific disciplines and is of an entirely different nature in some areas of the humanities, where most scholars are still focused on the book literature. The Modern Language Association (MLA) describes a different kind of crisis in the area of language and literary studies:

> university presses, facing loss of subsidies, are less able to bring out low-selling specialized monographs. Libraries, bound to commit shrinking funds to cover spiraling costs of journals (primarily outside the humanities) are a less reliable market for the specialized scholarly book. At the same time, academic departments in the humanities are more fixated than ever on the book, possibly even two books as the 'gold standard' for promotion and tenure. (Modern Language Association, 2002)

The Modern Language Association goes on to state that in the humanities, broad dissemination is *not* the goal. As library budgets for monographs in humanities shrink, fewer books are sold, and subsidies for university presses decline, while their costs continue to increase. Numbers of submissions continue to rise (Davis et al., 2004; MLA, 2002). In some respects, humanities disciplines clearly do not have a need to move as quickly to an open access model. However, humanities disciplines, rather than focused on freeing the journal literature, may find special interest in supporting open access monographic efforts. Librarians serving those disciplines will have to tackle the issues of open access books as they relate to other issues of erosion of the businesses of some publishers. Librarians may want to find new ways to support scholarly presses, possibly as collaborators in the digital production of monographs. As LIS collections are part of the social sciences, this literature must continue to move to more open models at least at the pace of the rest of the social sciences disciplines.

The rapidity of the move to open access is hampered in some disciplines by a slow movement toward developing new views of acceptable types of digital materials to be put forth for promotion and tenure. Many university committees as well as associations are engaged in ongoing dialogue about acceptable publications for faculty seeking promotion and tenure as part of new focus on scholarly communication. Librarians can be involved in these conversations, especially those librarians who have a working knowledge of new digital formats and open access alternatives. Librarians will need specific knowledge of the disciplines in order to be effective participants. When it comes to the humanities, the *Report of the MLA Task Force on Evaluating Scholarship for Tenure and Promotion* codifies much of the discussion into some recommendations for action. One of these recommendations focuses on the need to 'recognize the legitimacy of scholarship produced in new media, whether by individuals or in collaboration, and create procedures for evaluating these forms of scholarship' (MLA, 2007). Still, there is a long way to go for acceptance of electronic formats in the humanities. The report surveys 1,300 English and foreign language departments in US universities and reports that '35–50 per cent of department chairs have had no experience evaluating scholarly work produced in these new forms by candidates for tenure and promotion' (MLA, 2007). An example of electronic monograph publishing was the Gutenberg-e project. When this free e-books initiative was developed and subsequently viewed favourably by promotion and tenure committees, officials of the American Historical Association (AHA) had to send out letters to department chairs containing information that would lend legitimacy to this type of e-monograph publishing (MLA, 2007). Another statistic contained in the MLA report states that fully peer-reviewed electronic articles counted for promotion and tenure in less than half as many departments as refereed articles in print (MLA, 2007). Print articles counted in some fashion in 97.9 per cent of cases, while only 46.8 per cent for electronic articles. Similar numbers were reported for monographs (30.1 per cent electronic favourability versus 87.6 per cent for print) (MLA, 2007). Clearly, this type of conventional practice has implications for libraries in both collection development and public services work as librarians seek to provide appropriate and desired research materials to humanities scholars and students. Librarians may also play a role in guiding the conversation toward a more electronic future if researchers are receptive to furthering ideas of enhanced accessibility through online access to scholarly materials, and if publishers move further toward digital production models. Traditions long routed in institutional and disciplinary culture will change slowly, and the continuum from what is happening in the STEM fields with journal articles to the situation in the humanities must be handled sensitively to avoid alienating the library's users who may still view electronic formats with some scepticism. Other science and some social science disciplines will struggle with changing promotion and tenure expectations to include the importance of data associated with scholarly article publication (Guernsey, 2008). Issues of supplementary data linked to commercial publications, as well as sharing of research data from open repositories are two of the issues on the horizon.

Librarians are seeing other examples of disciplinary differences in the move to digital libraries. It is no longer possible to take a one-size-fits-all approach to serials cancellation projects or to the weeding of print collections. Suber has published a list that details some of the disciplinary differences apparent in the move to open access (Suber, 2006b). Clearly, more success has been demonstrated in some disciplines than others. It is often stated that in the sciences, open access speaks to the need for the most current information. Science fields must now respond to funder mandates regarding public deposit of research materials emanating from taxpayer funding. With the LIS field changing at lightning speed, it would seem that it would also lend itself to open access publishing (especially given the supposed interest of librarians in moving to open access). Librarianship, the literature as well as the publication behaviour of many members of the profession, has been slower to change. With efforts focused in other directions, the library literature remains mainly available in traditional formats, and not necessarily accessible to a wide range of readers. Librarians are in a prime position to drive change for their literature if that is a priority of the profession.

Disciplinary differences in scholarly communication aside, librarians covering all areas have been assumed to be on the vanguard of this ubiquitous movement. In reality, how are librarians actually involved in moving the open access agenda forward? Has the activism displayed by librarians through initiatives such as those of SPARC, or the marketing efforts of the Association for College and Research Libraries' 'Create Change' campaign (*http://www.createchange.org/*) where librarians are asked to publish in open access journals, caused those involved in LIS to function as role models for other faculty? Are librarians actually exhibiting behaviour that supports open access in their discipline by starting open access journals focusing on LIS, submitting their own scholarly work to LIS subject repositories or their own institutional repositories? One would assume that open access activities would be a priority for librarians. Librarians have a long way to go in setting an example by transforming scholarly communications through open access initiatives in LIS areas. Even so, as Suber says, 'open access is not synonymous with universal access', and librarians must work to get information to all members of society (Suber, 2007b). Much of the library literature is still locked behind price and permission barriers. Morrison has also sounded an alarm for librarians and their associations in her article, 'Professional library and information associations should rise to the challenge and lead by example' (Morrison, 2004).

Many librarians may be uninformed, even though so much information has been published about open access in the library literature. Suber has published 'lists' of practical steps librarians can take to move the open access agenda forward (Suber, 2006c). The *SPARC Open Access Newsletter*, edited by Peter Suber is an online source for librarians who wish to keep up to date on all current open access publications and news (*http://www.earlham.edu/~peters/fos/*). In 2007, the Association of Research Libraries (ARL) published a SPEC Kit entitled 'Open Access Resources', which has a plethora of information but also details what librarians are actually doing in a practical sense to move open access into library workflows. Libraries have developed policies for institutional repositories and for integrating open access into collection development strategies. Even here, however, it is stated of a few libraries that 'time constraints prevent them from assigning a significant priority to open access resources; instead they focus on their purchased resources' (Hood, 2007). Another SPEC Kit, entitled 'Scholarly Communication Education Initiatives', includes a discussion of how the ARL/ACRL Institute on Scholarly Communications has allowed hundreds of librarians to come together for programmes designed to allow participants to become campus leaders in developing outreach programmes for colleges and universities. The information in SPEC Kit 299 is freely accessible to all librarians through the Freely Accessible Institute Resources (FAIR) website (*http://www.arl.org/sc/institute/fair/index.shtml*). This represents another important useful tenet in maximising engagement – that information resources for librarians about open access must themselves be freely accessible. Campus outreach tools are available from the FAIR website, and are created under the Creative Commons Share-Alike License. Further assessment will be needed to determine the efficacy of campus outreach efforts and the follow-up result of librarians' participation in leadership programmes as described in SPEC Kit 299. It will also depend on how the library profession decides to measure the success of the open access movement. Many have lamented that just because libraries are publishing more born-digital journals and books, or encouraging faculty to deposit accepted articles in the institutional repository, this does not mean that open access has translated into success for the library and for society. Success may be measured in the future by some sort of ongoing cost savings, or by some tangible evidence of the effect of library promotion of open access as a 'value'.

Studies will show whether certain types of libraries, individual countries, or other populations have in fact benefited from resultant cost outlays by cash-strapped libraries undertaken in promotion of the open access effort. Official statements in support of open access, often focusing on the STEM literature, have been published by many library organisations including ARL, the Association for College and Research Libraries (ACRL), the International Federation of Library Associations and Institutions (IFLA), SPARC, and SPARC's Create Change (with ARL) and Declaring Independence initiatives. SPARC is an international group of 200 institutions in North America, Asia and Australia created under the auspices of ARL. SPARC, together with SPARC Europe and SPARC Japan (and other partners) now form an international alliance of more than 800 academic and research libraries (SPARC, 2009b). SPARC's open access campaign is the most visible of its educational initiatives, and offers support and information for interested librarians. SPARC has distributed brochures to universities, offered programmes and workshops focusing on open access, and published a business planning guide to assist libraries and others who are operating open access journals (Tananbaum, 2005). SPARC also sponsors and publishes the *SPARC Open Access Newsletter*, formerly the *Free Online Scholarship Newsletter*, created and edited by Peter Suber.

Librarians are on the front-lines of the 'helping' function here, but the questions remain as to where the open access publishing initiatives are developing within the LIS literature, or within the daily work of academic librarians. Librarians have been asked to 'get on board' but may still be unsure how to do that in their everyday work. How do librarians integrate open access initiatives and all of the educational materials produced by the aforementioned groups into work on the reference desk or in information literacy efforts, for instance? How can these campaigns by the major library organisations filter down to the daily work of busy academic librarians?

Many libraries and individual librarians have signed on to open access advocacy initiatives. The Budapest Open Access Initiative (BOAI), convened in 2001, offers a statement in support of open access that is relevant to many of the players in the movement. BOAI applies to all academic fields, and is sponsored by the Open Society Institute. A search of the signatories to the initiative, which attempts to 'accelerate progress in the international effort to make research articles in all academic fields freely available on the internet' shows many individual librarians as well as library-related organisations represented (BOAI, 2001). BOAI publishes guidelines that can apply to librarians as authors and researchers, and assists in advocacy for self-archiving of the peer-reviewed literature. Librarians involved in reference services, and those working with faculty as library liaisons may want to keep up with the advocacy position that prominent librarians and library organisations have signed onto with BOAI. Librarians are in a position to follow recommendations in the BOAI by asking would-be authors to remember open access journals when choosing journals to publish in, by becoming editors and reviewers for open access journals in their field, or by expanding library publishing efforts in support of BOAI initiatives. The BOAI has a mandate to help open access journals launched at libraries to become more well known. This type of work might fall to subject-specialist librarians who have access to relevant communication channels and expertise in the publication norms of the individual discipline or subfield. These librarians may not be well integrated into open access publishing teams. Individual libraries may not have subject specialists who can bring discipline-specific information to scholarly communication discussions.

The Medical Library Association has also issued a statement on open access and made the transition of its journal to open access (Medical Library Association, 2003). ARL has made a serious commitment to moving its members to what it calls 'open access scholarly models' (Quint, 2004). ACRL has published its 'Scholarly Communication Toolkit' to provide more practical information on managing copyrights for academic librarians (ACRL, 2007). ACRL and ARL also publish a free online guide to developing a scholarly communication programme in one's library (ARL, 2009a). IFLA has issued a statement on open access in a global sense: 'IFLA is committed to ensuring the widest possible access to information for all peoples in accordance with the principles in the Glasgow Declaration on Libraries, Information Services, and Intellectual Freedom' (IFLA, 2004). A joint statement, entitled 'Enhancing the debate on open access', has been published by IFLA and the International Publishers' Association, suggesting collaboration for all parties in going forward (IFLA/IPA, 2009).

Individual libraries will have to decide how deep their advocacy roles should extend into workflows and everyday practices. A strong advocacy role will demand a stronger voice from all librarians, even at the risk of getting into adversarial discussions with the institution's researchers, who may not understand or care deeply about the library role beyond providing access to much desired traditional subscribed and owned collections. Erica Linke, ACRL President for 2008–09, 'sees open access as trying to encourage ... authors to understand that they can manage their intellectual property' (Salisbury, 2008). Prominent library organisations such as ACRL clearly envision the dialogue between the library and researchers as necessary and vital. Others may see that the library should only provide the materials that the researcher needs and demands, and that the conversation needs to start at another place in the institution where researchers engage, especially at the provost level. Copyright and intellectual property issues, as well as issues affecting students must be part of the open access discussion at a local level. Librarians may be unclear as to how these roles to 'encourage authors' work at a micro level in the library. Advocacy at any level in the institution is made easier because there is not much opposition to the actual idea of open access. In a special issue of *Genome Technology* on open access, Salisbury defines the 'central conundrum of the open access debate':

> you can't find anyone opposed to it. Really. For all the grandstanding and arguing, the fiercest opponents and supporters alike tend to support the underlying principle – that freely accessible data would be a boon to the greater scientific enterprise. In an ideal world, most everyone agrees, there would be no restrictions on scientific results. It's the real world practical concerns that provide the point of contention. (Salisbury, 2008)

An international group of library organisations coalesced around the issues inherent in open access advocacy. The International Scholarly

Communications Alliance has offered a vehicle for more broad communication of open access issues (Buckholtz, 2002). It is clearly evident that many library organisations worldwide are rallying around issues of open access, and it will be at the local academic library and individual librarian level where change will really take place. Each library will need to decide what level of priority to give to open access activism even as it is a major focus of the profession today. Librarians may be listening carefully and looking for the relevance of the rhetoric to their daily work with library users.

Keeping up with legislation mandating open access

Library organisations have also supported legislation that involves taxpayer-funded research that is published in journals, and the movement of that literature toward open access. Worldwide, there are many mandates and policies that are fuelling open access, and librarians may follow the international list of such actions through the *SPARC Open Access Newsletter*, which continually updates the information. This newsletter is a goldmine of information for the librarian interested in keeping up with the latest news and issues on open access. In predictions written in December 2007, the newsletter lists 'more progress on every front in open access in 2008 including new open access policies from many countries' (Suber, 2007c). There is a truly worldwide list of open access mandates at play and many countries are signing on to the potential public benefits of open access to scholarly research literature, especially that which focuses on the biomedical sciences. Academic research libraries, as the traditional source of that literature, of course sign on as well. Signing on signifies the playing of a major role going forward.

Legislation has provided an important touchstone for library and public participation in discussions on open access. One early example of important library support for open access includes the American Library Association (ALA) belonging to the 'Alliance for Taxpayer Access'. A further example is the endorsement of the American Center for Cures Act 2005, known as the CURES Bill, by five library organisations, namely the ALA, ARL, MLA, Special Libraries Association, and the American Association of Law Libraries. The bill sought to 'expedite development of new therapies and cures for life-threatening diseases' (ALA, 2006). The bill required expanded public access to articles emanating from research funded by the National Institutes of Health (NIH) and other government agencies. ALA then passed a resolution to support the Federal Research Public Access Act 2006 (FRPAA). The FRPAA affected over 65,000 journals annually where the NIH provided at least a portion of funding for scientific research associated with the published results (ALA, 2006). A coalition of 75 nonprofit publishers opposed this legislation (Frank, 2007).

Librarians in academic libraries may need to become more aware of, and become advocates of, legislation potentially affecting collections work and scholarly communication trends but may be unsure how to become involved other than being part of discussions. 'Public access to federally-funded research' is listed as number two in the priority list of the 2009 ACRL legislative agenda, demonstrating the high emphasis being placed on this effort (Malenfant, 2009). Librarians may want to be more engaged in the legislation that their organisations stand behind, not only because of shared library values, but because of the potential impact from successful legislative initiatives on work practices in academic libraries. Following legislation allows libraries to track trends in open access that will have implications for collections and public services work. Such fallout from legislation might involve an increasing role for the institutional repository, librarians being designated to work with constituencies on issues of copyright, or a new focus by librarians on observing publisher response to new mandates in case there are implications for collection development. Even reference and liaison work may be affected by new policies requiring deposition of funded research materials. Researchers may certainly expect reference librarians to answer questions and offer advice about many issues of open access and scholarly communication, especially as more public relations campaigns from library organisations reach into the institutional community. Science libraries may find this newer participation in scholarly communication through response to open access initiatives more pressing. Ideally, studies will show exactly how science libraries and all librarians are being affected by the open access movement in its various iterations.

Some librarians may be directly involved with assisting patrons dealing with mandates, such as the NIH mandate in the USA. The NIH mandate requires all articles emanating from federal funds to be deposited in the National Library of Medicine's publicly available database, PubMedCentral. Such deposit of federally-funded work was initially optional (Grillot, 2008), but from 7 April 2008, it became mandatory for researchers to submit a 'final electronic version of the manuscript as accepted by the publisher' to PubMedCentral. Legislation requires 'an electronic version of the final peer-reviewed manuscript upon acceptance for publication, to be made publicly available no later than 12 months after the official date of publication' (Kaiser, 2008). There was an unsuccessful challenge to the legislation from publisher groups and others, notably through the Conyers Bill, also known as the Fair Copyright in Research Works Act. Since the policy was made mandatory in 2008, 'submissions are on track to reach 56 per cent of the 80,000 eligible papers this year, many submitted directly by journals' (Kaiser, 2008). On 11 March 2009, President Barack Obama signed this bill into law as part of the Consolidated Appropriations Act 2009, making the NIH Public Access Policy permanent (McLennan, 2009a). Librarians will want to understand the ramifications of these policies for the individual community of researchers in the institutions that they serve.

Many librarians, especially those working with institutional repositories see a role for the library, but publishers may be stepping in to take care of the deposition process. Other public access policies come from the Wellcome Trust and the Howard Hughes Medical Institution (Nguyen, 2008) and more can be expected to follow. One mandate from the Research Councils UK emphasises protection of author rights, and in this wording from a Rand Europe report:

> it is argued that the establishment of access regions for research outputs from public funding in particular should be 'based on a set of objectives and principles including openness but also protection of intellectual property' (OECD, 2007). In other words, taxpayers should have the right to access publicly funded research. (Hoorens et al., 2008)

The Canadian Institutes of Health Research (CIHR) requires open access to CIHR funded research after a six-month period. Another recent statement from Australia is not a policy, but a declaration. The statement is known as the 'Brisbane Declaration', and endorses author self-archiving at the time of acceptance for publication (immediate deposit) (Suber, 2008b). Around the world, funding agencies, through mandates, have spoken to the necessity of open access to research. The library is at a unique crossroads in terms of its ability to forge a place in the scholarly communication chain that is pushing researchers to consider issues of open access that may not have been of interest in the past. Librarians have got the message that the mandates are important, but need to reaffirm their own roles in the research process. How is this best accomplished?

Instead of the usual practice of evaluation, purchasing, and ensuring access to scholarly journal articles in STEM areas, librarians may now find they need to be able to consult in a different area of the research process – that of advising on aspects of the submission process for researchers. These funding mandates can give librarians anxious to embed themselves into the process, especially those desirous of increasing deposits to an institutional repository, a 'hook' if they can simplify, or even handle completely, the process for researchers. Librarians will be involved in the relationship that evolves between self-archiving initiatives in subject or disciplinary archives and the institutional repository. Researchers may need guidance about archiving their work, and choosing which type of repository for deposit. Many faculty and other researchers publishing work not under government mandates are unsure whether they should archive at all, are weighing risks and benefits, and feel that they need information on copyright issues. Librarians, besides being early adopters themselves, would need to be advocates of the repository initiative if it is to find an integral place following mandates for deposit of scholarly articles. A library focus on scholarly communications and open access may require teams of librarians to be brought together to plan appropriate programmes and outreach efforts while watching opportunities to leverage changes in the publishing world to best financial advantage.

Other types of mandates of importance to library work come from university bodies. An example is the action taken by the Faculty of Arts and Sciences at Harvard. The faculty voted to adopt a policy that authors must 'send an electronic copy of their scholarly articles to the university's digital repository', and that 'faculty authors automatically grant copyright permission to the university to archive and distribute these articles unless a faculty member has waived the policy for a particular article' (Nguyen, 2008). It has often been mentioned that leaving an 'opt out' may be problematic in moving to open access, along with the reader frustration about the 12-month embargo on the NIH side (Lowry, 2008). University policies may serve to engage librarians in the institution more directly in the process, seeing such support among faculty for open access becoming newly embedded in institutional culture. A SPARC/Science Commons white paper published in April 2008 discusses practical steps to be taken in 'establishing a binding institutional policy that automatically grants a copyright license' (Nguyen, 2008).

A great deal of coordination and teamwork must go into the adoption of broad-based policies or mandates. At Harvard, it is reported that it took 'nearly two years to build consensus, working with university administration, its library, faculty, and the University's Office of General

Counsel' (Nguyen, 2008). To assist researchers with the policy, the Harvard Library will create a new Office of Scholarly Communication to 'support faculty, encourage deposit and develop the repository' (Nguyen, 2008). In Harvard's, case, in the practical plan of action offered by SPARC, the library's part in the system in place is stated to be realised 'once a policy is adopted' (Nguyen, 2008). Furthermore, the library's part sounds rather like a housekeeping role, rather than a chance for engagement with faculty as they examine new scholarly communication patterns and challenge traditional practices. SPARC suggests a role for the library such as one to 'identify and secure resources that will be needed once a policy is adopted, such as the capacity to manage the deposit of scholarly articles and to make them available online'. Libraries, especially science libraries, must take into account the relative value of the most recent 12 months of articles still possibly available under tolls, but still in the greatest demand due to their currency. These articles may have great economic importance to publishers, and may change how librarians need to collect, make available to researchers, and preserve these articles and their journal 'package' over the long term.

SPARC's description of the functional library role may not be appealing to academic librarians, and subject specialists, library researchers, collection development and public services librarians (to name a few) may see this role as one for a repository manager working somewhere outside of the day-to-day flow of work with library users. The repository and its role in compliance with mandates may not be seen as an integral part of every library service and every librarian's professional mindset. Librarians may assume that the repository is now the place for open access, and the transformation of public services and collection development may not be a reality. The work of the rest of the library may go on as before, while the repository develops as a parallel service, and librarians do not engage with the broader issues. The institutional repository, rather than being integrated with all library workflows, including reference, instruction and collection development, risks becoming 'out of sight, out of mind'. Reference, collections, and liaison librarians may now also be expected to become experts in promoting the institutional repository (Bailey, 2006). Policy-making and the eventual success of the institutional repository may now be part of the role of the librarians working with the potential depositors of scholarly work. This is a new role and one that will need to be well thought out. Librarians, especially those in liaison roles, may be hearing that the success of the institutional repository depends directly on them. If institutional repositories struggle with issues of content and role in the organisation, librarians may be held accountable. Librarians may feel unsure how to influence the success of the repository. If they are authors in their own right, they might not have deposited their own work in the repository for any number of reasons. As with those in other disciplines, librarians make highly individual choices when it comes to submitting their own work to various publication outlets.

Even if institutional policies or mandates ensure a higher degree of participation by the university community in the repository or other open access initiatives, it is clear that leadership must come from a team that includes the library, but does not emanate only from librarians. Individual librarians may sign on to open access advocacy positions without any real support from the necessary larger community. In this case, librarians may feel marginalised if the conversation does not spread too far from the library itself. However, the library can become a place, either physically or virtually, for talk of open access and scholarly communication, but only if librarians have the time and some incentive to step outside traditional roles. If departmental faculty and other researchers are not pushing librarians to act, then it may simply be easier to respond to already stated service and collections needs of library users than to step out into a new dialogue. Librarians may be vulnerable if they go out alone without institutional support in carrying the message of open access to departments or research centres. The message may be unduly fragmented, lacking clarity of purpose or relevance to the particular audience. However, to be truly effective at the disciplinary level, many librarians would have to spend a great deal of time becoming the experts on open access behaviours in the specific disciplines. Outside of time pressures, many academic librarians are covering multiple areas with traditional services and may not want to carry out this extra advocacy work without concrete practical direction for working with departmental faculty and students. Different roles for librarians, especially roles not covered in library education programmes or previous library positions, may require a great deal of information and backing from the library and the institution in order to ensure efficacy.

Librarians in many institutions may be waiting for the type of consensus formed at Harvard before becoming involved in changing workflows, and may only then desire to be an integral part of the team going forward. Rather than eagerly taking on new roles, librarians may choose to continue with business as usual, and library leadership will be needed in decision-making on extending the boundaries of traditional librarian roles. Librarians are used to responding to what researchers desire in terms of publications; this may not often include new forms of scholarship. As a service profession, librarians may find most satisfaction in responding to the stated needs of faculty, students and other constituencies. Librarians must decide whether to be proactive in promoting open access materials in encounters with library users. One wonders if many academic librarians are asking whether mandates, or even open access policies are coming to their institutions, or whether they are at least discussing what their response to such actions will be in their everyday roles. Librarians may wish to push university leadership on the issue of mandates and take a proactive stance. Library leadership can foster communication up the levels in the institution, but also make sure it percolates down to all interested and potentially affected librarians and staff. The learning curve may be steep in both directions, and other university priorities may be more pressing.

Assisting researchers with new open access concerns

There may be new niche public services roles for librarians who may be sought out by library users interested in open access issues. Researchers may need to understand the differences between publishers when it comes to conferring author rights, how to handle submission of articles when the publisher will not be the depositor, whether to take advantage of institutional repository services, or how to interpret new terminology related to versioning. With publishers having many different strategies for working with authors, confusion is created, and librarians may be consulted about differences in the solutions offered by publishers (Grillot, 2008). Even as some charts have been made available detailing the different publisher requirements, making such information available from the library and keeping current with updates is a daunting task. Analysing the charts which provide an overview of what authors are allowed to do for each specific publisher, one can see how complicated the situation is for the researcher submitting an article (Grillot, 2008). The library community may need to rely on SHERPA/RoMEO (*http://www .sherpa.ac.uk/romeo/*) or develop a more complete searchable database which could be consulted by librarians when questions are raised. It may be possible for a commercial entity to include this type of information when describing each serial publication as part of background information such as rejection rate, editorial board contacts, impact within discipline or other descriptive information helpful to authors. Librarians will need a constantly updated online source for information from copyright transfer agreements or licensing information if they are to be the 'go to' source. Giving out information that may affect authors' publication choices may be a newer role for academic librarians, even as some are used to discussing journal impact factor, citation analysis or journal ranking mechanisms with potential authors. Liaisons to departmental faculty may struggle to be the most visible source of information on complying with mandates and other open access questions. Authors may not be used to consulting librarians on these matters, and librarians are not used to providing this information. Pulling together information in a convenient online resource on an institutional level may be necessary. Provision of excellent current advice on open access publishing may require the expertise of a dedicated position in each institution.

Even within a single academic discipline, keeping up with publisher requirements may be seen as outside the scope of the librarian's role. This new aspect of the librarian's skill set may not be reflected in position descriptions or taught in library school programmes. Some publishers charge fees, others place embargoes on content, and still others allow unusual versions to be deposited. The resulting scenario on the publisher end quickly becomes complicated for the researcher. Development of National Information Standards Organization (NISO) versioning language may be of assistance to the library world in its quest to simplify terminology both for librarians and researchers. Managers of repositories may need to work more closely with front-line and subject-specialist librarians to create seamless workflows and prevent redundancy of work and complications in public service information. This is another area where it will make sense for different types of librarians to work across boundaries to make the institutional repository's role in open access as simple as possible for the researcher. Artificial walls between librarians with different roles will have to be broken down and teamwork established for optimum communication within the library itself, and also out toward user groups. Librarians working in collections, liaison work and public services may prefer to have repository personnel handle all aspects of this process, knowing that those managers may not have the same level of experience with the norms of the disciplines when it comes to scholarly communication. Ideally, and if possible, it would seem that a team approach may work best. However, the library may be passed by completely when funding requirements are met more easily by publishers. If librarians are as interested in being part of the changes in scholarly communication, it would seem that the deposit process would be a natural extension of librarians' work with publishers and researchers. Even if librarians wholeheartedly embrace these new roles, it remains to be seen whether faculty will require or desire these services in large numbers.

Librarians may also need to find a new dialogue with publishers in their attempts to understand the pressures within the scholarly communication system as well as to find solutions to the concerns of researchers. The onus is now on busy authors to navigate the areas of permissions, addenda, versions, and other possibly unfamiliar territory. Librarians see an opportunity here but may be unsure whether a role is appropriate and whether they should be proactive in offering advice, much of which involves areas of legal expertise. The learning curve for the busy librarian may be steep and changes in information constant, especially as librarians are being asked to 'do more with less' in other areas of their jobs. Librarians who are authors themselves may be more familiar, not necessarily with the process of complying with mandates, but with the issues of signing away copyright or providing access to supplementary materials, or occasionally by being asked to pay author fees for print journal graphs and charts. It may make sense for librarians to be able to gather advice from those colleagues in the library who regularly publish their own work or self-archive their own publications. Some libraries may find that having a librarian with a law degree or other background may be most valuable in dealing with copyright and intellectual property issues as part of a larger scholarly communication expertise situated in the library. Institutions that require or value active publishing behaviour by faculty librarians may find that they will have to take more of a lead with transforming the LIS literature toward open access if that is the will of the profession.

Librarians can market the institutional repository, but may be much more effective at that effort if their own work is deposited first as an example. Further study is needed to ascertain whether librarians are enthusiastic depositors in their institution's repository. Initiatives like Cornell's VIVO can include librarians and LIS faculty in vast networks that may embed them further in the research networks of the institution and give them new ability to connect such efforts to the repository. The use of a system like VIVO may be valuable if there is a desire to maximise collection of information about faculty publications and following that with exposure of full text in the repository, showcasing and preserving the institution's total scholarly output (Cornell, 2009). Updating such an effort at collecting information about faculty research and publications alongside a corresponding repository effort presents a challenge for any library. Handling enquiries about issues such as author rights, incentives, and versioning may consume a great amount of time.

One major impediment to greater numbers of deposits has been confusion around versioning, and especially about the deposit of postprints, usually not an established practice for authors. The term 'postprints' has itself caused some confusion. Librarians embedded further into research teams through use of a VIVO-like system will have greater opportunity for dialogue and collaboration with researchers, and the chance to be involved in the research process at whatever level they desire. Failure to populate the repository with faculty and student work will result in another missed opportunity in the institutional plan to move a scholarly communication agenda forward. Faculty in all subfields are bound by disciplinary conventions and traditions around promotion and tenure. Librarians alone cannot provide incentives to departmental faculty and researchers for deposit in the repository. Often, the rhetoric of library organisations exhorts librarians to be the ones pushing change when researchers are not demanding, or even desiring it.

Copyright and licensing issues

Peter Suber coined the term 'permissions crisis' to describe the other issue of importance to academic librarians that goes along with the familiar serials pricing crisis (Suber, 2003). A move to open access, helping to solve the permissions crisis, will simplify the everyday life of any librarian involved with the complicated issues of contracts, licences, implementation of software to block unauthorised users, and authentication issues for remote access. Librarians working with licensing issues thoroughly understand the implications of tolls and permissions, and related problems for users. Copyright law and licensing agreements prevent librarians from fully using the material in journals for which they have paid (Suber, 2003). Statutes and contracts hamper the ease of use of research literature, putting many restrictions on the access, use, and sharing of material.

In the library literature, librarians seeking to publish their work still routinely sign away their copyright to publishers, often including their right to self-archive their own work. The publisher then sells back the librarians' work to the library through traditionally published journals, and then receives payment for this work via expensive subscriptions. Librarians certainly see the irony in these practices. Liberal permissions are another crucial tenet of open access journal publishing – the freedom to share information by circulating it freely among interested researchers (Frankish, 2004). Returning copyright to authors, and all authors choosing to publish in certain types of open access journals, or, especially to deposit their work in subject or institutional repositories will begin to change this situation. Librarians, in their quest for prestige and impact, may give away their work to publishers because they are not used to getting paid for what they write. Librarians may not see economic value to their writing.

Discussions of open access among librarians must include at least a basic understanding of underlying copyright and permissions issues. In 2001, libraries saw the emergence of the Creative Commons licence, allowing a compromise between the public domain works and works with all rights reserved (Kleinman, 2008). Creative Commons makes content more usable, and allows potential readers to find shared work more easily. Authors retain some rights but have the ability to share their work. Libraries may want to publicise Creative Commons as an example of a more open approach to works of scholarship. Creative Commons licensing has been used in many different open access initiatives, such as the publication by Yale University Press of James Boyle's work, *The Public Domain: Enclosing the Commons of the Mind*, which was published as an open access work using a Creative Commons licence alongside production of a print edition (Boyle, 2008). In addition, Bloomsbury Academic plans to make all of its titles immediately available using Creative Commons licences, while simultaneously selling print-on-demand versions (Harper, 2009). This reserving of some rights by authors may be very appealing in open access projects and attracting authors to alternative types of publishing. Librarians will need to build collections using different types of resources and this open access material provides choices for library users in terms of format, and is free to libraries to add to collections.

Recent policy changes noted in the LIS literature

In recent years, there has been focus on the copyright policies of the publishers of the major LIS journals. The traditional commercial publishers of some of the library journals, such as Elsevier and Emerald, although making major strides toward more liberal permissions for authors, still appear to be charging libraries large amounts of subscription money to include the librarian authors' own scholarly articles in academic library collections. Librarians, themselves seeking publication in their own discipline's top-tier journals, may not have much incentive to advocate for change. Journals such as Elsevier's *Journal of Academic*

Librarianship still hold a high place on lists of perceived prestige according to practising academic librarians as well as recent surveys of LIS deans and directors (Nisonger and Davis, 2005). Clearly, although librarians push faculty and researchers to move their work to lesser-known open access journals, the 'prestige factor' appears to still hold sway for librarians and library scholars in respect to their own LIS journal literature. Librarians are not moving their own major journals to true open access models by demanding change from LIS publishers. Librarians have not changed their own publishing behaviour, even as they continue to advocate for open access among other faculty. Librarians at institutions with faculty status for librarians are under the same pressures to publish as other teaching faculty, and have the ability to transform some aspects of their literature. In general, there appears to be some lethargy and apathy in terms of a changing paradigm for librarians' publishing behaviour. Academic librarians may be largely uninformed, or they may be uninterested in changing the traditional system that is in place. It is not exactly clear who is pushing this change, or whether it will ever take place in the academy. Librarians have been aware of the issues for some time, and there has not been large-scale change in the LIS literature.

Open access initiatives for library research promote more visibility of LIS topics on the web and allow researchers to control the fate of their intellectual output. Moving more of the LIS literature onto the open web through open access journals and repositories would allow for crawling by Google Scholar, OAIster (*http://www.oaister.org/*) and other search engines, further increasing visibility and hence impact. The impact of open access for the library literature extends to personal impact for authors, but also to the potential value of maximum dissemination of publications about library issues to the greater society. Holding the library literature behind tolls would not seem to be in librarianship's best interest, especially now as open access advocacy by librarians has ratcheted up. Maximising readership of the library literature would give it more visibility through free web access. Librarians may want to advocate for openness in their own literature as a primary example of direct action.

Open access, increasing research impact, and libraries integrating free search engines

There are many recent studies on the increase in impact that comes from open access. A very helpful webliography from the Open Citation Project pulls together the many studies showing that open access increases research impact (Open Citation Project, 2009). As putting material on the free web allows an author maximum visibility, libraries must consider issues of access to those resources. In order to maximise discovery, academic libraries are now showing a trend toward including free web-based search engines such as Google Scholar that crawl open access journals and repositories on their websites, web lists and OPACs (Mullen and Hartman, 2006; Hartman and Mullen, 2008). Integrating these free web resources can provide access to quality peer-reviewed journal scholarship alongside the subscribed-to journals. With a move to more article-level (or digital object) searching in the Google era, the benefit will be to individual authors and their articles, as well as to the LIS profession as a whole. Libraries wishing to truly integrate open access materials must include resources that index them alongside other subscription discovery tools. Along with listing on weblists of indexes and databases, libraries will need to include the records themselves in library catalogues or integrated library systems. However, librarians may wish to continue to be cognisant of the increasing reliance on Google as a search engine, considering the lack of transparency regarding its algorithms and development plans. Librarians should continue to engage with the issue of search engine development and consider what would happen to the searching of open access literature if popular free search engines can no longer provide the service libraries are accustomed to. A study at the Centre for Publishing at University College London showed that search engines increase online journal usage even more than open access, and in the case of *Nucleic Acids Research*, the introduction of an open access publishing option resulted in an additional upturn in journal use (Mayor, 2006).

Maximum web visibility for authors and effective searching by librarians require excellent search engines. Librarians working in public services roles cannot become complacent and take the availability of effective search engines for granted. It is possible and beneficial for librarians to engage with issues related to search engine development as they greatly affect the search and discovery of scholarly open access material. Examples of ways librarians can engage further would be by attending conferences relating to search engine development or by producing library web pages that point users to good sources of open access material. There are many conferences on this topic where librarians could mix with developers or do presentations on search engine use in academic libraries. An example would be the annual Search Engine Meeting (Infonortics, 2009), along with many other venues where librarians are welcome. It is also important for librarians to know whether free internet search engines such as Google are indexing scholarly materials from the 'deep web', thereby making them available to researchers (Hagedorn and Santelli, 2008). Librarians may be making decisions to leave free web search out of their library offerings, instead sticking to subscription products. In a 2007 study by the Research Information Network (RIN) and the Consortium of University Research Libraries in the British Isles (CURL), it was found that librarians expect that researchers are 'highly conservative in the range of tools they use', and this study confirms that researchers use a narrow list of discovery tools in their work. Over 70 per cent of researchers routinely use Google to access scholarly content (Swan and Brown, 2005; RIN/CURL, 2007). Most importantly for librarians developing repositories as a large part of their library outreach effort, it is found that searching the web accounts for the 'vast majority' of access to institutional repositories (Carr, 2006). Repositories not crawled by major search engines such as Google will miss most searchers' attempts at finding scholarly literature. Building library services that do not take advantage of popular search engines will not maximise effectiveness or discoverability.

Librarians need to understand the value of web search engines as part of common researcher behaviour in their daily work. Librarians may need to take a broader look at open access and how it can be incorporated into library services now that the web can be seen as part of the library. The ability of librarians to take a holistic look at the entire picture of the available scholarly resources in each discipline (regardless of fee or free) will also create value for the role of public service librarians engaged in the presenting of the whole spectrum of choices to a possibly overwhelmed researcher. Simply presenting a traditional grouping of resources to library users will not be enough; instead, librarians will have to pick through the plethora of choices (both free and subscribed) to speak quickly to the needs of the individual researcher. Organising a vast amount of scholarly information found on the web can be a great value-added service of librarians. Individual academic libraries will have to decide whether to extend the whole range of free as well as subscribed resources to library users seeking information. Best practices will have to be changed to integrate open access materials found free on the web into reference work. Reference training could put emphasis on incorporating the whole corpus of scholarly research resources into any potential answer to a query, while taking care to give a specific targeted response. With such a complicated milieu of quality information available, it will be a challenge to condense possible resources into manageable lists of citations. The 'reference interview' can once again take centre stage as important training for information professionals tasked with matching the most appropriate resources to each researcher, taking into account a dizzying array of choices of resources of all types and formats, both subscribed and free. The librarian will need to make sense of the total array of scholarly literature for the researcher community.

Due to the rapid pace of the digital revolution in libraries, librarians are functioning in new relationships with publishers, vendors, teaching faculty and researchers. Librarians are in a position to steer researchers toward the most relevant scholarly information both in the library and on the web, whatever that might be. This new information world requires librarians, traditionally the information access experts, to be knowledgeable about all the many ways of discovering and accessing scholarly information. This is highly subjective, and requires an unbiased viewpoint on the part of the librarian, as well as a great deal of understanding of the current state of scholarly information dissemination. Librarians may need continuous education about scholarly communication models in the disciplines that they serve in order to stay up to date. There is confusion as to the role of the librarian in promoting the scholarly communications agenda in the academy from the reference desk and in classes of students and faculty on a broad scale.

The concept of open access, popularised by Harnad, beginning with his 'subversive proposal' in 1994, has now become a recurring theme of conferences and LIS literature. In fact, as early as 1989, Harnad launched and edited *Psycoloquy*, the first toll-free (no subscription price) journal (Okerson and O'Donnell, 1995; Kaser and Ojala, 2005). As Velterop states, 'there are no technical barriers to open access; just barriers of habit such as restricted-access business models based on the legal construct of copyright' (Velterop, 2008). In those earlier days, it seemed time to discuss the opening up of the scholarly literature in terms of access, discovery and price. For reasons of values of universal access, as well as the need for budget relief from serials threatening to engulf the library budget, librarians seemed well poised to jump on board as advocates for open access. There was not necessarily a roadmap, but the combination of budget issues, new library technology and the promise of the internet made the open access movement seem a perfect fit for libraries. For many, the self-archiving of articles and other papers in repositories, and the establishment of new 'born-digital' open journals (many free to both readers and authors) seemed to be an excellent fit for academic libraries' missions.

As part of the 'subversive discussion' on the internet almost 15 years ago that is often referred to as the jumping-off point for the open access discussion, a question was posed that still resonates today. An ARL paper states that:

> the simplest answer is that the problem is not technical, but sociological. How do we get the right user community interested and committed to communicating in this way? The first step is to talk up the idea, talk it through, and talk it out to the point of practical application. (ARL, 1995)

Librarians have been talking ever since, but there has been no broad-based answer to the serials crisis still facing libraries, or to really changing the scholarly communication traditions of most disciplines. There has been no open access answer as of yet to the budgetary problems of academic libraries, and no end of large 'big deal' commercial journal packages or price increases of other types of journals. Many librarians have not, as was once thought, accepted this new challenge with great enthusiasm. It could also be said that librarians have not maximised their own contributions to the movement in their everyday work and scholarship behaviour.

Open access and implications for peer review

Hundreds of articles about open access can be found in the literature of many disciplines, including the scholarly publishing literature. Still, the basics of what makes an article scholarly have not changed and need not change due to open access. The four essential components of scholarly communication have been described as: registration of the idea, concept or research; certification of the quality and validity of the research; awareness through dissemination; and archiving for the future (Roosendaal and Guerts, 1998; Crow, 2002).

The peer-review system retains its relevance and importance. It must be reiterated that open access does not signify any lack of peer review. However, there have been recent discussions about new forms of peer review, and the possibility of experimentation within certain disciplines. Library patrons want to be assured that research literature, whatever its format, retains credibility. Researchers look to librarians, editorial boards, indexing and abstracting services, and journal publishers to retain the traditional peer-review system. Traditionally, researchers know that scholarly material is found in academic libraries, where it is expected that librarians have vetted materials for certain standards of quality. Librarians' roles will continue to include the collection and organisation of material for the use of scholars – still a gatekeeper role. With so many other ways for researchers to discover materials away from the library website, the library must struggle to be known as the 'place' for collections of quality scholarly material, regardless of format or business model. Librarians need to be consistent and cognisant when organising information in the library and on the website so that peer-reviewed status is obvious to users. Students have recently expressed their desire to have some sort of assurance that what they are using in their research papers is peer-reviewed. Many library users may not understand that the process of peer review is no different for open access journals. Open access archives, however, do not usually mandate peer review, and this may cause some confusion for library users. Library instruction programmes will have to deal with this issue, and in the future, it may be that all scholarly work will carry some sort of metadata indicating whether or not it can be considered peer-reviewed, and, ideally, the level of peer review. This will be especially important for materials residing in repositories away from the recognisable package of the traditional journal. A change to open access does not necessitate making any changes to systems of peer review or the makeup of editorial boards. Behaviours such as self-archiving and publication in open access journals are not an attempt to move away from rigorous peer review in any way. Learned societies and professional associations are being called on to encourage universities to give peer-reviewed online publications the same weight as they give to print publications (BOAI, 2006). The actual activities involved in managing the peer-review process are actually easier in the online environment due to enhanced communication and ease of e-mailing manuscripts.

Librarians in everyday reference and instruction roles must keep up with discussions about, and changes to systems of peer review, including some of the newer models, such as 'open peer review' or expedited versions of traditional peer review practices. 'Open peer review' may provide a mechanism for scholars to review and sign each other's papers. In the extreme, even Google Peer Review offers an alternative (Google, 2009). The traditional information about peer review that librarians have relied upon is changing. Many studies are being performed both on new models of peer review and the efficacy of established norms. One helpful blog that attempts to encourage discussion of new issues surrounding peer review is published by Nature, and is entitled 'Peer to Peer: for peer-reviewers and about the peer-review process' (*http://blogs.nature.com/peer-to-peer/*).

Discussions of open access literature must involve issues of peer review as the basis of its credibility as research material emanating from scholars.

According to a report by the Publishing Research Consortium based on consultation with more than 3,000 authors, editors and reviewers, 'most researchers are not in favour of changing the current system of peer review for journal articles' (Mark Ware Consulting Ltd, 2007). In another large study, the Centre for Information Behaviour and the Evaluation of Research (CIBER) reviewed feedback from 5,513 academics, and found that 'a massive 96.2 per cent of academics support the system of peer review for publication of scholarly articles' (Thomas, 2005). Of course, with the open access community and the publishing community sometimes at odds, it may be difficult to stand behind surveys sponsored by one group or the other. Other studies have found both readers and researchers to be satisfied with using the free repository author version of a journal article, as long as it is fully peer-reviewed – even if it is not completely copyedited or publisher branded. Certainly, librarians will have a role in educating researchers and students about changes to peer review and will need to work closely with departmental faculty to understand what will be acceptable to instructors in terms of which articles will be acceptable for citation by students in writing research papers. Individual departments will grapple with setting standards for publications deemed acceptable and desirous for presentation in promotion and tenure cases. It may be the tenure track junior faculty who cannot afford to take risks with their choices of publication outlets. Librarians will continue to respond to the stated publication needs of students and researchers and may not be able in all cases to suggest new types of open access alternatives.

Discussions about peer review may be the catalyst to really move an institution's scholarly communications agenda forward. Without changes in established culture, researchers and prospective authors will stay within the prescribed and often narrow definition of 'quality', often labelled by impact factor or other metrics. The discussion will have to involve the senior scholars in order for the system to move in the interests of the junior faculty needing to shoot for top-tier journals when tenure is at issue. Opening up conversation about peer review and issues such as journal ranking may allow scholars to consider new forms of scholarship for their own publications. Staying only with traditional titles and formats may not allow the open access movement to gather momentum in an institution, or on a global scale. Harold Varmus has commented that 'scientists have a lot of respect for their journals' (Salisbury, 2008). Libraries may be speaking to an audience that is not receptive to the pleas for change, as discipline-based researchers may feel protective of established journals. Librarians may feel the same about the traditional and well-respected LIS journals and publishers.

Departmental faculty may need information about newer forms of scholarship in their disciplines and may wish to clarify why they want students to be pointed only to traditionally published literature, sometimes even specifying 'print'. Teaching faculty, in many cases, are specifically asking students to use peer-reviewed literature in writing research papers, and librarians are asked to direct students away from Google where much of the open access material can be found, in favour of searching for topics in the commercial subscribed-to databases. There is confusion about peer-reviewed materials that are born digital. Electronic publications are still sometimes felt (even by faculty) to be less scholarly than their paper counterparts. Such misinformation may be widespread. As more libraries acquire their journals in online format, and more publishers drop print production, this may soon begin to change. There is confusion abounding about what constitutes 'scholarly enough' in terms of publications. There is, however, evidence that researchers are citing electronic journals more than traditional publications. For a study done for the ARL and the Ithaka Group, field librarians conducted interviews with researchers and reported that, of the eight types of electronic scholarly resources studies, 'e-journals turned out to be the resource that scholars cited most often' (Howard, 2008b). Keeping this type of reader preference in mind can help librarians in making decisions about collections and services. Librarians must be aware that the way they teach using certain materials, display resources on library websites, or otherwise make resources available can push user behaviour in certain ways. Librarians have great influence over user discovery of resources when users start at the library website or other portal. Librarians must reach consensus on how to display and integrate new open access materials. With decision-making about electronic resources often dispersed among groups in a library (technical, collections, public services), more vetting and dialogue across boundaries may be beneficial to ensure best representation of electronic materials on library websites. The organisation and presentation of electronic materials (both open access and subscription) by the library can greatly influence patron use and satisfaction.

There is much misinformation that librarians may be able to address through communication and presentation about open access, new models of impact, and the rationale for increasing electronic content, both subscribed and open access, in collections. It may be extremely difficult for teaching faculty and others to keep up with this rapidly changing landscape, and they may appreciate the consultation and services that librarians can provide. This may be a new and expanded role for librarians, and it remains to be seen how many academic librarians will take on this role proactively, and in what type of institutions this librarian behaviour may become most common. Mainly, academic librarians will need to make sure that the library retains its excellence and relevance in delivering content seamlessly and remotely to affiliated patrons.

What do researchers want from their libraries?

Librarians may need to study closely what researchers actually want from their libraries and what they expect them to provide. This will be very specific by institution and by discipline, but some larger studies can be informative. In 2007, RIN and CURL completed a survey of 2,250 researchers and 300 librarians with a focus on academic libraries in the UK. Results showed that a 'majority of researchers think that their institution's libraries are doing an effective job in providing the information they need to do their work' and that 'nearly all researchers think that funding the library should be a priority'. Particularly among the arts and humanities, the researchers surveyed suggested that libraries should fight for increased funding to buy more traditional subscription products. Librarians in the survey did not agree with this position; they did not want to fight for more journal funding, they did not want their libraries to pay open access publication charges, and they really supported self-archiving in institutional repositories (RIN/CURL, 2007). This does not describe an environment conducive to reaching consensus on the successful role of the future library, and does not provide librarians in everyday roles with a roadmap to serving constituencies without conflict. In this study, researchers were not focused on open access solutions. Indeed, as with some other studies, there appears to be a disconnect between stakeholder groups in terms of advancing a more open publication library agenda.

The RIN/CURL study reports that, as we know, researchers want online information when they need it, but also that they are able to bypass barriers to get information in creative ways. The report further states that:

> there are some significant differences between researchers' and librarians' views as to the future roles of libraries in supporting research, and there is a need for dialogue between them to ensure that library services and expertise are developed and deployed in the most effective way. (RIN/CURL, 2007)

In addition, 'researchers' awareness of new developments in scholarly communications, particularly issues to do with open access to research outputs is low' (RIN/CURL, 2007). This does not bode well for library efforts at outreach and advocacy in the UK (or elsewhere) when researchers do not see open access behaviour as a priority. It could be that researchers are not currently pushing librarians for change, and that librarians may be ignoring the 'parallel conversation' about open access advocacy until the time when they hear interest from constituencies. Some might say that when the journals are cancelled, the researchers will take notice and support open access. It has not been proven that researchers will indeed move to different models just because important disciplinary journal titles are cancelled. Librarians are aware that support for and enthusiasm for the library comes from the researchers' ability to access subscriptions that they need for their work.

A study by Dill and Palmer (2007) looked at a group of academic librarians and their attitudes regarding open access. A strong majority of respondents to their survey felt that librarians 'should educate faculty and administration about open access and copyright issues'. It was felt that having the open access discussion helped the library remain relevant. One of the survey findings was that public services and acquisitions librarians had the least positive attitude toward open access, and it was hypothesised that those categories of librarians may see open access as a threat to their jobs (Arch, 2007). Librarians also were not supportive about the funding of open access projects by the library (Arch, 2007). Another viewpoint by Arch, an acquisitions librarian, in a review of the Dill and Palmer study, was that the 'idea of scholarly works online for free raises questions for these librarians about how quality control will be maintained and how these open access projects will be funded' (Arch, 2007). Clearly, more research needs to be done, and universities might want to have conversations with librarians to ascertain whether librarians on the front-lines actually do support and want to promote the expansion of open access into all aspects of the library. A more fulsome report of the Dill and Palmer research on librarian attitudes about open access has been recently published, and will be able to provide more background for the translation of statements of support into actual changes in librarian practice (Palmer et al., 2009). It becomes clear that there is an apparent disconnect between stated mission in support of open access and actual practice by librarians in many academic libraries. It is curious that more studies have not sought out librarian opinion about the changes that large-scale open access behaviour might bring to library work. Evidence that librarians may not be entirely 'on board' would give advocacy organisations and other library leaders another avenue for discussion.

Publishers are eager to continue dialogue with librarians and counter that 'In all debates about access, the fact that publishers in partnership with librarians already provide some degree of near universal access to STM literature is often lost' (Regazzi, 2004). Public libraries serving 97 per cent of people provide access to electronic indexes and interlibrary loan, and it is sometimes stated that many people have access to an open state university library in the USA (Regazzi, 2004). Whenever the conversation turns to open access for the public and onsite access to expensive subscriptions, this allows publishers to promulgate the idea that the library is providing everything the public needs and wants. If there is free access at the library, why use the web for this purpose? This comes at a great cost to the university library, and with budgets dwindling, these claims about universal access may ring hollow. Librarians know the barriers to most people in getting access to the fruits of taxpayer-funded research if it is not made both discoverable and available online. This access also depends on reliable access to search engines that expose the research articles and often the ability to travel to get library access or assistance with accessing the information needed from the publications. Simply making research material available to the public does not solve all issues of full access to needed information.

2

Librarians and their own open access publishing

Self-archiving by librarians

Open access initiatives useful to librarians and library and information science (LIS) faculty may include library-published, LIS-focused peer-reviewed open access journals, LIS subject repositories for author self-archiving of preprints and postprints, inclusion of work in institutional repositories, and integration of LIS open access journals in subject-focused indexes and abstracts. Of course, any definition of open access would take into account mounting articles on authors' personal web pages, and development of open source software for libraries. There are many opportunities for new roles for librarians in the movement of the library toward open access.

By definition, self-archiving is 'the practice of depositing one's work in an OAI-compliant archive' (Coleman and Roback, 2005) or the act of depositing 'a digital document in a publicly accessible website, preferably an OAI-compliant Eprint archive' (eprints, 2006). The actual process of depositing takes the researcher an average of ten minutes (Carr and Harnad, 2005). In many disciplines, self-archiving is not a common mode of sharing scholarship. For librarians, even though disciplinary archives exist, few librarians follow this behaviour. Even if librarians are not able to fully support a transition to open access journals at the present time, they can still support the concept of open access by self-archiving their work in one of the publicly accessible, OAI-compliant e-print subject repositories that are currently available to accept their deposited work. E-prints are defined as 'digital texts of peer-reviewed research articles, before and after refereeing' (eprints, 2006). Deposited work would usually be the author's preprint (before peer review) or postprint (post peer review). Postprints are increasingly being called the 'accepted version' to distinguish them from the final branded publisher PDF. Using the term 'accepted version' denotes that the peer-review process is complete, thereby certifying the work. The article, if going on to traditional journal publication, has not yet been through final copyediting or branding by the publisher. This branded version is often held behind subscription barriers.

A librarian publishing a scholarly article in the traditional manner may only produce minimal research impact unless the article is widely acclaimed and cited, or published in a top journal with wide readership. Whether an article in a top journal, or a less visible peer-reviewed LIS article, self-archiving produces maximum impact for the author for all versions of the work. A common misconception may be that self-archiving somehow equals self-publication, evoking thoughts of the old vanity press. Acceptance for publication by a peer-reviewed journal is the characteristic that gives these works stature, and most would consider the refereed version to be the one that qualifies as the scholarly publication. Each publisher has its own rules for self-archiving of accepted articles, and this information is usually found on the journal's website, or through a search of the SHERPA/RoMEO database. Library organisations or library research committees may want to follow the situation with LIS self-archiving, and market opportunities to interested librarians. Certain LIS publishers could be singled out for liberal archiving policies and this may be excellent public relations exposure if these companies seem to be responding to librarians regarding open access author permissions. Indeed, librarians might do more self-archiving of their own work were more information about the LIS journals available from an easy-to-access source. Librarians may wonder where this information about publisher and journal policies is pulled together in one convenient place for their discipline. Copyright transfer information is often buried, if available at all from many journals' websites.

In all fields, authors have most likely found it difficult to understand their rights in terms of permissions and copyright. The SHERPA/RoMEO site now lists permissions information for potential authors in an easily searchable format. Librarians in their daily work are now able to show potential authors how to search SHERPA/RoMEO by publisher to get clarification of policies about the permission to self-archive work in repositories or on web pages. Unfortunately, many publishers are not included in this convenient tool and constant updating is necessary for currency. A 2004 publisher survey representing 7,169 journals in all fields reported that 49 per cent permitted publication of the manuscript or the finalised paper on an open access server (Bjork, 2004). Such wording generally refers to the preprint or any version of the postprint, for instance the author's finalised word-processed or PDF document.

Times are changing in terms of publisher permissions, albeit slowly. In 2008, the RoMEO database reported that 65 per cent of publishers in all disciplines were allowing self-archiving of some kind (Morris, 2009a). A study by Cox and Cox reveals that 48–86 per cent of publishers already allow self-archiving of either the submitted or accepted versions, but only 5–19 per cent also allow deposit of the published version. There is also some evidence that some publishers may be moving to requiring an embargo on the accepted version even if they allow archiving of postprints (Cox and Cox, 2008; Morris, 2009a). RoMEO paints a less rosy picture of the situation for the branded publisher version, showing that in 2009 only 11.7 per cent of publishers allowed author use of the published version, with 4.2 per cent more after an embargo period, and a further 0.4 per cent after an embargo plus a fee (Morris, 2009a). Many researchers will want to put only the publisher's branded PDF on the web (against most publishers' policies), often due to the easy electronic dissemination of electronic journal articles. Researchers, including librarian authors, may want to have only one 'final' or 'official' version circulating online, and this may cause resistance to self-archiving other versions in repositories.

Librarians may wonder whether publishers are increasingly allowing authors to self-archive their scholarly work, and where. In another recent study by the Publishing Research Consortium, which analysed the Association of Learned and Professional Society Publishers' 'Scholarly publishing practices' report, it was reported that 53 per cent of publishers, and 86 per cent by number of articles published, allow authors to 'self-archive the submitted version to one or more of the following destinations: own or department website, institutional repository, or subject repository' (Morris 2009a, 2009b). Sixty per cent of publishers and 90 per cent of the number of articles published allow this for the accepted version, while only 39 per cent of publishers and 10 per cent of articles allow deposit of the branded publisher PDF version. That said, '60 per cent of authors misunderstood the misleading term "postprint" and believe that they can always or sometimes self-archive the published PDF' (Morris, 2009a). This study found that authors overestimated what they are allowed to do with the publisher-branded final version, and underestimated their rights concerning the 'accepted' or 'postprint' version. One half of authors thought that archiving the publisher's version was allowable even though very few publishers actually allow this practice (Morris, 2009a). This highlights the steep learning curve for communities of academics, researchers, and even librarians when it comes to understanding what exactly constitutes green open access, that is, the self-archiving of research articles on the web. It has been well-publicised by Harnad and others that the idea of open access does not require changes to traditional journals, or even necessarily the need to start new journals, but just the practice of all authors of scholarly peer-reviewed journal articles to self-archive copies of their papers on the web for others to read.

When researchers learn the limitations that exist on the branded final article, they may then look to librarians for advice about depositing other versions, as well as how to cite such alternative versions of articles. Front-line librarians may worry about giving incorrect advice, especially as it relates to copyright, or the use and citing of multiple article versions. Researchers often have difficulty with constantly changing norms in citation style, and producers of style manuals as well as the online citation management tools have had to play 'catch-up' to remain current with the changes inherent in the new forms of online article publication. To complicate matters further, the various disciplines have decidedly different norms when it comes to scholarly communication, and the library may not have subject specialists or others adequately versed in disciplinary conventions to be able to advise faculty and students in matters of archiving. On the other hand, there is tremendous added value in a library whose librarians are able to be a source of credible information for authors and researchers in these matters.

Swan and Brown (2005) interviewed scholars from all disciplines who had not self-archived their work and found that library and information scholars rated highest (60 per cent) in their awareness that self-archiving their work was a possibility. This may be because LIS authors have become well aware of open access through the profession's advocacy efforts; as such, this result shows that many are choosing, for reasons other than a lack of awareness, not to self-archive their work. Further study would be able to determine why these LIS scholars do not choose this method of open access, and are not overly concerned about self-archiving. The same study shows that LIS scholars archived postprints in 33 per cent of cases, preprints in 23 per cent, and technical reports in 22 per cent of cases. In other disciplines, preprint archiving may be more common, but in LIS, postprints (final, accepted author copy of a word-processed document) are the version that authors prefer to archive (Swan and Brown, 2005). It has been reported that even against publisher policies, many archive publisher PDFs (Antelman, 2006).

It could be postulated that if librarians and LIS faculty are not depositing their own work, they may not be suggesting this avenue to others. What do librarians feel is expected of them in terms of promotion of self-archiving from the desk, and in other contact with other faculty? Should academic librarians be able to advise faculty, students and researchers in the process of archiving their work, both in the institutional repository and in available disciplinary archives? It is unclear whether academic librarians at this time are acting in this advisory role to other faculty. Do librarians stand behind open access advocacy positions by following personal self-archiving behaviour? One wonders whether it is the voice of many librarians that are heard on this issue, or just a vocal few that are in strong advocacy positions. Librarians that are liaisons to departments may be more involved; subject specialists and collection development librarians may follow trends, but in reference and instruction roles; librarians may be seeking guidance about how to participate in the open access movement in their public services capacities.

Distinguishing the term 'postprint' from the new NISO term 'published' may reduce some of the confusion relating to the branded final version. Some may believe that 'postprint' denotes the final publisher version. It is unclear whether publishers will go after such researchers with 'take down' orders, or whether this practice will continue to grow and become common practice. Librarians may be wary of giving out definitive information about the various policies and possible penalties that authors may incur for using final published versions on the web, especially the posting on an author's personal website or use in coursepacks. Certainly, one place librarians know that researchers look for copies of articles is on scholars' individual websites.

A study by Cox and Cox in 2008 details what authors say they want when it comes to dissemination of their scholarly journal articles. Authors want to provide copies of their articles to other researchers outside of their home institutions, use all or part of their work in other publications that they author, and deposit their articles on a personal or departmental website, or in a subject or institutional repository (Morris, 2009a). The new NISO terminology will hopefully provide clarification regarding the names given to various versions: submitted (the author's original or submitted and under review), approved (the accepted manuscript) and published (the branded version of record) (Morgan, 2008; NISO, 2008). Librarians must move to incorporate this simplified and clarified terminology in all communications with constituencies in order to reduce confusion and start to normalise and standardise some of this language within the research community. Librarians always struggle with reducing library jargon and may see the simplification of language to be something that is very important when trying to reach interested audiences outside of the library and the world of open access advocacy.

Other studies have investigated author motivations for open access behaviours. A 2004 survey conducted on behalf of the Joint Information Systems Committee (JISC) and the Open Society Institute (OSI) surveyed journal authors about their publishing activities in open access publications as well as in conventional publications. The poll of 200 published authors investigated authors' awareness of open access journal publishing opportunities. This survey showed that awareness was high for the group not taking the open access publishing route (Swan and Brown, 2004b). Two-thirds of respondents chose not to publish in an open access outlet even though they were aware of the possibility, and one-quarter of authors who chose not to pursue this route had been made aware of open access alternatives by their institutions. Reasons for choosing open access publishing included: principle of free access to research, speed of publication, larger readership, and greater number of potential citations to their work. In contrast, within the group of authors choosing conventional non-open access publications, three-quarters felt that open access could negatively affect the impact of their work, that there was an expectation of slower publication times, a smaller readership, and fewer citations to the work (Swan and Brown, 2004b). Clearly, there are some misperceptions that librarians may be able to help allay if they choose to be a source of information and expertise for open access. It would be interesting to see an update of this study to see if there have been more inroads made on authors' attitudes to open access alternatives for their work. Are librarians influencing the conversation, or is any appreciable change due to other factors, such as strong statements, mandates or policies from institutional leadership?

As regards the question of author costs in open access publishing, more than 55 per cent of the authors choosing this route had not paid a fee. Only a small minority of both groups (the open access and non-open access authors) had ever self-archived their articles in either an institutional repository or a subject repository. The highest level of archiving could be found on the authors' personal websites (Swan and Brown, 2004b). Archiving on individual websites is the least attractive in terms of long-term digital preservation and web discoverability. It is not clear whether authors care so much about preservation, counting on the commercial and society publishers to take care of this concern. One of the major selling points for the trusted institutional repositories in terms of self-archiving has been the preservation aspect of the digital copy.

According to the aforementioned survey and others, there is still a lot of misinformation and confusion in most disciplines about self-archiving and other open access publishing alternatives. With many traditional publishers offering open access alternatives, such as 'author pays' options, researchers are getting mixed signals about the term 'open access'. This is true even among academic librarians. Specific libraries whose librarians choose to self-archive and use 'free to authors, free to readers' open access journals to publish their work could be identified as forward-thinking and cutting-edge. Academic librarian authors hailing from research libraries, especially those where faculty status, promotion and tenure are tied to scholarship pressures would seem a natural fit to become leaders in this area. Certain libraries would be known to place scholarly communication advocacy at the forefront of priority lists, especially if open access behaviour is common among librarians at the institution. This position assumes librarians want to change their modus operandi, and a consensus could be reached even among librarians at a single institution regarding their self-archiving behaviour. Such voluntary behaviour may depend on many factors in order to reach a critical mass where action would match advocacy.

Authors in LIS and permissions to self-archive

Many library journals that are listed in SHERPA/RoMEO still do not allow certain versions to be archived in LIS subject repositories such as E-LIS and dLIST. Some publishers do not differentiate clearly between types of self-archiving possibilities, only mentioning, for instance, institutional repositories or personal web pages. Institutional repositories and personal web pages are often included in permissions for self-archiving by LIS authors. However, the SHERPA site may not mention subject or disciplinary archives, as seen, for example, if one searches the site for the policies of LIS publishers such as the American Library Association (ALA). This is true even if librarians have two robust subject repositories available for deposit of articles. Vague statements from societies or publishers lead a librarian author to have to spend extra time in investigation by e-mail or phone to contact the editor or journal's offices seeking clarification about expanded self-archiving permissions. This type of hurdle may discourage authors from pursuing open access, seeing it as just too difficult, confusing and time-consuming. Many LIS publishers and journals are certainly not on the cutting-edge in terms of policies for both copyright and universal accessibility on the web. Many LIS journals do not have a copy of their copyright transfer agreement (CTA) available on the web for potential authors to consider as they are making decisions regarding where to submit their work. Some seem to hide this information, and LIS authors may want to move away from publishers that do not allow self-archiving of preprints and postprints of accepted articles. In a survey of the availability of CTAs on the web, Coleman (2007) observed that 62 per cent of ISI-ranked LIS journals did not publish their copyright policy on the open web. Of these journals, 40 per cent made no mention of self-archiving. Twenty of 52 publishers covered in Coleman's study made their CTAs available on the web, but even then, the self-archiving information was ambiguous.

Even if librarians choose to submit their work to traditionally published journals for reasons of prestige or preference, a liberal archiving policy on the part of the publisher of the non-open access journals would still allow librarians' work to be available open access through self-archiving. Self-archiving the postprint would allow the author more visibility and impact while advertising the publication in the traditional journal. The journal would still exist as the 'package' and the repository copy would refer to that journal title with every download. Librarians wanting to publish in traditionally well-known titles but still desiring open access visibility and potentially increased impact can now check each LIS publisher in SHERPA/RoMEO in order to determine whether it has restrictive copyright policies or licences or whether it does in fact allow archiving in subject or institutional repositories, or on personal web pages. If librarian authors decide that self-archiving of all of their work is important, as is often the message they promote in the academy, then they will have to be persistent in dealing with the unclear policies of LIS publishers. It is possible that publishers may be intentionally vague in their statements in order to discourage self-archiving. It can also be difficult for potential authors to find self-archiving information on journal websites. Librarians must insist that LIS publishers make copyright information readily available in an obvious place on every journal's homepage. Librarians have not organised in any way against publishers and journals that exhibit a lack of cooperation with the open access movement by developing more liberal self-archiving policies. As there have been no obvious repercussions, publishers have no incentive to change their permissions or business models in any way. Librarians will need to be proactive about open access in dealing with LIS publishers of all types. This statement assumes that librarian authors as a collective really care to demand change from LIS publishers.

Some publishers that cover in part the library literature have become more liberal in their open access practices. In response to continued discussion about the permissions/copyright restrictions hampering authors and libraries, some society and commercial publishers have very publicly declared more open policies for those who decide to entrust their scholarly work to their publications. Contrary to popular belief, some of the most liberal archiving policies may be associated with some of the large commercial publishers. In 2004, for instance, Elsevier adopted a policy allowing preprint and postprint self-archiving on authors' personal web pages or institutions' web pages (institutional repositories). This permission does not extend to archiving of branded publisher PDFs (Peek, 2004). These permissions to self-archive are similar to those given for ALA publications (SHERPA/RoMEO, 2009).

In LIS disciplines, membership organisations such as ACRL have been called upon by librarians to adopt open access publishing models. High-profile library membership organisations such as ACRL have recently had to examine their policies thoroughly to respond to the crisis in scholarly communication, and make the effort to lead by example. Funding is an important facet of the discussion, as publications have been shown to be an important reason for librarians to purchase membership in the organisation. By making prestigious publications free on the web, membership may drop and dues may be increased. In June 2003, ACRL endorsed open access as one of its strategies for dealing with the scholarly communications crisis and published a white paper examining its position (Orphan et al., 2004). By 2003, librarians had called on ALA and ACRL to 'walk the walk' and make their publications open access. In ACRL's case, according to Mary Ellen Davis, then Executive Director of the ACRL Board of Directors, on 10 June, 2004, the issues were 'potential impact of open access on membership, workflow, and cost' (Orphan et al., 2004). Subscription and advertising revenue remain considerations for ACRL, as publications provide its largest net revenue. In a survey of readership, a large proportion of respondents spoke to the value that members place on publications. Since June 2002, ACRL has been a signatory, along with 3,400 others, of the Budapest Open Access Initiative (BOAI). ACRL's journal *College & Research Libraries* has adopted a modified open access model where electronic access to PDFs is free following a six-month embargo period, during which time this current content is restricted to members. Some have considered this to be an 'incomplete realisation of open access' (Suber, 2006b). As a library organisation that advocates for open access, ACRL continues to face criticism for its lack of clarity about author self-archiving policies for its journal *College & Research Libraries*, especially as preprints are now being made available (Suber, 2008a). ACRL now goes one step further by allowing self-archiving of postprints in repositories. While ACRL does not specify subject archives, only institutional repositories, in its statement on the RoMEO site, it may be assumed that subject archives are included. Therefore, a librarian could archive a postprint of an article published in an ACRL journal in a LIS subject repository like E-LIS or dLIST. This self-archiving of the accepted refereed postprint allows the librarian's work to be made available on the web as a Word document (or PDF) while waiting to be published in the journal in both paper and electronic format. As this ACRL literature has moved to a modified open access model, it will take time to see whether fears of declining memberships and funding prove unfounded. For institutional subscribers, an issue arises as to whether stressed library budgets can continue to justify payment of subscriptions for the six months of the publication still behind tolls.

If librarians realise the possible implications for the financial sustainability of their own literature, it is surprising that they advocate so strongly for the opening up of other disciplines' literature, especially the work of cherished scholarly societies who may struggle in an uncertain publishing market and worsening economy. Members of many organisations value their journals, and will continue to pay for membership as long as these journals come to them in a convenient format. Some membership organisations have found that this preference may even extend to print journals delivered to the home. Librarians may not want to advocate for the potential death of their most valued journals in the name of open access. Librarians may be conflicted about support for open access while understanding the plight of the society or smaller publishers. Extensive self-archiving may serve open access while stressing smaller publishers without the reserves or resources of the commercial entities. Publishers, including those in LIS have many concerns about open access. One of the major issues regarding the open access movement for all publishers is the sustainability of funding for new publishing models. In 2007, the Washington DC Principles for Free Access to Science Coalition issued a statement urging caution in order to prevent the erosion of the published literature. The coalition of 75 medical and scientific nonprofit publishers 'opposes any legislation that would abruptly end a publishing system that has nurtured independent scientific inquiry for generations' (Frank, 2007).

Jan Velterop of BioMedCentral has said that by restricting to 'members only', we are not tapping into unusual markets. The question for societies seems to be whether publications should be seen as fundraisers to further the works of the society, or as vehicles for making research more visible and useful. Velterop mentions that open access 'would take science out of its ivory tower isolation by letting non-scientists in' (Velterop, 2003). In library and information science, wider visibility of publications might stimulate more interest in the library field by non-librarians or aspiring librarians. Some librarians, however, may still feel that the traditional library and information science literature may be adversely affected by open access initiatives. Librarians may not be anxious to change their own professional reading behaviours, or may see open access as more of a 'science' issue. More study is needed to determine whether librarians are actually anxious for a change to open access with their own literature, or whether they prefer traditional formats. Once again, librarians may be advocating for other literatures, but not their own.

Cheryl Knott Malone and Anita Coleman (2005) have begun to look at the impact of open access on library and information science. Their study is one of the few that is focused on the LIS education literature, and makes an important point that LIS research is also used widely by librarian practitioners, and hence may need to be studied differently for impact. Librarians often use the LIS research literature to inform their daily decision-making about services and collections, and citation patterns may differ from those in other literatures. More study of the LIS literature as a whole, including citation patterns, might provide insight into the overall potential for open access experimentation by librarians. A few distinct publications or niche areas may be identified for trial of new forms of librarian scholarship. Experimentation on a small scale might be a place to start for the production of new forms of LIS scholarship using open access principles.

Adkins and Budd have studied the scholarly productivity of US LIS faculty to investigate their productivity in terms of research and publication (Adkins and Budd, 2006). Adkins and Budd used citation counts from Social Sciences Citation Index (SSCI) to measure productivity. Using narrow citation metrics to measure the productivity of LIS authors is a concern, however, as many open access publications, especially in the social sciences, are not well represented by Thomson Reuters' SSCI. Adkins and Budd found 'an increase in LIS research productivity, suggesting an increase in faculty effectiveness' and their study lists the most productive researchers and programmes. If some of these more productive researchers adopted a focus on open access, it would send a message to the profession, as these most senior scholars hold great clout in putting an imprimatur on such open access behaviour. A follow-up study could examine the publication outlets of these prominent LIS authors to determine whether they are taking an advocacy position for open access in the library literature. Top LIS programmes could be studied to see if they are leaders in open access advocacy. In addition, faculty in library schools could be modelling and teaching this behaviour to their students, the future academic librarians who will need to publish and share open access advocacy with patrons. LIS teaching faculty and librarians who work as editors are also operating in positions to effect change, unless they are also protecting the journals from changing to new models. Incentive is still an issue for all except those promoting the open access conversation from a library-values perspective, and those pushing for changes in the hope of offsetting the serials crisis that continues to threaten library budgets.

Librarian authors may be choosing a more traditional path to publication, feeling that it may increase their chances of getting positive results from the editor. Having to enquire about posting on the web may be a difficult choice for all authors to make, and librarians may not be any different. Authors may fear that an enquiry about self-archiving might affect acceptance of an article to a top-tier journal. Publication in a high-prestige journal still holds great importance for authors in most fields, including librarianship. Where CTAs are vague, or comprehensive information from a publisher website is lacking, potential librarian authors may not wish to pursue self-archiving. They may worry that even an enquiry regarding web posting might be construed as potentially less than ideal from the editor's or publisher's vantage point, thereby possibly lessening the chances of the article's acceptance.

In 2008, a prominent publication in the LIS arena, *Journal of the American Society for Information Science & Technology* (JASIST), began allowing authors to deposit postprints in repositories with links to the final published article and to the journal. The journal did an extensive survey in 2007 intending to study, in part, whether members of the American Society for Information Science and Technology (ASIS&T), JASIST authors and other information science researchers were participating in the open access movement. Results indicated that, among the 581 responders, 95.7 per cent knew about open access journals, with 60.4 per cent knowing 'a lot' or 'quite a lot' about open access, and only 4 per cent knowing nothing about open access. Interestingly, even with this high level of awareness, 64.7 per cent of the respondents had never published an article in an open access journal (Johnson and Roderer, 2008). This particular study did not report on the self-archiving behaviour of the published LIS authors. This has often been a criticism of studies of the open access movement; that really it is the critical mass of self-archived articles that will tip the scales in favour of changes to current paradigms. For this, authors must be reminded that most of the time they can publish in the journals they want, just making sure to retain rights to post in repositories. As JASIS&T offers LIS authors this option, it will be interesting to see how many of the authors self-archive and whether the journal is affected in any way. As it has not yet been proven that journals will be negatively impacted by a certain degree of self-archiving, more publishers may allow liberal rights for authors. Librarians are able to study their own literature while watching trends in the disciplines they serve.

Feliciter, the newsletter of the Canadian Library Association (CLA), is openly accessible after a one-issue embargo period, authors are encouraged to self-archive, and no embargo period is imposed on self-archived content. Monographs from CLA are 'considered for open access on a case-by-case basis' (Morrison and Waller, 2008). Library associations in particular are in a position to make statements about open access that set a tone for members. In 2008, the CLA put out a strong statement in its 'Position statement on open access for Canadian libraries'. Once again, it remains to be seen what type of accountability, change in actual workflows and assessment will follow the statement that 'Canadian libraries of all types strongly support and encourage open access' (Morrison and Waller, 2008). It may be advantageous if the library community would spell out all of the practical ways that librarians could make a difference in their work in the library, as well as in their writing for publication, and make these lists readily available through national and international membership organisations or other venues. Librarians may be becoming fatigued by advocacy initiatives that make strong statements while not offering practical solutions to library authorship and daily workflows with patrons and collections.

Librarians may have to be able to discuss aspects of copyright and permissions with some of their users. Many researchers and authors in an institution may find keeping up with changes in this area daunting and time-consuming, and may turn to librarians for consultation. More experience with their own archiving of publications would enable librarians to develop expertise, making it easier to assist and develop best practices for other faculty in the institution. Conversely, librarians who may not write for publication themselves may be unfamiliar with the whole area of author rights, CTAs or fair use, and find that these topics lie outside of their skill set and knowledgebase. All academic librarians will have to become aware of the mechanics of self-archiving in all disciplines with which they interact in consulting roles. Each library would need to have a knowledgeable point person to offer assistance to other librarians and faculty seeking information in these areas. More training, even integration into public services initiatives, may be needed to bridge any gaps in understanding of open access strategies if library advocacy efforts are to be effective and widespread. Programmes targeted at student and faculty groups as part of advocacy campaigns may still not change the daily practical work of librarians.

Institutional repositories and subject archiving for LIS authors

One of the biggest initiatives promoting and affecting open access potential in many universities and colleges is the library's development of the institutional repository. As more libraries develop institutional repositories, librarians may feel pressure to be the early depositors in the fledgling services. Without librarians as role models, or at least participants, it may be harder to 'sell' the repository to other faculty and potential depositors. Policies and information about institutional repositories as well as other digital archives may be listed in the Registry of Open Access Repository Material Archiving Policies (ROARMAP; *http://www.eprints.org/openaccess/policysignup/*) or in the Register of Open Access Repositories (ROAR). ROARMAP lists the existence of open access archives and policies as well as displaying a complete listing of institutional, departmental and funder mandates.

Librarians may be depositing their work in institutional repositories alongside teaching faculty, and this type of archiving would help return ownership to authors and institutions. Librarians using institutional repositories to make their own publications available and including these services in informational sources like ROARMAP would allow more vocal advocacy with other potential depositors. Librarians who wish to self-archive accepted articles in support of open access will have to decide whether to use the institutional repository (as long as its contents are exposed to Google or other search engines) or to archive in one of the popular LIS subject repositories. Librarians will need to understand the implications of their choices; including whether to archive and where. Motivations will differ for each librarian and for each piece of scholarly writing.

Current examples of subject-based open access digital repositories available for self-archiving by librarian authors and library researchers include E-LIS: The Open Archive for Library and Information Science' (*http://eprints.rclis.org/*) and the Digital Library for Information Science and Technology (dLIST) (*http://dlist.sir.arizona.edu/*). These two major subject archives allow librarians to deposit their work, whether preprint, postprint, or unrefereed. E-LIS, opened in 2003, is based on GNU Eprints archive-creating software, and states its purpose as 'to make full text of LIS documents visible, accessible, harvestable, searchable, usable by any potential user with access to the internet. Also supports individuals who wish to publish or otherwise make their papers available worldwide'. E-LIS has been established as a community service by Research in Computing, Library and Information Science. The E-LIS website also describes its aim as being 'to further the open access philosophy by making available papers in the LIS and related fields'. E-LIS has features that allow librarians to gather their research output in one place on the web to be accessible from anywhere. It can provide a URL for each item that can be sent to anyone, and can provide download statistics by country. Number of downloads can be reported by librarians as a potential measure of impact. E-LIS allows a librarian to contribute research material to a common archive and to share work with the community of scholars in the discipline (Machovec et al., 2006). E-LIS contains 9,000 full-text documents from more than 5,600 authors as of April 2009, and has worked on standardising and communicating its policies. Showing the international scope of its LIS contributors, E-LIS contains documents in 37 languages from 90 countries (De Robbio and Katzmayr, 2009).

DLIST describes itself as a 'cross-institutional, subject-based, open access digital archive for the Information Sciences, including Archives and Records Management, Library and Information Science, Information Systems, Museum Informatics and other critical information infrastructures' (*http://dlist.sir.arizona.edu/*). It has a distinguished advisory board, allows simple and advanced search, provides detailed usage statistics for individual e-prints, and has a registered user area for authors to submit their work to the archives. Subject archives have different levels of collection development oversight, and an editor or group of subject experts vet submissions. Generally, the archive would accept original author submissions that fit scope and purpose. Few studies have focused on the usability and usefulness of open access digital libraries specifically, but it would make sense that subject repositories would need to focus not just on content but on user satisfaction with the interface and search capability. Tsakonas and Papatheodorou (2008) have described a study of usability and usefulness factors in E-LIS. It is important for librarians interested in the success of repositories to move away from simply discussing economics, scalability and deposit issues, and to remember that digital library systems will not be successful if the user experience is not placed at the forefront. Librarians are reminded that 'one of the major challenges that e-prints face is to become self-sustainable systems closely linked with users' work tasks, instead of gradually transform[ing] into graveyards of invaluable documents' (Tsakonas and Papatheodorou, 2008). These systems need to provide web discoverability and interoperability, or risk becoming yet another 'silo' that is not obviously integrated into the library.

Potential librarian contributors to LIS subject repositories may feel conflicted when choosing between depositing in the institutional repository or a wider library subject archive. Individual library leadership should provide clear guidance about the benefits or expectations regarding the archiving behaviour of librarians, even discussing whether contributing librarian work, whether preprint, postprint or presentation is considered a library 'value' or a beneficial behaviour for librarians seeking promotion and tenure. Again, incentive is important for researchers of all disciplines in choosing which type of repository will be best for individual or institutional purpose.

As for the actual process, archiving work in either of these LIS repositories is a simple ten-minute process, and the archives are searchable by the DL-Harvest search engine. DL-Harvest is a federated archive, and brings together full-text scholarly materials from different repositories, including selective harvesting from arXiv, E-LIS and dLIST. DL-Harvest has basic and advanced search, and includes LIS pathfinders and other material of interest to LIS researchers and readers. Librarians may begin to use DL-Harvest to do a targeted subject or author search of LIS material (Coleman and Roback, 2005). DL-Harvest may be seen as a subject portal for the LIS discipline that links to quality free content. Of course, it is important to remind fellow librarians that all major search engines, such as Google and Google Scholar, also crawl both disciplinary archives and most institutional repository content. Librarians choosing to archive their work in repositories would make their work more visible to the world while increasing their personal research impact. In addition, by depositing their own work, it would be easier for librarians to sell the idea of the institutional or subject repository as a useful tool to increase web visibility of scholarly work and by extension promote open access. There are some disciplines where subject archives have become part of the scholarly culture (such as arXiv for physics) but this does not seem to be the case quite yet with LIS. It would seem that any discipline could be well served by having one or two prominent disciplinary repositories serving as a 'one-stop shop' for the corpus of the field's research literature, making it available to researchers on a global level. These repositories could become as well-known as other popular LIS tools if critical mass could be reached and librarians worked to market such a concept.

Librarians who have access to major LIS indexes and databases might be satisfied to search for background literature in a traditional manner, and may not want to seek out repository content that may or may not have been peer-reviewed. Repository material may be considered valuable for librarians as background reading, but may not be seen as a source of definitive citable articles that can be easily used in LIS writing and scholarship. As with some other subjects, repository content might not be considered the top priority for researchers, except for those who do not have access to research libraries or LIS collections through their institutions or interlibrary loan. Librarians and other researchers alike may be finding repository content through searches of major search engines such as Google, and not necessarily take note of the archiving behaviour that made the articles available. As researchers 'search and find' using Google, many are already utilising disciplinary or institutional archives for 'informal' research purposes.

Integrating LIS and other disciplines' repositories into the library

Librarians will also have to give some real thought to bringing the subject repositories with their search capabilities and content into the library web space. Repositories can be searched separately, or their contents discovered via search engines such as Google Scholar. Where scholarly literature in many versions is found on the web, as in repositories, librarians need to be cognisant of how this material meshes with existing collections as well as what type of discoverability the library can and should provide. Integrating subject repositories will need to be considered along with issues of the institutional repository in terms of library collections and services. This is an issue for public services, instruction, and especially in the discussion about new scholarly communication practices in a very discipline-specific manner. Further study is needed to understand how academic libraries are handling these newer sources of scholarly materials, making them discoverable and accessible, and consulting on their citation and use. Along with the LIS subject repositories, librarians handling various disciplines will need to work to integrate the repositories of those disciplines into library collections and services. The library website, reference services, instruction and collection development will need to make plans to integrate and promote these sources of important scholarly material.

It remains to be seen how extensive the practice of author self-archiving in repositories has become to this point, or could be expected into the future. Knowledge of uptake trends would allow librarians to plan integration of repository materials into collections and services. One ongoing initiative investigating effects of green open access (self-archiving) in terms of 'user access, author visibility, and journal viability' is known as Publishing and the Ecology of European Research (PEER). PEER is a collaboration of publishers, repositories and the research community studying at least 16,000 peer-reviewed manuscripts per year (for three years) with European first authors from ISI-ranked journals (*http://www.peerproject.eu/*). This is an attempt to understand the roles that repositories are playing and how journals might in turn be affected by green open access practices. Librarians must keep an eye on all such studies in order to determine whether there will be implications, especially when it comes to potential availability of repository alternatives to relieve some of the cost of traditional peer-reviewed journal scholarship. This critical point where journals are being affected by self-archiving would vary by discipline, and this is something for the subject-specialist librarian to be monitoring.

Publishers are quick to respond with information about the value-added content and services that repositories cannot provide. These publisher features important to library users include such things as sophisticated search platforms with linking out to supplementary materials, and a lot of capital invested in ongoing technological development. Publishers have also commented that open access will not increase library funding, decrease costs of publishing peer-reviewed scholarship or generate the kind of increased revenue that can be invested in future development (Regazzi, 2004).

SPARC lists eight disciplines where subject-based repositories have emerged as 'digital extensions of existing peer-to-peer research communication practice'. These disciplines are: 'high-energy physics and mathematics (arXiv); working papers in economics (RePEc); cognitive science (CogPrints); astronomy, astrophysics, and geophysics (NTRS and ADS); and computer science (NCSTRL)' (Crow, 2002). Humanities scholars have not had a prominent subject repository, but in 2009 the Social Science Research Network (SSRN) created the Humanities Research Network, and will be starting with philosophy, classics, and English and American literature (Howard, 2007). Even without an established culture of preprints, librarians could be more proactive in moving their LIS literature to a model where self-archiving would be more common. It would involve changes in behaviour and culture among librarian authors as well as library and information science researchers. Many assumptions can be entertained about the slow uptake of self-archiving behaviour by librarians, and more study is necessary in evaluating the behaviour of a group that has advocated so strongly for open access at the institutional, national and international levels.

Librarians as authors in the journal literature

In many fields, it has been shown that authors submitting articles to the peer-reviewed journal literature have concerns about the quality and prestige of open access journals. The main reason for not publishing their work in open access journals is that these authors are unfamiliar with the open access journals in their particular fields. In their comprehensive study of self-archiving behaviour, Swan and Brown (2005) report that the most important reason that authors report for publishing in open access journals is the 'principle of free access' and that their main concerns are 'impact and grants'. In addition, more rapid publication was cited as another reason to adopt open access behaviour. There are many available options for LIS authors, including fully open access journals or the traditional journals that allow liberal self-archiving. Librarians keeping up with the open access debate will be able to make informed decisions about submissions of their own articles to the professional literature. Over time, other librarians will see whether increased visibility of individual librarians' or LIS researchers' work has benefited the individual or their library or institution in some tangible way. Librarians who have successfully self-archived or used open access journals should either anecdotally or quantitatively report results back to the profession. Showing increased web visibility, or research impact would encourage other librarians to pursue open access choices for their published work.

In some fields, such as medicine, there have been recent legislative initiatives to mandate the open access publishing of research results. Obviously, these initiatives result from demands for quick access to medical breakthroughs that are financed through taxpayer funding. Grant funding can be designated for open access publication charges in 'author-pays' journals. The LIS literature has no such mandate pressure, and very little library research receives funding. Lack of grant funding of library research would also doom the 'author pays' model of open access publishing for librarians. Fees to publish scholarly work would not work for librarians unless the academy supported such efforts with dedicated funding. Because librarians are not often funded in their research, they would most likely avoid any journal that charges fees either for publication or submission, regardless of reputation or stature. The 'partial author payment model' where page charges are levied to authors, although tolerated in some disciplines such as life sciences where many of the journals are published by society publishers, would not be a viable model for the library literature (Davis et al., 2004). Librarians may be attracted to certain open access journals for reasons such as the absence of submission fees, page charges or other publication fees.

Librarians must advocate for the LIS literature. Librarians may not have forged a place at the table in the discussion as scholars. Librarian authors are often not referred to as scholars. Suber says that 'If I'm right that librarians have the best understanding of the problem, and that scholars control the solution, then collaboration is highly desirable' (Suber, 2003). Practising academic librarians may have an enhanced role as facilitators and consultants for other scholars, alongside a role (with library school departmental teaching faculty) for scholarly communication in the subject areas of LIS. Besides responsibility for management, Geyde describes the significant role of librarians in open access as 'crusaders, educators, investors, aggregators, and developers'. These roles would have the 'ultimate goal of supporting an easily accessible, interconnected international network of quality research, available to all who might need to use it' (Gedye, 2004). Geyde's list of roles ascribed to librarians does not include authors, researchers or publishers. These are all increasingly common roles for academic librarians today. Goodman (2004) mentions 'the ability to assist in and observe the process of research', rather than seeing librarians as a group conducting actual research. Some members of the library profession may be promoting the viewpoint that practising academic librarians are really not the scholars and researchers, but some other type of participant in the research process. This will be reflected in the library literature and its inability to be considered truly scholarly material. In some ways, it may become peripheral as open access models evolve. Waters (2006) advocates for the advancement of discipline-specific standards and practices in terms of particular applications and technologies that will advance open access. Librarians, if divided on the identity of their scholarly purpose, will have a more difficult time coming together to advance the LIS disciplines in terms of open access to their respective literature. While focusing on open access to STEM literature, and building institutional repositories, have librarians forgotten to focus on the literature of their own discipline?

Montanelli and Stenstrom (1986) argue that librarians who do research are more responsive to change and innovation. These librarians may be more aware of discussions in the literature and at conferences about changes in scholarly communication and how these are affecting the LIS literature. Pressure to publish may encourage librarians to keep up with new paradigms, and to attend conference presentations about issues such as open access or institutional repository development. Librarians with faculty status seeking promotion and tenure in academic institutions (as well as LIS teaching faculty) are required to pursue important current scholarly research for publication. Their literature, and the business models used in its publication, should certainly reflect the most current models of scholarly communication available in the academy, especially given the prominence of librarians' advocacy for open access.

Librarians in their roles as journal editors

Librarians working as editors or reviewers for some of the LIS journals are giving away expertise free in many cases, and must keep an eye on changing publication models. Although some editors are paid, many are not, and their libraries must, in turn, purchase back the material in the edited journal. In their relationships with commercial publishers as journal editors, librarians and LIS faculty are well positioned to become advocates for a move toward more open access, as they will not only see visibility and impact of individual articles increase, but the visibility of the journal's brand will also become more widespread. Librarian editors and reviewers may not have taken a stand for open access with the publications with which they are affiliated.

Editors have sometimes become advocates for new business models by walking away from a commercial publisher, even taking the editorial board with them, and starting an entirely new journal. In a movement of support, some academic libraries may choose to cancel any journal where the entire editorial board has resigned. The new journal, although starting with a new name and publisher, may have a long way to go to reach the name recognition of its former iteration. Still, this move away from the runaway profit motives of certain commercial publishers may be more in line with the mission of the journal and the interests of its audience. This is especially true for LIS journals, where it may become difficult to struggle with the bills for the largest publishers as they engulf the library's budget, and then give away expertise and professional time through editorial work to the same publishers. The adoption of more liberal self-archiving policies on the part of the commercial publisher may assuage much of the concern that authors and editors may have over the lack of visibility of published work on the open web. Librarians and LIS faculty working as editors can have influence on individual journal open access policies.

Within LIS, the most notable example of the exodus of almost an entire editorial board was in 1998, when the editor and board of the *Journal of Academic Librarianship* departed to form *portal: Libraries and the Academy* (Swan and Brown, 2004b). *Journal of Academic Librarianship*, published by Elsevier, has recently relaxed its copyright restrictions for authors, allowing some forms of self-archiving, and within the LIS field is still a successful publication in terms of prestige. *portal* has also developed a reputation of excellence, and was listed as the title 'most left off the list of most prestigious journals' in a recent survey of library literature (Nisonger and Davis, 2005). While these moves in support of open access are certainly laudable and understandable, the end result was that libraries now must be able to access two journals, for which the cost is higher. This was a statement, but not a solution for libraries.

It has been suggested that editors of LIS journals would find value in meeting as a group to discuss open access issues. This would allow a conversation about the unique place that the library literature holds in the discussion of open access alternatives and the pressure that could possibly exist for that collective literature to adopt forward-thinking policies. In an effort to meet to discuss best practices for LIS journals, a small group of LIS editors was brought together by Charles Lowry, Editor of *portal*, and Joseph Branin, Editor of *College & Research Libraries* (Branin and Lowry, 2008). Future forums of LIS editors are planned, and this type of collaborative discussion may lead to some common understandings that will serve prospective librarian authors well and provide a framework for possible action in a collective sense for the LIS literature.

Hierarchy and prestige of LIS journals

As in other disciplines, there is a hierarchy of prestige among LIS journals. The study by Nisonger and Davis (2005) lists the top journals as rated by both LIS deans and directors, as well as by librarians. Although the two groups rate the prestige of certain journals differently, there is a consistency with previous studies. The findings of the current study replicate the study by Kohl and Davis (1985). These studies used the journal ranking criteria of citation data (impact factor and total citation counts) as well as the recorded perceptions of domain experts in LIS. Six of the top ten journals overlap between the results from the two groups (LIS deans and LIS directors). Many have held this elite status for the past 20 years (Nisonger and Davis, 2005). Of course, these studies do not take into account any of the new journals, whether traditional or born-digital open access. Even with changes in scholarly communication, and the large amount of discussion about open access advocacy by librarians, ratings of journals in LIS areas have remained remarkably stable over time. It would seem, due to consistency of stature over time, that these 'highest prestige' journals would need to take a lead in moving to open access in their publication models, and in their relaxation of copyright restrictions. Further study of the publishing patterns of librarian authors submitting work to these top journals would be able to determine whether authors are self-archiving and seeking more visibility for their work alongside reaping the benefits of the added prestige of the branded journals. A study of librarian self-archiving behaviour restricted to top journals may be illustrative in terms of whether librarians really feel that open access to scholarship is of utmost importance. It may be that publication in a specific journal regardless of web availability is the goal of many librarian authors. Librarians may be aggressively promoting open access behaviour in conferences, symposia and in their everyday work with other user groups, while not practising it with their own literature. Changes to promotion guidelines for librarians mandating open access of their work prior to assembling a tenure dossier may change behaviour. An interesting note regarding the survey by Nisonger and Davis is that 13 of the libraries approached could not complete the questionnaire because their libraries did not collect LIS literature and there was a 'lack of knowledge about the journals', with one dean reporting a desire for some of the journals to 'cease' (Nisonger and Davis, 2005). There may be a feeling that there are enough LIS journals in the market at the present time. This may not be the case with the research corpus of other academic disciplines, where the journals of the discipline may be more uniformly highly regarded. It would seem that librarians in a collective sense must take ownership for the quality and the economic sustainability of the LIS literature. Subject-specialist librarians may be more involved in analysis of the journals in the disciplines for which they are responsible in their everyday jobs. Most librarians may not follow the LIS literature closely. One wonders how many academic librarians intend to submit their work to any of the new or established LIS open access journals, and how well these journals are marketed to librarians both for adding to collections as well as for article submission. Only a few of these publications can be considered well-established within the LIS community. Adding to difficulties in making generalisations about trends in library publishing is the fact that librarians publish in many interdisciplinary areas, such as information and computer science, psychology and business.

While working for Elsevier, Tagler (2005) spoke with librarians about open access and alternative publishing models and found that 'reaction has been mixed'. He also stated that libraries might fear budget cuts if open access were to become a successful alternative and wondered whether open access would cause libraries to lose buying power and result in 'declining influence'. Another commercial publisher's representative, Oxford Journals' Richard Gedye, felt that librarians need to adopt a 'crusader role' and

> lobby for change (both within and outside their institutions), and to educate their researchers to understand all the issues surrounding OA (and Oxford Journals' research with authors shows that there are still a majority who know and understand very little). (Gedye, 2004)

Still, moving toward open access may represent a conflict of interest for many in academic libraries.

Many LIS journals do not have an impact factor as reported by Thomson Reuters in its Journal Citation Reports. This makes it more difficult to talk about journal 'success' in terms of the tradition of impact factors. As impact will be measured in many different ways in the future, and new metrics are currently emerging, there may soon be more ways to quantify the impact of LIS publications. Eigenfactor (*http://www .eigenfactor.org/*) has now been added to the citation analysis toolkit for journal impact, and is also currently reported in Journal Citation Reports. Librarians are some of the experts in studies of citation analysis, and there are entire LIS journals built around scientometrics, informetrics and other related areas of information science. This makes the LIS community an obvious one to enhance citation studies of the discipline, and take a lead in evaluating all types of open access journals for quality.

Besides Web of Science, citation analysis for articles in LIS publications can now also be found in Google Scholar, Scopus and some subject-specific databases. Google Scholar covers open access materials, listing all versions of an article, including those deposited in repositories. A study by Meho and Yang (2007) has studied the citations to the work of 25 LIS faculty members as a case study using Web of Science versus Scopus and Google Scholar. They conclude that for LIS, a more accurate and comprehensive picture of the scholarly impact of authors can be found by using all three citation analysis sources. In the future, institutions and libraries may need access to all of these tools in order to assess scholars' work if their open access publications will be taken into account alongside any traditionally published works. Tools such as Google Scholar, free on the web, will also aid discovery of open access materials, and more of an author's total output including archived e-prints will be visible when reporting impact.

LIS abstracting and indexing services

Many of the most well-known abstracting and indexing (A&I) services in many fields, especially those covering the STEM literature, are now including open access journal publications. Have the LIS indexes, most notably Library and Information Science Abstracts (LISA), Library, Information Science & Technology Abstracts (LISTA), and Library Literature & Information Science Full Text followed suit or been mavericks in this area? It appears that all of these major LIS subject indexes are including some open access journals in their coverage of the literature. A cursory look at coverage lists of citation indexing sources that include LIS journals also shows that Elsevier's Scopus and Thomson Reuters' Web of Science now include coverage of open access journals from many fields. Other popular indexes, such as PsycINFO, have included open access journals that meet their stringent criteria (APA, 2007). Indexes do not need to discriminate based on business model or format when vetting journal titles for coverage in selective indexing services. Open access journals can be evaluated using similar criteria as more traditional titles. Librarians can promote indexes that include open access resources, thereby reiterating the fact that open access does not mean not peer-reviewed. Google and Google Scholar also provide searching of open access LIS publications and subject repository content. These search engines for the LIS open access literature can be useful to librarians and researchers wishing to conduct comprehensive searches of the scholarly literature of librarianship.

LIS weblogs covering open access topics

Librarians are increasingly keeping up with important trends, as well as participating in the open access discussion in real time by reading and commenting in the LIS weblogs, of which the list is long. There are now library weblogs entirely devoted to open access for librarians. It is possible for librarians to keep up with scholarly communications news as well as the current state of the art by following the open access library blogs. Some notable examples found through a web search are Open Access News, DigitalKoans, OA Librarian, Open Access Archivangelism, and Heather Morrison's Imaginary Journal of Poetic Economics. An example of a useful blog dedicated to copyright and scholarly communications issues which highlights an institution's activities is Kevin Smith's Duke Scholarly Communications (*http://library.duke.edu/blogs/scholcomm/*).

With so many choices as regards LIS blogs, it is even possible to find one in a niche area. Some are group efforts, while others, such as Suber's Open Access News, are the work of a single person. Many allow recent material to be pushed to e-mail through RSS feeds, and this allows news to come to the reader as developments occur. Open Access News attempts to provide more news and less commentary, and is very useful for any librarian wishing to remain current on open access issues. LIS blogs can pull together much of the burgeoning literature of the open access movement, making it possible for busy librarians to keep up with the exponential growth of the literature now devoted to scholarly communication concerns in academic libraries. Web 2.0 tools associated with blogs help librarians to interact with others interested in open access and to expand their network of interested parties. It would be best to see the broadest possible international conversation represented in reactions to blog posts. Without broad representation from more librarians on the front-lines, the open access discussion often seems somewhat of a niche conversation. Facebook, the immensely popular social networking site, includes a group labelled 'Librarians who support open access' (Facebook, 2009). Even Facebook can be a gathering place for librarians interested in open access, and may attract a new group who can translate rhetoric into action. A wiki for the open access community is currently hosted by the Graduate School of Library and Information Science at Simmons College in Boston. The Open Access Directory wiki seeks to provide a site for anyone interested in open access to participate in the dissemination of information on the movement as it affects libraries (*http://oad.simmons.edu/oadwiki/Main_Page*). With so many venues for conversation, surely the open access conversation can translate to action and change in libraries.

LISZEN: Library & Information Science Search Engine, the new aggregator blog search, crawls more than 600 specific LIS blogs and is helpful for subject-specific background reading (*http://liszen.com/*). Librarians must become increasingly aware of search and discovery tools outside the traditional indexes and abstracts for their own literature as well as that of their constituencies. Even blog postings may be considered 'publications' by some, and librarians will be interested to evaluate all types of new entrants into publication about research topics. Sustainability may be an issue with many free tools available to the library world. Funding and manpower shortages may impede some efforts even as the web provides space for international discussion of open access.

As useful as blogs are, there is some evidence that due to information overload or other factors, librarians may not be reading as many blogs on a regular basis as is often assumed. Librarians wishing to be consultants to faculty in the disciplines as well as accurate in the information they share in public services capacities will find it essential to keep up with current LIS literature on open access. This is a fast-moving area, very discipline-specific, and today's academic librarians may be busier than ever before as libraries respond to budget concerns and retirements. According a recent study of librarians' attitudes about 'keeping up', only 28 per cent of respondents to a large-scale survey used blogs to stay current, and only 15 per cent used RSS aggregators or XML readers (Hardesty and Sugarman, 2007). This survey of over 700 librarians studied the ways that librarians attempt to keep up with new trends and technologies in this time of information overload. A combination of reading listservs and journal articles along with attending conferences proved most popular, while reading blogs and following up on RSS feeds proved less popular. Keeping up with listservs allows time-pressed librarians to keep sufficiently up to date with the open access movement to remain conversant with their constituencies.

There are many listservs (or electronic mailing lists) such as Liblicense where trends in scholarly communications that affect LIS disciplines are discussed on a daily basis (*http://www.library.yale.edu/~llicense*). Librarians desiring to follow the open access discussion in real time would benefit from accessing Liblicense, a moderated list where many of the most prominent names in the worldwide discussion of open access weigh in on a regular basis. This list and others also bring together related stakeholders in one conversation. To truly understand open access and how it might affect libraries, the dialogue would have to include all of the major stakeholders in a more or less ongoing conversation as participants react to a currently changing landscape. Liblicense includes this variety of voices. Although the many high-profile contributors make this list one of the best ways to keep up with open access trends, it is also possible for academic librarians to post questions or concerns to the list. For those librarians interested in researching open access topics, the Liblicense list might be the first place that new trends are spotted. This informal online open access discussion is another manifestation of the intersection of interests of publishers, librarians, attorneys and researchers in working together to understand new scholarly communication paradigms. Curiously, because readers see the same names as contributors on popular open access discussion listservs, it becomes difficult to gauge whether there is widespread interest on the part of academic librarians generally. Interested librarians have access to other lists and social networking tools where open access topics can be broached and the conversation widened to other groups of librarians, or niche disciplinary areas.

Open access journals for librarians

Beyond discussion of informal communication channels for librarians to keep up with open access, there is a growing outlet for librarian publication of more formal scholarship in the form of quality born-digital open access journals that accept submissions without fees, and provide peer-reviewed articles free to readers. It would seem that librarians would want to move their many discussions of all LIS topics (including open access) to these publications, especially articles formerly destined for toll journals. An optimal situation for supporting new scholarship forms exists through submission of scholarly articles to one of the open access peer-reviewed journals produced and edited by librarians. Communication would be facilitated, ideas shared more ubiquitously, and the library literature would be in the hands of librarians and authors without the burden of the profit agendas of commercial firms. Commercial publishers must reinvest any money made back into product development and there is risk of failure for journals that are not money-makers. With different motivations, society publishers may use any surplus not only to support the journal but to finance meetings or fund research (Drake, 2007). Librarians may, on the other hand, understand how their own organisations need to monetise their activities and be on board with support for publications emanating out of their membership organisations, even if there are embargoes or tolls levied.

The library literature, categorised within social sciences, has been slow to join the move to open access. Librarians seem willing to move scholarly communication forward for others in related fields while in some ways ignoring their own. Librarians who work with LIS collections in major research libraries know the history of price increases through the 1980s and 1990s that have affected their ability to subscribe to many of the journals covering the field's scholarly output. Some of the advocacy surrounding LIS price increases may have fallen on deaf ears as the price of STEM journals was skyrocketing into much higher ranges. Important early born-digital LIS journals were started in 1995 and 1996. *D-Lib Magazine* was originally published by the nonprofit Corporation for National Research Initiatives and funded by the US Defense Advanced Research Projects Agency and the National Science Foundation, and is still a successful open access journal focused on digital library research and development. *Ariadne*, published in the UK by UKOLN with funding from the Museums, Libraries and Archives Council, the Joint Information Systems Committee (JISC) and other government bodies, also continues as a successful LIS open access journal based at the University of Bath (Wilson, 2005). These two journals stand as examples of success in LIS open access publishing. Another interesting case study of the development since 1999 of a successful open access journal serving the LIS community is that of *E-JASL: The Journal of Academic and Special Librarianship*, which is described as an example of the 'platinum' or 'voluntary, collaborative, no charge model' of publishing (Haschak, 2007).

Recently, more open access LIS journals have been emerging, such as the debut of *Open Access Research* (*http://ojs.gsu.edu/index.php/oar*), which, although sounding promising as a library-published journal on exactly this topic, has not published any issues as of this writing. Undoubtedly, many librarians have wondered why there has been no open access LIS journal devoted solely to the topic of open access, especially knowing the current capability for LIS publishing out of repositories or other team-based library publishing programmes.

E-JASL and the *Journal of Information Literacy* are other examples of members of the LIS profession starting valuable journal publications using open access formats and open source journal systems. Other open access journals that focus on LIS areas are *LIBRES: Library and Information Science Research Electronic Journal*, *Library Philosophy and Practice*, *Webology* and *School Library Media Research*. Still, one wonders why there are not more library-published and edited open access LIS journals. Many academic libraries' academic open access journal publishing efforts focus on the literature of other disciplines. Librarians possess the unusual ability to utilise the support of their libraries to become publishers, authors and editors of their own literature. Librarians are able to assume major roles in publishing library-related journals while sharing important scholarly library literature free with a worldwide audience online if they so desire, and if their libraries and institutions support such publishing efforts. Creative solutions have been utilised when sustainability of funding has become an issue. *D-Lib Magazine*, a popular journal for libraries, at one point adopted a reduced publication schedule and asked institutions to support the journal in a time of funding uncertainty going forward (Lannom, 2007). In 2007, *D-Lib Magazine* created the D-Lib Alliance and began accepting donations in order to ensure the financial stability of this 'free to read' open access LIS journal. A list of supporting organisations (including academic libraries) is listed along with the amounts of their donations (*D-Lib Magazine*, 2007). Will librarians feel they should support these initiatives, even if it means redirecting funding from other areas? In this interesting case, library support for open access has meant that some libraries have paid a fee for all readers worldwide to have access to the literature of *D-Lib Magazine*. Library advocacy groups would applaud libraries that 'put their money where their mouth is'. Someone has to pay for open access, and if not authors, then libraries will decide whether they can and should pay to support journals in this way. Library budgets may allow for redirecting money from commercial journals, or this may be another add-on cost for stretched academic libraries.

Librarians as publishers of open access journals

Even though librarians and other authors may be eager to send their work to well-known publishers, whether society or commercial, they may also be interested in supporting the libraries that have taken on the role of publisher. Librarians, especially, may wish to publish their work under the imprimatur of a high-level research library. If libraries ultimately become the publishers of their journals, then librarian authors may worry less about sustainability, editorial continuity, solid metadata development, knowledge of indexing, and digital preservation of content. On the other hand, this type of system may be viewed as too insular, especially if the editors, reviewers, readers and authors are all from the LIS community. Some of the journals are new, and librarians may not wish to submit articles until these journals show longevity.

The number of open access journals in LIS continues to increase, and titles may be found in popular directories and indexes. By 2009, the Directory of Open Access Journals (DOAJ) included 94 social science journals under the heading of 'library and information science' (*http://www.doaj.org/*). Many major subject indexes also now include open access journals. Open access publishing and business models do not preclude full acceptance into any sources of scholarly journal listings or collections. Librarians may have to keep pressing for the pulling together of all scholarly resources, regardless of business model or format, into catalogues, weblists, indexes, databases, and any other common sources of information related to scholarly journals. This may be the model for the future library, no different than in the past; the 'place' for vetting, gathering, organising and making the scholarly literature discoverable and accessible.

By becoming publishers of open access journals, librarians would be following a mission to make the journal literature more accessible to all. However, librarians must be concerned that there are still problems with access to electronic material due to issues of availability of technology and adequate policies related to free electronic access to information. Librarians have a great interest in the lessening of the 'digital divide'. Suber (2007b) reminds librarians that there are still impediments for many readers. Access issues for some include filtering, censorship, language, handicap access, and connectivity barriers. A move to open access would be a step in lessening the digital divide, but is only part of the solution to the complex issues of information equity and democratisation.

A few academic libraries have taken on the role of open access journal publisher for faculty editors in other disciplines. Librarians, using their digital expertise and open source software, have undertaken a new role in assisting faculty editors with the start-up of scholarly, peer-reviewed journals. In most cases, these journals are born digital, although in some cases the journals have transitioned from a former print format. Librarians are often acting as the publishers in these cases, and in a few cases, the editors. There is no impediment to any role for an academic librarian with open access journals, whether editor, author, reviewer or publisher, even as issues of sustainability and funding remain. Especially for libraries that have developed a robust institutional repository, publishing journals for departmental faculty can be a highly desirable extension of the library mission and librarian roles. To some librarians, the library as publisher can seem a conflict of mission as well as an expensive proposition. Traditional publishers wonder how libraries can become publishers, seeing the skill set as decidedly different.

A new role for the subject specialist in open access journal publishing

In the case of the library-published open access journal, a subject-specialist librarian can be a great asset to the publishing team. These librarians use their knowledge of subject-specific indexes, databases and open access directories to assist in increasing the visibility and credibility of the library-published open access journal. This type of marketing effort can be an interesting new role for liaison librarians who are seeking new ways to collaborate with teaching faculty editors. The success of the journal will depend on the quality of submissions, as well as the visibility and potential impact that potential authors can anticipate. Subject indexes in many cases are actively seeking quality peer-reviewed journals to cover, and more are indexing open access journals all the time. The climate is good for the marketing of library-published journals to the abstracting and indexing services.

Subject-specialist librarians would ostensibly know which indexes would lend credibility to a new open access publication, and would also be able to make contact with these database producers through established contacts. The subject librarian may have a working relationship with those at the publication and production offices of the subject index. Library conferences provide an opportunity for librarians to network with publishers and vendors of indexes and databases, and to discuss the new journals while engaged in committee work, as well as more informally with colleagues working in the same subject area. Subject-specific librarian listservs are tailor-made for the advertisement of new open access journals both within the home institution and in the greater scholarly community.

A librarian acting as faculty liaison may be seeking these new opportunities to use subject-specific library expertise, and may market the use of repository digital publishing capability as a new way to connect with departmental faculty. The librarian becomes a consultant and liaison on scholarly communication issues while actively increasing the visibility of the open access journal. The journal can expect to attain more success as measured in visibility and downloads through added marketing assistance by the subject librarian. Adding indexing and marketing, along with the existing web-crawling by major search engines, ensures maximum visibility and credibility of the library-published open access journal. Through the librarian's outreach efforts on behalf of the journal, the home library and institution gains visibility as an active supporter of open access.

Academic libraries would also be expected to have a librarian who is a known expert in copyright policy, and this person would be able to consult on such matters for the fledgling journal and advise the faculty editor. The open access journal team could include digital library publishing specialist, library copyright specialist, teaching faculty or library faculty editor, subject specialist as marketing consultant, scholarly communications committee chair and budget officer. Digital specialist librarians and bibliographers will increasingly work together using complementary expertise. This is an example of a new paradigm of librarian teamwork and exciting expansion of roles for librarians looking for new challenges. Journals may decide to feature the 'librarian consultant' on their web page, giving further credibility to the publication.

Many libraries have decided to support open access initiatives by publishing open access journals for scholars in other fields from within their home institutions, thereby increasing the type of services that the library can offer. For instance, the Rutgers University Libraries publish *Pragmatic Case Studies in Psychotherapy*, an open access journal that covers an area of psychology. A statement about the publishing activities of the Rutgers University Libraries is presented on the journal's homepage (*http://pcsp.libraries.rutgers.edu/*). Libraries will need to identify sustainable funding for publishing efforts, or risk losing credibility as publishers of open access journals. Libraries must be careful about redirecting money from traditional collections while those resources are still in demand from researchers.

Open access journals published by the Rutgers University Libraries

At Rutgers University, two of the peer-reviewed open access journals published by the university libraries are now included in many indexing sources. Both *Electronic Journal of Boundary Elements* (EJBE) and *Pragmatic Case Studies in Psychotherapy* (PCSP) have found entry into high-level indexing services, and have become successful journals. PCSP is now indexed in PsycINFO, and has applied to other major indexes. EJBE is indexed in Chemical Abstracts Service and Mathematical Reviews. In the case of PCSP, the present author has also acted as a contact for the faculty editor for any issues regarding subject indexes, online directories and search engines, cataloguing issues, and inclusion in specific areas of the libraries' website. Potential authors want to ensure quality, credibility and potential for impact, not only by evidence of peer review by a distinguished editorial board, but also because the open access journal is indexed in the major subject indexes covering the discipline. Once a new journal has passed through the stringent review process for inclusion in prominent indexes, librarians will feel more inclined to add it to collections, and authors will be assured of a level of continuity, credibility and quality. Examples of emerging issues for journals might be the inclusion of new types of content such as data or video, or relationships with initiatives such as CrossRef, if including digital object identifiers (DOIs) is considered important for the journal. The subject librarian has the expertise to act as consultant to the faculty editor and the rest of the journal team, all of whom are invested in seeing the journal become a success. This is a natural extension of the liaison role for librarians.

Subject-specialist librarians involved with the indexing and marketing effort for the new open access journal also have access to listservs and other communication channels to alert other librarians in the subject field to the existence of the journal. In the case of PCSP, it was possible to put information about the journal on. a national listserv for psychology librarians, and then enter into a dialogue about the title with interested librarians at many other institutions. Librarians were able to add a new free high-quality peer-reviewed journal in a niche area of psychology to their holdings, catalogues and web lists. This further enhanced the visibility of the journal, while the libraries adding the title to collections gained access to a new scholarly title at no cost. PCSP was listed as an "up and coming title" in the 2007 "Core Journals in Psychology" on the website of the ALA/ACRL Education and Behavioral Sciences Section. This type of exposure indicates interest in the title among other psychology librarians.

Usage statistics, often reported as numbers of downloads by geographic area, are easily accessible when publishing open access journals. Statistics can show growth following marketing efforts by librarians, and PCSP has shown increasing downloads of its content. Simply starting a new library-published journal with open source software will not ensure that the journal will see usage and become a success. Marketing and indexing will make the difference. The subject librarian on the publishing team will be aware of all of the library-related issues that the journal must be concerned with in order to be truly integrated into collections and read by as many scholars as possible.

Of course, new open access journals need to be listed in DOAJ, be included in Ulrich's Periodicals Directory and OCLC WorldCat, as well as have their content crawled by Google Scholar and other similar free web search engines. Contents of issues must be available through searches of institutional repositories. Authors seeking impact may also want to see the open access journal covered by citation indexes such as Web of Science (Science Citation Index, Social Citation Index and Arts and Humanities Index), and Elsevier's Scopus. Google Scholar also provides citation impact information and crawls open access journals. Currently, Web of Science includes approximately 200 open access journals, while Scopus presently covers approximately 500. Association of the journal with the large aggregator indexes may be another entry point for journals into libraries through subscription products, further driving traffic to the publication (Morrison, 2008b). The journal will need the maximum coverage afforded to other traditionally published journals seeking to increase discoverability by researchers as well as the public at large.

In many subject indexes and aggregators, open access journals are treated no differently from traditional journals in the review process and they must meet all of the same criteria for inclusion. Criteria include the usual evidence of peer review, continuous quality publishing schedules, and stature of editor and board members. As with any fledgling journal in most fields, however, it may take years for the new open access journal to reach a level of prestige. Of course, traditionally-published journals could also transition to an open access model. An example of this in the field of librarianship would be *Journal of the Medical Library Association*, which started as a traditional publication and has made the successful switch to open access (Morrison, 2004).

Capability for publishing open access journals now exists at many academic libraries. The websites of open source library publishing platform products provide extensive material on library publishing programmes, and give rationale for libraries taking on digital publishing of journals and other scholarly material as evidence of continued support for open access. There are now at least two open source electronic journal management systems for publishing open access journals, including the Public Knowledge Project's Open Journal Systems (*http://pkp.sfu.ca/?q=ojs*) and the Digital Publishing System of Cornell University Library and Pennsylvania State University Libraries and Press (*http://dpubs.org/*). Another open source publishing platform is HyperJournal (*http://www.hjournal.org/*; Barbera and DiDonato, 2006). Another system where advertisements may appear is the platform hosted by Scholarly Exchange (*http://www.scholarlyexchange.org/*). Some may feel that publishing is not an appropriate activity for librarians and that it may redirect funds from other important core services. There may be concern that librarians do not have the necessary skill set to tackle a new mission and create a sustainable manpower situation or funding stream to support this new library activity. Academic librarians as a group may not be in favour of moving the library's resources to publishing activities. Libraries may see that publishing activities may not sit well alongside their traditional and published missions. Gedye (2004) advocates new roles for librarians in the open access movement, and believes that 'there are many excellent reasons why librarians should adopt a financially supportive role within the open access journey that scholarly publishing is beginning to take'. Librarians may wonder what the cost of publishing an online journal would be to the institution or to the library itself. Based on anecdotal data in 2004, Cornell University Library estimated that to cover operating expenses for a 'modest-sized' scholarly journal, the annual cost to the library or to the provost's office would be in the range of $200,000–225,000 (Davis et al., 2004). Other sources estimate costs to be much lower but would have to take into account staffing and the redirecting of librarians from other roles.

Commercial publishers ask whether academics have the necessary publishing, financial and technical skill set to create, launch, and most importantly, sustain an open access journal (Greco et al., 2006). Open access journals must gather momentum and achieve success against great odds and funding challenges. There is still a major need for continuous funding and editorial stewardship in order for a new open access journal to survive. Not surprisingly, many new open access journals fail. It has been reported that, out of hundreds of new open access journals begun in the first few years of the movement, approximately one-half have ceased (Bjork, 2004). Funding is a perennial problem for academic libraries, and adequate monetisation would be essential for sustainability of library-published open access journals. In a web survey by the Hanken School of Economics, in terms of business models for open access journals, results garnered from 55 open access journal editors showed that only 10 per cent had budgets. Editors and publishers tend to minimise costs by funding journals as open source projects (Bjork, 2004). Academic libraries will have to decide whether publishing journals is cost-effective, and within the scope of their missions. This discussion will take place against the backdrop of the voices of open access advocates who wish to showcase and enhance this aspect of research library capability. Starting new journals may have great appeal to departmental faculty in the institution and librarians will grapple with prioritising projects and funding them.

In the case of open access journals in general, many are created by a single person or a group of academics. Sustainability is a major problem when the person in charge stops working for the journal or chooses to move to another institution (Bjork, 2004). In the case of librarians as publishers, there would need to be a commitment by library leadership to publishing as a librarian activity in order to ensure sustainability of a particular journal or other scholarly publication or series. Workload issues may arise where an institution may wish to utilise librarian time to accomplish other more traditional tasks. How does publishing a journal 'count' in terms of the traditional areas of librarianship, scholarship and service? The voices of the open access movement exhort librarians to take on new roles. One wonders how much the library would value publishing as an activity for librarians.

The launch of the Open Access Scholarly Publishers Association in 2008 is an attempt to provide a central information and advocacy source for all publishers of open access journals (Sutton, 2008). Libraries publishing open access journals may join as long as they are signatories of the BOAI and publish at least one journal. Which librarians will be involved in these publishing activities beyond the production of the journal out of the repository? The publishing arm of the library may operate outside the understanding of the other librarians in the institution, and may take up valuable resources and staffing. Communication between the technical services librarians and the public services groups will be paramount or there will be a risk of separate missions, possibly diluting the effectiveness of the whole organisation.

Library-published open access journals and publishing programmes must fit in with collection development strategies and policies in order to be fully integrated. In collection development and other areas where impact is important, BOAI reminds librarians of the importance of open access when 'weighting journals for importance' (BOAI, 2006). Librarians can push readership of open access journals by including them in any tool or resource that can increase visibility to patrons. The library can help an institution's faculty keep up with open access journals being published in different fields. Librarians can include (after careful vetting) open access journals in OPACs, electronic journals lists, subject research guides, web lists and newsletter items. Mainly, the librarian can use the same criteria for vetting open access journals for inclusion into library collections and services as is used for all traditionally-published journals.

3

Collection development and open access

Librarians' relationships with traditional publishers

The representatives of publishing companies have written many articles expounding their beliefs regarding the role of libraries in this new world of open access. For instance, on the subject of libraries' migration to online-only publications, Robert Campbell, former President of Blackwell Publishing, has stated that 'overall, the UK performs well in research and it could do better through publishers and librarians working together, and persuading faculty to understand the benefits of online-only', adding that 'in any public debate librarians are seen as more worthy than publishers' (Campbell, 2004). Campbell quotes Alastair Dryburgh as stating that 'I have left the library out of the list of players for the author-pays model as it is unclear what its role would be in an open access world' (Campbell, 2004). There is clearly speculation as to the role of libraries in the changing online publishing environment and librarians need to take the lead in carving out new roles. One such role may well be in open access publishing. There have been comments that publishers would like to see libraries 'justify their funding' by publishing measures of success and efficiency (Campbell, 2004). Clearly, this attempt by publishers to challenge libraries may drive a further wedge between commercial publishers and librarians. On the other hand, if certain open access models are truly successful, then both publishers and librarians would seem to have much to lose, whether in terms of declining subscriptions or losing users to the web. It may be that traditional publishers and librarians share some common fears. The disruptive nature of open access and library publishing may actually necessitate increased dialogue between publishers and librarians in this time of transformation. Increasingly, there are venues set aside for these conversations at conferences and places for librarians on the library advisory boards of publishers and vendors. Collaboration between publishers and librarians is becoming more commonplace. Librarians may have a new place at the table in the creation of working relationships and information sharing with the representatives of publishers and vendors. A difficult economy can also accelerate some changes for both publishers and libraries and force new dialogues.

Some representatives of large commercial publishers have called for further enhancement of collaboration between librarians and commercial publishers (Tagler, 2005). The Council on Library and Information Resources (CLIR) has been suggested as a possible vehicle for collaboration between publishers and librarians, and represents a source of information for 'providers and preservers of information' (*http://www.clir.org/*). In 2007, CLIR received a $2.19 million operating grant from the Andrew W. Mellon Foundation for a range of initiatives in programme areas including 'the emerging library', and its role has been described as helping to 'create services that expand the concept of "library"' (CLIR, 2007). Librarians will want to maintain awareness of how this new definition of the library might end up affecting their positions and daily work.

The often adversarial relationship between commercial publishers and librarians colours how librarians must look at the various publishers of library and information science (LIS) literature. Groups of scholarly publishers have engaged in public relations campaigns in order to improve their relationships with librarians (Carlson, 2002). There is some distinction to be made between the commercial and society publishers when it comes to relationships with libraries and librarians. Librarians sometimes deal with publishers in a more contentious climate when forced to take on cancellations projects. Library budgets and difficult negotiations processes do not always promote harmonious relationships. Open access, especially large-scale self-archiving has at times been suggested as a mechanism that would allow cancellation of expensive subscriptions. Although it is yet to be reached, there is a tipping point at which it is postulated that 'green' open access (self-archiving) of all research articles will alleviate the 'serials crisis'. Many suggest that the worst thing that librarians must deal with is the commercial publisher that takes authors' work and resells it to the academy at an increasingly escalating price. According to estimates by the Association of Research Libraries (ARL), there was a 227 per cent increase in the cost of journal subscriptions from 1986 to 2002 (Frankish, 2004). Researchers are aware of journal reputations, but are not always aware of the cost of their journals to libraries. As long as researchers are being provided seamless access to information on their desktop, and even at their homes via remote access, subscription costs to libraries are often not known or considered. However, librarians who submit their work for publication are often well aware of the publishers with the most egregiously escalating costs. There are many costs passed down in the system outside of libraries, including publication fees, page charges, and even submission fees. Many of these charges are handed down to authors in scientific disciplines where grant money is a funding source; the LIS literature is not known for charging authors for publication.

When librarians are making decisions as to where to send their own scholarly work to be published, they cannot divorce themselves from their impressions of the publishers they deal with in their daily work. Some commercial publishers have had contentious relationships with the library community due to pricing structures. Only recently have there been calls from the library world to seek more transparency and disclosure in publicly revealing the true costs of doing business with some of these publishers, and how expensive it has been, not only in terms of the bottom line, but in terms of a stranglehold on collections work. In lean budget years, the system seems often stressed to its breaking point, and crises are barely averted. Large commercial publishers, such as Elsevier, publish some of the most prestigious LIS journals. Editors and editorial boards comprised of well-known LIS faculty and librarians are at the helm of these journals. Librarians have preconceived opinions about these large publishers, but may be swayed to submit articles to them if their policies toward self-archiving become more liberal, as has been the case with Elsevier. This liberalisation of permissions is very attractive to those wishing to self-archive while still wishing to be published in the more traditional and prestigious titles. There may still be an attraction to seeing one's paper in a print publication, especially for librarians who have sometimes fought to retain print journals at many institutions. These traditional print (or print/online combination) publications may still hold more appeal for some librarian authors as they may be indexed in more and higher-level databases and indexes, and have long histories and established prestige in the profession. Open access journals, however, are making inroads. One might have expected LIS to have been one of the first disciplines to change to more open access models, but instead it is lagging some way behind.

Publishers provide complex editorial and other production processes that include sophisticated platforms and search capabilities. Other value-added features may also be attractive, for example, Elsevier publishes a list of its '25 hottest articles', provides an 'articles in press' feature, and its 'author gateway' allows authors to track the status of their publications. As for the publisher's perspective, a survey by Elsevier of its authors in 2004/05 found that, as far as what a publisher can do for authors, the worth of 'value-added' is 'immense' (Lankester, 2006). Those publishing open access journals need to remember the high value that users place on features such as being able to format citations in bibliographic management programmes, set up alerts and RSS feeds, comment on articles, and use other Web 2.0 tools while accessing and reading the publication via a professional and attractive website. Emphasis on high-level peer review and assuring the reader of that status is of vital importance to the open access journal competing for readers and submissions alongside established journals in a discipline. Journal recognition and status in the discipline are difficult to attain for any newly-formed journal.

There are other reasons that authors are turning to open access journals; one is the issue of research impact. Authors from many disciplines have received the message that open access increases research impact. However, institutional subscriptions to journals deemed important by the disciplines are in great demand in academic libraries, and are still difficult for librarians to cancel. In the journal *Science*, one study that used much more extensive citation data than previous studies did find that 'across subfields, the impact of commercial online availability was positive, statistically significant, and on average 40 per cent larger than the OA effect, suggesting that most researchers rely on institutional subscriptions' (Evans and Reimer, 2009). Librarians will always need to respond to what researchers need and want, and these studies show that in many disciplines, that remains the traditional journal literature. If open access articles reach a critical mass either through green self-archiving or open journal publishing, this may change. Librarians may not have any vested interest in pushing that change. If researchers demand traditional subscriptions, then rather than preach an alternative, librarians will likely try to provide them, either onsite or through rapid interlibrary delivery. Most front-line public services and collections librarians respond to requests for information for specific articles from named journals, and always attempt to provide excellent service by meeting user requests. Librarians seeking harmonious working relationships with the teaching faculty and other researchers may continue to work to provide the publications these groups desire.

There has been difficulty in determining just how extensive an inroad open access has made into the total amount of peer-reviewed scholarship on the web. It is possible to count the number of open access journals, but some feel that in terms of declaring the 'success' of the movement, it is the total number of scholarly articles available on the open web that really matters, even in a limited sense of having changed the journal landscape to any great degree. A study by Bjork et al. (2009) aimed to determine the percentage of journal articles available on the web in 2006 that were open access. The study took into account scholarly articles made available through both green and gold open access routes. The results of the study indicated that for 2006, of the approximately 1,350,000 total articles, 4.6 per cent became immediately available on the open web, with another 3.5 per cent available after an embargo period (typically one year). It was also reported that 'usable copies of 11.3 per cent could be found in subject-specific or institutional repositories or on the home pages of authors' (Bjork et al., 2009). More studies will be able to estimate the worldwide effect of open access on the scholarly publishing system and allow librarians to analyse hard evidence when promoting open access behaviour to their constituencies. With evidence of trends, librarians will be able to understand how open access might provide relief to serials budgets or be in a position to change how reference or instruction services will represent open access alternatives to library users. Without evidence, librarians may choose to stay with established workflows. As the economy worsens and budgets tighten, open access may still not be the answer for libraries' collections woes. It may be difficult for librarians dealing with budget realities to envision how open access will really provide an answer, especially without rendering the library obsolete as more free material is found online through popular search engines.

Threats that open access may pose to libraries

In their daily work, librarians are used to purchasing, organising and providing access to publishers' scholarly output. According to Goodman (2004), 'Libraries are only intermediaries. They act as transfer agents for the money that goes to publishers.' In some ways, librarians advocating for open access models may risk having to explain to constituents why often dwindling budget resources need to be spent to sustain traditional subscription models if open access provides such a satisfactory alternative. Conversely, librarians know that cancelling traditional journals is unlikely to promote open access behaviour among faculty and other researchers. Indeed, although open access adds another dimension, it has not yet freed librarians from their struggles with traditional publishers. Open access has forced librarians to stretch their skill set and deal with a whole new category of resources. Funding from the institution or state may be lessened if open access emerges as a viable alternative. If librarians are continually touting open access as the preferred way to go in the future, why should the taxpayer (in the case of the state) or the institution still be asked to continue to pay high prices for traditionally-subscribed journals? Librarians may find this position to be tenuous, and may want the ability to continue to fund commercial purchases, support society and scholarly publishers such as university presses, as well as add open access alternatives to their collections. Collections librarians may prefer a diversified approach, with some real flexibility to selecting materials, rather than dedicating their entire budget and planning to one format or another. Librarians may prefer to keep their advocacy for open access limited for fear of losing budgetary support for collections from the institution and promulgation of any idea that the library does not need funding for research journals. There may be confusion among librarians as to the possible effects on collections funding of advocating too openly and too aggressively for open access alternatives.

On the other hand, especially with new government mandates in place, there may be pressure from funding bodies to see librarians aggressively pursue the construction of digital libraries that focus on quality free open access publications. There may be librarians who see this possibility as threatening. Some may ask 'what is a library any more?' A definition of the library would include being the place of scholarly record. In the words of Keller et al. (2003), 'a web page with a set of links is not a library'. Academic libraries' collections are becoming more focused on access instead of ownership. This fact makes it easier to consider web materials a part of the library. It does however become harder to define or quantify the library's collection – always a cornerstone of demonstrating excellence.

Even in these changing times, many are tied to the 'library as place'. There are stark disciplinary differences that may determine maximal uptake of open access opportunities. There may be a misperception that open access takes away from the identification of the scholarly journal literature with the library itself. Visits to the physical library by researchers continue to decline. Arts and humanities scholars visit the library more often as books are the objects of their research, and those researchers may work with a longer timeframe. Physical sciences and life sciences researchers, however, are the least likely to access information at the library in person (RIN/CURL, 2007). These types of behaviour affect the librarians that serve those communities as well as the expectation of uptake of either self-archiving behaviour or interest in open access journals.

Researchers are accessing more scholarly material online all the time – both free and subscribed. Outside of disciplinary differences in open access behaviour, there may be other factors that come into play, such as the age of researchers. Younger students who have grown up using electronic journals and books may not readily recognise the paper journal volume, and it will become less important for the article to be a facsimile of that product. In time, the terms 'book' and 'journal' may not be known as the basic building blocks of academic libraries. When discussing the digital objects comprising scholarship, librarians will need to take care to use consistent and current standard terminology to avoid confusion for all library users. Open access to scholarship will push the boundaries of libraries collections even further with various digital versions of scholarly output available to researchers.

Inertia for the LIS journal literature

Many articles illustrate the fact that if scholars had to pay for information, they would change their research habits. Individual researchers do not have much incentive to change habits if the library provides what they need (Davis, 2003). Librarians, especially those involved directly with collection building, are well aware of the cost of traditionally-published journals, yet they are not moving their libraries toward open access models as quickly as some might expect. There is a well-established 'serials crisis', especially apparent in the scientific literature, but the LIS literature may not be under that same kind of financial pressure. Is there a true serials crisis affecting the LIS journal literature? As many library journals are not as costly as those in other fields, even the titles from the commercial publishers, librarians may be more comfortable with continuing to pay for these subscriptions. Alternative models are sought much more often for costly journals in other fields, especially in the areas of science, technology, engineering and mathematics (STEM). Should price really be the deciding factor in changing to the more open business models that would make the LIS literature more accessible to all? As costs are involved in all types of publishing, librarians must decide what constitutes value for their money. There is not an absolute understanding of what information is worth, and how much librarians and other researchers should be willing to pay to read and publish articles in the journal literature (Davis, 2003).

Swan and Brown (2005) note that scholars in engineering, materials science and technology publish the most papers, while those in humanities and LIS publish the fewest in a given year. There may not be a critical mass moving the corpus of LIS journal literature to open access. The total amount of the LIS literature may be too small. Even though the community of scholars in library and information science may be said to be relatively small in terms of other social sciences fields, and the literature relatively inexpensive compared with some others, those factors should not preclude a thorough examination of the state of the literature when it comes to potential changes such as the lessening of permissions and moving to open access models. As librarians are used to focusing on more expensive literature, especially in STEM fields, and talking about the pricing crisis in terms of those disciplinary areas, it may not seem crucial to discuss changes to the relatively small and less expensive library literature. Librarians must always keep in mind the cost to the reader of inaccessible scholarship and try to work on democratisation of information. Librarians need to be as concerned about their literature as a body of work. The library literature could find a wider audience, and greater disciplinary impact through movement toward open access.

A study of librarian publishing behaviour by Peterson (2006) gives a snapshot as to how librarians view open access titles in their own field of LIS. In May 2006, a survey was sent to librarian authors whose work had been published in a print LIS journal seeking feedback about their choices when submitting their own work for publication. Most of the authors surveyed (70 per cent) considered 'relevance' and 'peer-reviewed' to be of highest value in choosing a venue for their work. This was followed by prestige of the journal, and also of paramount importance was how widely read the title was. Of course, relevance, peer review, level of prestige, and wide readership are all possible for open access journals in LIS and in all other fields. Librarian behaviour, especially at the senior ranks, is key to raising awareness and/or status of open access titles.

Studying the self-archiving behaviour of librarians may be able to show the extent of knowledge of open access strategies that librarians possess. If librarians are highly knowledgeable about open access, and have experience in self-archiving or publishing in open access journals, it would stand to reason that they would try to keep such strategies in mind when doing collections and faculty liaison work. Librarians would also be expected to employ various strategies when submitting different types of articles to ensure impact and web visibility. Each article may have a different 'purpose' and could be submitted to different types of journals, but if librarian authors self-archived all their articles in a repository, they would not be considered 'nonsupportive' if they decided to use a more traditional journal. Librarians could find it useful to know web visibility strategies, both for their own work and that of others. One wonders whether librarians are serving as consultants for faculty, graduate students and researchers when those researchers are choosing venues for publication. Various categories of scholars will have different motivations when it comes to web visibility; junior faculty may have less room for experimentation away from traditionally ranked journals.

The literature of some disciplines has proven more amenable to moving to an open access model. Most of the progress is taking place in the STEM literature, but many open access models used in the STEM community would be applicable to LIS publications. Even with so much information available to researchers, and especially to librarians about their own literature, the switch to open access journals and the practice of self-archiving in institutional and subject repositories may still be said to be a marginal phenomenon in the global scholarly communication system. There is still strong growth in the commercial publishing world in terms of the journal literature. Bjork (2004) remarks that the old model continues to hinge on customers' willingness and capacity to pay. How long will librarians be willing to support the current system for LIS journal literature? Librarians may want to actively discuss scholarly communications specifically related to LIS, or even as part of the broader conversation about the social sciences. This topic has been suggested for future library conferences where most conversations about scholarly communications and open access have been restricted specifically to issues with the sciences. Social sciences may not be far behind the sciences, and library conferences will start reflecting this fact; indeed, more programmes incorporating social sciences topics have been noted.

Curiously, in a study of the ten most popular topic areas for open access, information science appears at number ten (Bjork, 2004). In a study of self-archiving behaviour in six social sciences disciplines, findings showed that authors in these fields are indeed depositing materials on the web. Although authors in these related social sciences disciplines are self-archiving, they are not necessarily aware of publisher 'rules' or other important issues related to open access behaviour (Antelman, 2006). As the information science portion of the library literature is faring so well, it might be postulated that the rest of the associated library literature may not be far behind. However, this may be how LIS literature splits – the information science literature behaves more like the STEM literature. Library journals are, for the most part, inexpensive in comparison with publications in many other disciplines, reducing pressure to change the business model. Some are society publications that are dependent on journal subscriptions to keep membership fees down. The LIS literature is comprised of social science-related topics, but the large information science component makes it difficult to define the corpus of research literature.

Librarians engaging in business with traditional publishers

Complicating the relationships between librarians and commercial publishers is the lack of transparency about pricing and negotiations, and the faculty liaison librarian may not be able to weigh an open access publication against a subscription one without adequate information. All of the negotiating takes the process to another level, often leaving those with the disciplinary knowledge on the sidelines. Transparency in all negotiations would help collection development librarians understand the real costs to the academy of continuing commercial subscriptions. Unfortunately, it is becoming more difficult for subject librarians to participate in the business of negotiating price with publishers and vendors. The discipline's readers and researchers are even further away from the discussion of journal costs. Publicising actual cost might resonate with researchers.

Subject-specialist librarians run the risk of losing touch with the business end of electronic resources negotiations, making it more difficult for them to participate as consultants on author rights or open access addenda in a meaningful way with their constituencies. As new positions such as electronic resources librarian or scholarly communications librarian move the pricing discussions away from the faculty liaison librarians, it may become a parallel conversation. Discussion of open access and other changes to scholarly communication paradigms needs to permeate the library organisation, not just remain with certain librarians who make deals with commercial and society publishers. In considering journal options, librarians must have all tools available: usage statistics, domain expertise, published assessment tools, and an understanding of the particular library within a consortium or network. Teamwork may be essential for the conversation to extend not only throughout the library organisation, but out into the institution. To perceive the problems that librarians have traditionally dealt with, departmental faculty, provosts and even students need to know the cost of library materials. Business as usual will not promote uptake of open access options by faculty and students.

Commercial versus society publishers: different relationships with librarians

Librarians may be conflicted about supporting both types of open access, that is, self-archiving (green) and open access journals (gold). Academic libraries have traditionally been supporters of the nonprofit and society publishers. For instance, the Association of Learned and Society Publishers (ALPSP) has had a positive relationship with library organisations. ALPSP is an international organisation for nonprofit publishers and those who work with them, and is comprised of 340 members in 36 countries who collectively publish approximately 10,000 journals. In its mission to work alongside libraries and librarians to preserve the role of learned societies and nonprofit publishers, ALPSP sees a possible peril in libraries treating smaller nonprofits and society publishers in the same way as they deal with large commercial publishers in the move to open access. ALPSP also does not see libraries moving into the role of publisher of open access journals as problematic. In fact, these libraries may even turn to ALPSP for certain skills training and sharing of information (Tananbaum, 2006). Publishers are working hard to understand 'information production', and are watching what users do with the information that is delivered to them. Librarians have a great role in determining which publishers, and which philosophies and business models they will continue to support. Enhanced dialogue and collaboration with publishers will be necessary for each group to understand the other's needs. In recent years, both sides have called for greater collaboration in the development of new business models for library products.

ALPSP does not understand librarians' talk of supporting open access, thinking only that librarians see open access initiatives as a way for their libraries to save money. ALPSP feels that open access journals need funding, and 'if the money has to be redirected, it will be taken from libraries' (Tananbaum, 2006). In addition, if librarians push the move to self-archiving by authors, subscriptions will be cancelled, damaging journals and learned societies. ALPSP estimates that nonprofit publishers are responsible for publishing half of all journals, and on average, charge one-third as much per page as commercial publishers (Tananbaum, 2006). Do librarians agree that it is part of the library's mission to support the nonprofit publishers? The library may not be able to support everyone; the authors needing publication fees, the scholarly publishers, the membership organisations, and the open access experimentations. Most budgets will not allow such support, even for the stated 'library value' that is used to describe open access.

Roles of librarians in discussions of university press partnerships

Any discussion of open access and librarians must take into account the publishing of monographs. In recent years, university presses have also faced pressure to transform and embrace a more digital future due to well-known declines in the scholarly publishing environment, with particular respect to the humanities. With libraries moving toward digital publishing as a central or peripheral role, librarians have had to envision the library as not just a place to hold collections but as a possible creator of scholarly publications. Institutional repositories serve roles in digital preservation, archiving and searching for university output, and are increasingly publishing journals and monographs. While this is going on, universities that also have traditional presses find two different types of publishing houses on campus. Library-based publication may be seen as more experimental, but university presses may suffer from being too rooted in tradition, and may increasingly need to collaborate and to assert their role as mission-centric to the university. For the first time, many libraries and university presses have had to begin conversations based on collaboration and future vision. University presses have not been known as innovators or promoters of open access, but that is changing. Librarians may become more aware and more involved in issues of university press publishing and there will have to be a way to integrate university press issues, and even university/college store issues into the library conversation. A new relationship between libraries, IT departments, university presses and even college stores may prove beneficial to the institution. Remaining in silos promotes marginalisation, and this represents yet another opportunity for librarians to repurpose roles and integrate more into the wider university community. This will allow the discussion of library and user needs to percolate through more broad-based institutional conversations. University publishing efforts will move toward a more hybrid model including some open access initiatives if the library is always at the table. The library's experience in innovation and experimentation when it comes to digital publishing, allied with some of the more traditional functions of the press (such as recruitment of authors, peer-review functions and marketing) would seem to be of great mutual benefit. The library and university press can be a powerful alliance. Both serve a similar mission to promote the research and publication needs of local faculty while also facilitating the certification and dissemination of the scholarship of specific disciplines in the wider academy. Publishing collaborations between libraries and university presses may be one of the most promising aspects of open access and libraries. Still, some librarians may not see publishing as a library function and may be wary of this new role in assisting another university entity due to budget pressure or even lack of interest or incentive.

By collaborating with their university press, librarians may become more sensitised to the plight of the university presses, as well larger issues such as the need for marketplace diversification. With smaller nonprofit publishers losing market share to the large commercial publishers, collection development and subject-selector librarians may wish to consider supporting university press publishing as a matter of principle. Repository developers and those in the library charged with prioritising digital projects may start with smaller collaborative niche projects so as to leverage expertise while planning for the future. As there is a cost to open access monograph publishing, libraries will be wary of a large degree of participation at first. However, using an open access model for some publications would allow the collaborative venture to have greater appeal to both researchers and librarians who have similar concerns about the humanities monograph, especially as the library budget continues to suffer due to the demands of commercial journal publishers. University press/library collaboration can broaden the open access discussion by bringing it to humanities scholars.

A recent Ithaka report considers the issues involved in this move toward collaboration between university presses and libraries. It suggests that the community needs to collaborate and see that a 'powerful technology, service and marketing platform would serve as a catalyst for collaboration and shared capital investment in university-based publishing' (Brown et al., 2007). This enhanced university publishing partnership could bring some focus to open access dissemination of research output resulting from local mandates or successful faculty involvement. Subject-specialist librarians may have a key role in passing on extensive discipline-based knowledge of research behaviour to those who possess more of the technical or production aspects of publishing expertise. There has been a possible disconnect and waste of valuable expertise in not involving librarians in planning efforts that involve faculty research output. Librarians are often closely involved with faculty and scholarly associations in the disciplines, and see incredible differences in scholarly communication and open access behaviours by disciplines and even subfields. There can be no broad-brushed approach to university digital publishing initiatives, either from the library or from new collaborations. Librarians can have useful insight and prevent misguided initiatives from proceeding. Librarians can be empowered to be spokespersons for the changes affecting scholarly communications in the disciplines. Academic librarians can communicate the real desires of researchers for new mechanisms and outlets for published research. Subject-selector librarians, often acting as liaisons to academic departments, will have a sense of what will be most effective in terms of potential publications due to their knowledge of promotion and tenure mores, and current topics of research interest in the disciplines they serve.

Subject selectors may find a new role with library publishing efforts. Librarians will also know which open access digital initiatives will make sense for the various disciplines, and this domain knowledge gained from working directly with researchers will be a valuable asset to any publishing venture. This has not been a traditional venue for librarian expertise, but roles can be expanded if librarians are to be considered experts in scholarly communication and open access. Libraries may want to reassert the value of the knowledge that subject-specialist librarians bring not only to publishing efforts but to any scholarly communication efforts university-wide. Budgetary pressures create closing of ranks, and selectors can easily become marginalised without a stronger voice and advocacy at the library and university level. Librarians need to exploit any opportunity for enhancement of roles within the university at large. Subject specialists, bibliographers and/or liaisons to university departments, especially in the humanities, know that scholars need more outlets for monograph publishing. This focus on establishing credible avenues for scholarly publishing in the humanities can be a positive move for the institution and involve the library and librarians.

The Ithaka report also mentions the fact that librarians may not have thought enough about library users as authors, instead focusing on the search and discovery, collection building or preservation aspects of the process. Authors have concerns regarding copyright protection, research impact, status of publication, branding, and potential income from publications (Brown et al., 2007). Moving an open access agenda forward requires librarians to connect with users as authors needing publication outlets for their scholarly work, and as researchers seeking certification for promotion and tenure. This may entail embracing open access publications or it may focus on the traditional route. Librarians will advocate for open access differently depending on discipline, and those differences will affect efforts at university press transformation. To move the issue of collaboration between libraries and university presses forward, Brown et al. (2007) call for 'a third party enterprise, or at least a catalytic force'. However, the librarians they surveyed also reported that they felt that the presses were 'anachronistic' and 'too small to matter'. Due to a convergence of technical capability and economic uncertainties, the time may be opportune for real discussion between libraries and university presses. Within institutions, new teams focused on library/press collaboration can be formed.

Moving university press published books to electronic formats should please librarians because it is assumed that researchers and readers want to access more content in electronic format. Libraries have had some challenges moving to e-book formats because of issues related to digital rights management, perpetual access, and business models that include packages too reminiscent of journal 'big deals'. Certainly, librarians involved in collection development and electronic resources would be able to advise those working in university press publishing about models that work best for library purchasing and which small niche areas might lend themselves to experimentation with open access publishing models. The issue of using Creative Commons licences for university press digital monographs is an idea whose time has come, and librarians may be able to promote this issue with a reluctant press. This is an opportunity to focus on the place of the monograph again in terms of library and publishing priorities. Monetisation will be a problem, and in the humanities areas served well by university presses, an 'author-pays' open access model is not likely to be successful.

Currently, there are examples of some successful and interesting collaborations between libraries and presses. Librarians at institutions with presses can become more aware of efforts at collaboration and seek appropriate roles. This is another way that librarians, especially subject specialists and repository managers, can support open access while focusing on areas of institutional excellence in scholarship. For example, the director of Pennsylvania State University Press reports to the university library, and together they have established the Office of Digital and Scholarly Publishing. Metalmark Press is the joint imprint of the university press and the library at Pennsylvania State University (Brown et al., 2007). The University of Pittsburgh's library has digitised 521 out-of-print Pitt Press monographs and made them freely available from the website of Pitt's Digital Research Library (*http://digital.library.pitt.edu/p/pittpress/*).

Leadership is needed at many levels to set an agenda for partnership that will be beneficial to the university at large. Institutional repository development and library publishing efforts initiated to address the larger problems inherent in the current scholarly communication behaviour of researchers have not had the necessary dramatic result. In December 2008, a special issue of the journal *Against the Grain* was published, devoted to library/university press collaborations. Writing in the issue, Furlough describes the situation thus:

> though there have been some shifts in stance and postures among libraries and publishers after ten years of advocacy and experimentation, I can't think of a single commercial academic publication put out of business by an open-access or alternative publication. Ultimately, we won't change that landscape; researchers will. (Furlough, 2008)

Librarians may not understand or know the publishing process itself and fully appreciate its traditional focus on excellence in copyediting and certification. Peer review is of vital importance, whether open access or not, and librarians may not be familiar with the process of certification for monographic publishing. Helpful information on potential partnerships between libraries and university presses may be found in information published by the Scholarly Publishing and Academic Resources Coalition (SPARC) in *Campus-Based Publishing Partnerships: A Guide to Critical Issues* (Crow, 2009). No matter how valuable university press partnerships with libraries become, it will still not positively impact the stressed budget in any substantial way, or change how information is delivered or collections built. Can libraries afford to assist university presses at this point in time? Individual libraries may struggle with the value of library-based publishing or partnerships. University leadership in reasserting the mission of both is crucial and dedicated sustainable funding streams must be established.

Dissertations as important unique open access materials

Another focus of open access efforts in libraries involves the publishing of electronic versions of dissertations. As unique institutional output, the corpus of dissertations is valuable to the academic library and its parent institution. Librarians may already be involved in consulting on dissertation publishing, possibly suggesting strategies to authors who wish maximum dissemination for these unique works. Many libraries are participating in successful electronic theses and dissertations (ETD) programmes utilising their institutional repositories. This option makes dissertations open access. Some researchers may be interested in paying extra fees to ProQuest for the open access option now available. Proquest makes available a guide to 'open access vs traditional publishing' (UMI Dissertation Publishing, 2008). Before making decisions, students may want to talk to librarians with expertise in their subject areas in order to discuss the issues of open access and research impact pertaining to dissertation literature. As more universities publish dissertations through ETD programmes, thereby making them available on the web, authors may find paying for the ProQuest open access option redundant. Open access brings no royalties, but does bring web visibility of consequence to a newly-minted PhD or junior scholar. It is important to consider the motivations of the author and the publication conventions of the discipline. Disciplinary knowledge about the advisability of sharing of materials from dissertations will be important in this conversation, and may be a new area of expertise for librarians. Beginning with helping students in searching for relevant citations while doing research for the dissertation's literature review, librarians may assist at the other end of the process by helping students with strategies for publishing their dissertations. Web visibility is a new concern for authors of dissertations.

With ETDs being crawled by Google, and ProQuest offering an open access option, students may wish to consider various options for making supplementary materials available through the repository or by strategically publishing the dissertation to maximise web availability. Data will increasingly become an issue for graduate students of both social sciences and sciences as they seek to preserve and possibly make data more visible and accessible.

Institutions may want to make the work of honours or other advanced undergraduates not only available, but discoverable through the repository, the integrated library systems (ILS), the web, or all three. Librarians can be consultants in these types of conversations that may lead to increased research impact for authors of dissertations, or simply identify issues that may affect the use or dissemination of their graduate work both now and in their future lives and careers.

Of course, not all disciplines find maximum web visibility of dissertation research or other works desirable. Subjects that involve creative writing, dissertations that seem promising to be published as books, or dissertations that have patentable contents might be areas where web visibility is not desirable for the authors (Foster, 2008). Subject specialists can work closely with departments and the institutional repository to create optimal situations for those completing dissertations and theses. This may become an important new role for library liaisons as well as adding an interesting way to introduce open access to graduate students as they begin their publishing careers.

Overall growth of electronic publishing

Electronic publishing continues to grow in all fields. Librarians must keep up with a publishing world changing at lightning speed. To truly understand market forces, librarians must make sure to converse freely with all stakeholders, most notably the researchers and the publishers. According to an ALPSP survey of all major society and commercial publishers, 90 per cent of journals were online by 2005, up from 75 per cent in 2003. The figure for online availability of social sciences and humanities journals continues to approach that of the STM literature. The study shows that 84 per cent of humanities and social sciences journals offer an online version, while the figure is 93 per cent for STM journals. One-fifth of publishers are utilising or experimenting with open access models (Cox and Cox, 2006). The growth trajectory for online availability has continued. (Cox and Cox, 2008).

In some fields, there has been discussion as to whether it would be satisfactory for publishers to stop producing print. Many fields have moved so much of their published scholarship to online formats that there may be a lessening demand for print. Are LIS journals also moving to online or clinging to print? The LIS literature must continue to evolve at least on par with other analogous social sciences fields. Online literature, taking advantage of scalability, quick access, linking with other research, and other value-added features has become the 'medium of choice' (Waltham, 2003). However, paper is still important for some areas of humanities, and may be the preference of librarians collecting in some of those areas. Librarians may prefer print in some cases for some of their own LIS journals. It may not be too long before publishers also prefer to drop print publication due to market forces.

A large international survey of academic and research library journal publishing by the Primary Research Group in 2008 sheds light on the actual practices of academic libraries in terms of purchasing decisions. This type of information can inform decision-making by librarians faced with myriad choices for serials collections. For example, according to the report, 'about a quarter of the libraries in the sample believe that open access has already slowed the increase in journal prices' (Primary Research Group, 2008). Such information may spur librarians to recommit to the conversation about open access ultimately providing some relief for budgets. Each library must examine how open access is influencing serials pricing at the institution and consortial level, and communicate that to others in the system.

As librarians continue to focus on user needs and desires, and open access becomes a force affecting the market, publishers are looking to get closer to their customers outside the library – the readers and the researchers. In the online world, profits will be made by publishers learning what the users want and delivering it (Waltham, 2003). Publishers will become more focused on becoming service providers, and the librarian may be left out. In addition, many publishers have reputations in their disciplines, and have developed relationships with the scholarly author community. Publishers are increasingly contacting teaching faculty about suggesting potential library purchases. The library must be aware of the enhanced possibilities for the formation of direct relationships between publishers and readers/authors, and the resulting marginalisation of the subject specialist or electronic resources librarian as initial contact. Libraries and librarians must position themselves to be able to take control of the fate of collections work and not let outside forces dictate the outcome.

Open access and the LIS book literature

Librarians are also dealing with issues of changes in the availability of books. There is discussion about e-books in every sector, and this is a hot topic in the academic library world at present. With current digitisation projects of public domain monographs, and librarians looking to increase dissemination of their work published in books, issues of electronic access to this material will become more important with time. While disciplines outside the humanities focus most on peer-reviewed journal literature in discussions of scholarly communication, material in books may not realise the same level of visibility or provide the same type of impact for librarian authors. Scholarly publishers are beginning to move toward publishing book content in e-book formats as well as experimenting with unbundling content. A 2003 study of readers' preferences for reading books in PDF format illustrated that there was still a great desire for printed books alongside increasing digital content (Pope and Kannan, 2003). Librarians will have to watch trends regarding the reading of e-books on mobile devices and react in institutionally-specific ways to the availability of new methods of delivering content to users. Librarians may wish to exercise caution in many disciplines with any large-scale move to e-book content, making sure that library users will be accepting of such change. However, librarians will also want to respond to the free e-book content on the web and take advantage of the availability of scholarly content that can be added to the library free of charge.

Publishers of LIS book material will be under increasing pressure to unbundle scholarly book content into chapters for electronic publishing, as well as to make digital monographs easily accessible for libraries. Authors having used open access solutions for their journal articles may begin to demand similar consideration for book materials. Authors will want to enhance the visibility and impact of their monographic publications, not just their articles in journals. It may be that librarian authors will want to self-archive book chapter materials as well as versions of their journal article publications (notwithstanding copyright challenges). If impact is much less with authors publishing in monographs, and the cost of these monographs also presents challenges to academic library budgets, libraries may purchase fewer books, or rely on Google's book scanning project or other types of free e-book initiatives. Academic libraries may add more public domain material to catalogues as purchasing of in-copyright books slows. Librarian authors will find a more limited readership for their chapters in books. With current book materials, search engines may not actually cover book chapters adequately, and librarian authors may be less willing to contribute their work to monographs. Chapters in books by LIS authors may find a greater audience on the web through self-archiving. Some movement toward open access by publishers of monographs has been recently noted, and self-archiving of monographs or book chapters may be the next phase of open access that will affect library collections and publishers' bottom line. Websites focused on this aspect of open access, as well as the development of metrics to measure the impact of self-archived book materials, have begun to crop up (Harnad 2008; OASIS, 2009). Librarian authors may begin to abandon some of their ideas for publications in traditional monographs as web visibility remains limited, royalties mean less than impact for many, and the books may only find their way to shelves in some of the larger academic libraries. With publishers producing fewer print books in some disciplines, there will need to be new outlets for monographic scholarship. Librarians covering LIS areas in collection development may only be able to continue purchasing books from the most prominent publishers, or whittle approval plan profiles to cover a smaller list. Librarians, wise to changes in scholarly communication trends, may change their own ideas about where to publish their research. Publishers may begin to struggle with provision of greater incentives for potential book authors, especially authors of chapters. It will be interesting to see how libraries, publishers and vendors deal with the coming chapter-level economy, and how library users and teaching faculty respond to the changes. Library users may be confused by the array of 'digital objects' in the library collection, not caring whether they represent book chapters or journal articles. Librarians need to study trends in the e-book situation closely (whether free or subscription) and take part in discussions of product development with publishers and vendors. What will the book collections look like in the coming years, and how will librarians differentiate between books, journals and other formats as they start to transition to chapter or article-level digital objects in collections?

With the movement of the journal literature in some areas (especially in the sciences) to more open models, the transitioning of the book literature to free access on the web has even been pronounced in the humanities. Many wonder whether the monograph literature will transition to open access in ways similar to what has happened with the journal literature. Search engines do not often reveal important scholarship in current books. However, libraries have seen the world of out-of-copyright (public domain) materials explode on the web, with services that can now expose the full text of an entire book to researchers and readers. The free public domain e-books that are scanned and placed on the web represent a treasure trove of material that librarians can begin to integrate into collections and services. Along with this new source of material will come other open access monographic material placed on the web by scholars.

Implications for libraries of large open access book digitisation initiatives

Libraries and librarians have recently had to make decisions about the benefits of partnering with large book digitisation projects. Libraries have opened up their collections to major initiatives, both commercial and consortial, including Google Book Search, Open Content Alliance, Million Book Project and Project Gutenberg, to name a few. With budgets always an issue, librarians worldwide have had to see this new open access material as another source for scholarly acquisitions. Print-on-demand models, partnering with Google, adding scanned public domain books to ILSs, effects on interlibrary loan, and availability of 'search inside the book' functions have engaged librarians in new conversations. Librarians dealing with collection development activities will have the ability to add many free books to their collections, inflating acquisitions statistics, and integrating more of the library with the web. The result of open access to books will benefit the user, notwithstanding some of the poor-quality scanning that has been a topic of concern to librarians.

Another concern may be that libraries will share the collections that have made them 'special', and the incredible wealth of public domain book material held in the world's premier libraries will be available and searchable by keyword on the desktop of every researcher. This is a truly transformative situation for the remote researcher and for readers who would never have access to the original owning libraries. Libraries can do their part to point students and faculty toward open access books and the services to search them. Often Google's 'search inside the book' is found to be valuable in answering reference questions about obscure topics, and librarians have eagerly taken to this type of search.

Scholars may approach librarians with questions of citing this material, wondering whether reading the Google Books monograph is the same as seeing the original. This may only be a problem for the humanities scholar completing a dissertation or for those citing books in bibliographies in other books. Students may also have concerns, and faculty will decide whether these materials, almost exact replicas of the original, will be acceptable for coursework. If the scan is complete, it would seem that the open access web copy could be considered the actual book. One wonders whether scholars will still travel to far-flung libraries to consult the actual text. Rare books and special collections materials will be made available to a wider audience, watering down the importance of the uniqueness of materials in certain libraries. On the other hand, owning the original copy may become more valuable as more researchers discover its existence through the web. In an open access world, and with electronic materials dominating, many libraries may have come to see their unique special collections as their strength in this world of collection 'sameness'.

As with any Google programme, librarians have had to decide whether Google's terms are too restrictive, especially the requirement that book contents will not be opened to other search services. Librarians have had to make decisions whether to allow Google to transport their books to offsite locations to be scanned and then returned to the library. Many libraries that partnered with Google for the Google Scholar initiative may now be more comfortable with working with this commercial entity. However, some libraries will always worry about a commercial entity dictating terms and holding a monopoly over scholarly material. There is concern about the sustainability of a single company that is integrating so extensively with traditional libraries. Google pays to do the scanning, does not profit directly from the process (except to enhance the value of Google search), and libraries are free to add the public domain scanned Google Books to their catalogues. No payment is required of the library. Librarians will also decide whether to expose the snippets that Google makes available from their in-copyright books to their users through the catalogue or through the library website. By October 2007, the libraries allowing Google to scan their public domain collections included Oxford, New York Public Library, University of Michigan, Stanford and Harvard. Google intends to scan 15 million books in the next ten years, and conceivably any library may add those books, as long as they adhere to terms of service (Pfanner, 2008). For those libraries that worry about what might happen if Google ends its relationship with libraries for some reason, some prominent universities have created the 'HathiTrust', a collaborative repository initiative (Young, 2008). HathiTrust holdings will be searchable by OCLC WorldCat, providing enhanced discoverability and access (HathiTrust, 2009). HathiTrust can also be considered a preservation vehicle for digitised copies of printed books, further securing their availability in case the original artefact becomes unavailable at some point in the future due to deterioration or other loss.

Libraries that choose a true open access option may decide to go with the Open Content Alliance (OCA). The OCA was started by Brewster Kahle, the founder and director of the Internet Archive, and has grown steadily as a community effort. There is a cost to the scanning of books in this cooperative effort, but this is shared by the group's members and benefactors. The OCA does not stipulate which search engines can crawl the material, and libraries are free to have books scanned again by another company. The OCA is a nonprofit initiative that aims to make copies broadly available; its main principle is open access. The Boston Library Consortium, made up of 19 academic and research library members, has signed up to the initiative. The consortium project is self-funded, and cost $845,000 for two years (ten cents per page, paid by the consortium). This consortium has the potential to put 34 million public domain books on the internet for readers. The OCA began in 2005, with collections from European Archive, the Internet Archive, National Archives (UK), O'Reilly Media, Prelinger Archives, University of California, and University of Toronto. At the time of writing this, some 80 libraries and research institutes, including the Smithsonian, are participating in the OCA (Pfanner, 2008). The OCA's prominent non-academic partners also include the British Library, Marine Biological Laboratory/Woods Hole Oceanographic Institution Library, Biodiversity Heritage Project, and the Natural History Museum – London, among others. As of October 2007, the OCA had scanned 50 million pages of 200,000 books. While Google has closed scanning facilities, the OCA has open scanning centres located in libraries. Having the scanning centre in the library may represent another advantage for the library in partnering with OCA. The 'Espresso Book Machine' is OCA's print-on-demand solution for those individuals and libraries that prefer a printed copy (Ashmore and Grogg, 2008). When making open access books more discoverable as an extension of the collections, libraries will want to provide services to go with them for the convenience of users, whether print-on-demand options, access on mobile readers or phones, ability to print from computer labs, or use of these books in whole or in part in course reserves.

Michael Hart's Project Gutenberg is another example of an initiative attempting to put more book literature on the free web. Project Gutenberg and its worldwide partners and affiliates make available more than 100,000 free e-books on the web. Even though Project Gutenberg started out with an English-language focus, as of April 2008, its books spanned 55 languages. There is a focus on worldwide coverage. Volunteer proofreaders hail from all over the world, and no doubt librarians may want to be involved in this kind of quality assurance of a major digitisation project in a show of support for open access to information (*http://www.gutenberg.org*). A counterpart to Google Books in Europe is the Europeana project (BBC, 2008).

Amazon offers other programmes to libraries, one being to scan and sell 'rare and hard to find books from library collections'. Amazon will scan copies of out-of-print library books, and sell copies on the web. The Amazon model includes the library retaining the digital copies along with a portion of any revenue from print-on-demand services. Librarians will want to decide whether this type of initiative can generate revenue for the library while assisting researchers uncover and read truly obscure materials. Another role for librarians in the open access movement will be to evaluate all of the various programmes for library participation (Ashmore and Grogg, 2008). Libraries may choose maximum scanning and open access by partnering with many projects. For instance, the University of California has used OCA, Microsoft and Google. Librarians will need to collaborate on best practices for addition of free open access scholarly monographs to library collections and services. Although open access may be a 'library value', joining any digitisation project requires careful deliberation about benefit and staffing cost, and use of library resources. Librarians in public services can point users to scholarly book materials, whether free or purchased. For users to discover all scholarly content, librarians must organise the books and integrate them into catalogues, weblists and other library portals.

Other digitisation projects of interest to academic libraries include the Million Book Project and smaller initiatives such as the University of

Michigan's digitalculturebooks (*http://www.digitalculture.org/*). The University of Michigan Press and the Scholarly Publishing Office of the University of Michigan Library have (at the time of writing) produced six free open access books, and also sell those books in print. It would seem that librarians would be on the forefront of experimentation with producing open access books with library publishing programmes developed as repository initiatives or collaborations between libraries and university presses. Monographs about open access or digital initiatives produced using library personnel and available library expertise and repository capability would be another active way to showcase the benefits of open access book publishing.

Some traditional publishers are experimenting with open access monographs, and librarians will need to weigh these products as they do any other books. Will subject specialists add free books more readily, or still look for reviews, and other traditional means usually used by librarians to evaluate new books for potential purchase? National Academies Press, for instance has introduced an open access science series, and Penn State University Press and Penn State University Libraries are publishing 'Romance Studies', a peer-reviewed monograph series offered in both print and open access form. In this case, Penn State Libraries has followed the model of libraries as journal publisher, but is now moving toward a role as a book publisher as well. Could a respected library become a major publisher of open access books in the fields of librarianship? With the capabilities of the repositories, LIS interest in open access, and availability of potential high-profile authors and editors, it certainly seems a possibility.

There are examples of success with open access book publishing found in some niche areas of scholarship. Because promotion and tenure are tied more closely to the book literature in humanities, there may be more of an interest in those fields in open access book publishing. In addition, difficulty with lessening dissemination of scholarly books to libraries in recent years has caused some difficulty for authors. Publishers are less interested in books that have a limited audience due to the cost of production. A study by a group of scholars in the field of composition and rhetoric has produced a model for a successful open access monograph. The book, entitled *Writing Selves/Writing Societies*, used to be published in print, and was a respected work in the field. When the authors suggested that the work move to online, most contributors agreed with this plan, except junior faculty who worried about how electronic book publication might look to the promotion and tenure committee. Again, senior scholars may have to take the initiative in making changes toward open access behaviour. In talking about open access books, the necessity of still utilising stringent copyediting has been often mentioned, and in the case of *Writing Selves/Writing Society*, grant funds had to be spent to hire a copyeditor. An article in *First Monday* details the process that led to the successful online publication of *Writing Selves/Writing Societies*, including tasks such as getting the book listed in Books in Print, acquiring an ISBN, and marketing the books to libraries. The author found that the fact that the book was free and had no price caused some issues with Bowker. Since it was published, the website associated with *Writing Selves/Writing Society* has proved very popular with readers, amassing 36,000 downloads of the entire work, and 108,000 downloads of individual essays as of January 2008 (Bazerman et al., 2008). The work has received positive reviews and has been regularly cited by other works in Google Scholar. The analysis of the process after the fact not only reported the necessity of hiring the copyeditor, but also described the potential value for subsequent projects of having assistance with electronic formatting and other services that could potentially be offered by university libraries. These books could be opened up to all who do not have access to print books or library collections. When it comes to evaluating digital open access monographs, Bazerman et al. caution that promotion and tenure committees need the same type of instruction as they have had in many fields as regards the measurement of quality of material in open access journals. In addition, edited collections and single-author books may have different issues. For books, the qualifications of the editorial board and reviewers are paramount. As with journals, marketing and details of the publishing effort can benefit from the consultancy of a librarian. In fact, the authors of the aforementioned work asked readers to contact their acquisitions librarian to ask to have the book listed in catalogues. This is another acquisitions stream, and one wonders whether the subject specialist would use the same criteria normally used, such a vetting the work through reviews, or evaluating the author's or editor's reputation before adding such a book to library catalogues.

Many publishers continually speak to the value of copyediting, especially those who have seen results of the work of many scholars throughout the years. There is argument with this as well, specifically, whether librarians and readers are satisfied with rigorous peer review without final copyediting when reading an article or manuscript. With journals, proponents of 'green' open access would argue that the author's final copy after peer review is acceptable. While more empirical studies of the real value of copyediting to the research process may be necessary, Goodman et al. (2007) undertook a pilot study of unedited articles from a small group of titles in social sciences and biology and found no errors significant enough to affect the results presented. Still, there are many publishers, readers and authors that care very much about excellent copyediting.

Cataloguing librarians would need to develop workflows for born-digital open access books. Would the librarian expect to follow available usage statistics on such an open access title? In the early going, will librarians tend to add born open access books to collections in order to support the concept of new types of scholarly output? Soon, teaching faculty may begin to develop digitally-produced 'open textbooks' as a response to frustrations with the escalating cost and business climate of the textbook industry. Interested faculty and students will find initiatives on the web promoting open access textbooks. Librarians also need to be watching the open access textbook trends and discussing the library's part in supporting, advocating or integrating these quality scholarly alternatives. Students would undoubtedly be highly appreciative of any move to lessening the cost and improving the availability of textbooks. As tuition rises and economic woes increase, textbook issues have moved front and centre for libraries and may benefit from even limited open access solutions. There is great support from students and faculty for open textbooks, but issues remain as to format as well as suitability and desirability for many disciplines that are used to taking extensive notes, such as accounting, for example.

In the end, librarians will struggle with ways to define 'the library' while adding web materials that extend their collections without adding cost. Along with readers, librarians will most likely welcome this addition of material. Use of the word 'library' has been applied to non-traditional players such as the Internet Archive, which uses the term 'internet library' to describe what it is building. This is a community effort, but the internet library exists on the web. The Internet Archive talks of countries building 'libraries' of their cultural heritage on the internet (Internet Archive, 2009). Clearly, the library is moving out of the building, and the institution, and into the community at large, and librarians will have to recognise and contribute to this transformation. Libraries will have to decide whether to move to publishing, whether to include free web book collections in catalogues, and most importantly, what will comprise the collection and the identity of each individual academic library. Along with their advocacy for open access for the journal literature, and if the book literature follows, librarians will have to grapple with what 'success' of the movement means for the future of the work of librarians, and for the library itself.

4

Librarians and their roles in the academy

Promotion and tenure issues for librarians and teaching faculty

Promotion and tenure concerns govern where many librarians in research institutions publish their work. The library may be promoting open access while expecting faculty librarians to stay with the traditionally prestigious titles for their own publications, regardless of the open access practices of these journals. Faculty promotion and tenure committees, when evaluating librarians, may not be paying heed to current recommendations for expanding the definitions of scholarly communications to include open access journal publications, or even liberal self-archiving of preprints and postprints in either library and information science (LIS) subject or institutional repositories. This may be the case even as librarians are managing the institutional repositories that may or may not be populated with librarians' work. Librarian authors, as is the case with scholars in other disciplines, may not feel completely comfortable moving outside the boundaries of the most prestigious of the LIS titles when promotion or tenure is the goal. As with other faculty, librarians on a tenure track may wish to stay with the 'tried and true' scholarly LIS journals when publishing. The journal article is still the currency of the promotion and tenure process for faculty librarians in many institutions. Promotion and tenure requirements do much to increase the submissions to peer-reviewed journals and may also be a key component of librarian scholarship making a collective move toward open access.

Senior librarians evaluating others for promotion and tenure may want to make strong statements in support of junior faculty's submission of work to open access LIS journals and relevant repositories. This may require a move away from only looking at prestige and stature as measured through 'impact factor' and other established metrics. LIS, especially the library literature that is not classified under 'information science', is not well represented by impact factor as listed in Thomson Reuters' Journal Citation Reports. Given the appropriate support, open access journals may in time become high impact. Having an open access business model is not an impediment to a journal's stature. In terms of impact factor, for example, open access journals within other disciplines have had success. Within biology, for instance, the journal with the highest impact factor in 2007 was, according to the Journal Citation Reports, *PLoS Biology*, an open access journal (Thomson Reuters, 2007). Caution is often urged when the talk of open access journals turns to the 'author-pays' or other researcher/institutional membership funded journals. These journals, although successful, do rely on stable funding sources, and expenses are covered in such a way. Open access journals that are 'free to authors' represent the option that librarians would most likely use for publication of scholarly work. LIS journals, like others in the social sciences, will have a longer path to the type of measured success demonstrated by the Public Library of Science (PLoS). Other values may need to be factored into the promotion and tenure process in order for the LIS discipline's journal literature to be able to make a more forceful move toward open access practices. When decisions are made about submitting for potential publication, it would need to become desirable and acceptable for librarian authors to choose newer, but still rigorously peer-reviewed journals. Some have called for an expansion of the definition of what can be considered acceptable publication types, including many new digital forms of scholarship, in evaluating librarians and others for promotion and tenure.

Open access and research impact

Many publishers do not allow self-archiving of a postprint to a repository until after publication of the article. Once any version of an article is available in Google Scholar or other search engines, impact can be shown, which may be helpful in promotion and tenure actions. Librarians may be attracted to prestigious peer-reviewed journals that allow self-archiving of both preprint and postprint, while providing quick turnaround time in the refereeing process (Suber, 2007b). Librarians should make sure that publishers accepting their work are participating with Google Scholar and other similar search engines so that their work, or at least a citation, will be visible on the web. If publications archived in an institutional repository are not visible through a Google Scholar search, it is possible that the repository making the deposited works available is not configured to be easily crawled by Google or other search engines. Librarians, even more than other faculty members, should be well aware of strategies to use in archiving their own work, but also in offering advice to others who may be less knowledgeable about changes in their discipline's patterns of scholarly communications.

Many studies continue to support the premise that open access, where research is available free to readers on the web, increases research impact. A helpful, continuously updated webliography from the Open Citation Project compiles all relevant references, and can be useful to any librarian considering studying issues of research impact and open access (Open Citation Project, 2009). Librarians may be approached by faculty authors and other researchers to consult on issues of impact. This type of role may be more in demand from all in the institution as time goes on. Librarians can use many methods to increase the web visibility and research impact of their own work, and also offer practical strategies to other researchers (Mullen, 2008). Whether self-archiving, publishing in open access journals, choosing journals with open models, or seeking journal publishers that participate with Google Scholar, there are currently many strategies to increase personal impact that librarian authors may want to consider before submitting their work and possibly signing away copyright in a traditional manner. This type of consulting role could be a new avenue for librarians eager to be part of the scholarly communication discussion in any discipline served. Offering other discipline-appropriate strategies for making researchers' work more web visible expands the librarians' offerings beyond simply advocating for deposits to the institutional repository. Placing the repository services more within the context of an informed strategy may be of greater interest to potential depositors, and ensure a more well-rounded service geared toward trying to entice more traffic to the institutional repository. Librarians may also wish to find methods to demonstrate the success of the 'informal' kind of impact that comes from greater web visibility of scholarly work. Informal impact from open access journals may include instances of the article being used as background reading for courses, referred to in the research guides of other institutions, or mentioned in blogs. This kind of informal impact furthers the reach of the scholarship, and pushes readership.

Measuring impact is as important as ever to deans, department chairs and provosts. Senior scholars can set the tone for acceptable publication activity. Faculty with tenure should be more able to expand their article submissions to include open access publications, and by doing so, indicate a commitment to publishing in more open publications. In addition, pressure on certain commercial publishers would be greatest if tenured faculty began to move away from publishing in their journals, affecting the all-important impact factor. For junior faculty, the stakes are greater in moving to publish in the possibly less prestigious and less well-known fledgling open access titles. It is less risky for tenured faculty to take the lead in the move to more open scholarship. Many of the current open access guidelines suggest that librarians ask teaching faculty to consider offering incentives for junior faculty to publish in open access publications, and it is hoped that committees evaluating librarians for tenure would also follow suit.

Librarians now have an array of open access publication options, both in terms of journals and available repositories. Articles about scholarly communication issues in LIS may be best included in open access LIS journals as there are now several to choose between. Another option is to publish in a prestigious traditional library journal whose publisher supports self-archiving of postprints, or a journal with a very short embargo period before all articles become open access. If advocacy is to continue, these issues must be discussed and practised broadly by librarians globally in order to send a message. Librarians will need to advocate through their own behaviour, as well as keeping all of these issues in mind when making acquisitions and cancellation decisions for collections, especially in LIS.

Timeliness is an issue for librarians in searching for an outlet for their publications. For those with a ticking promotion or tenure clock, the need to publish and show impact necessitates a faster publication cycle than is sometimes offered by traditional LIS publishers. Quality open access journals may be a good alternative for novice librarian authors, or even for senior scholars who wish quick, widespread dissemination of ideas. Mentors can be useful in advising less experienced librarians about publication alternatives. All librarians working as mentors in academic libraries can be a valuable source of information on open access and self-archiving alternatives for appropriate LIS publications. In LIS, librarians at institutions where there is a robust institutional repository will have to weigh the pros and cons of multiple deposits in both the disciplinary repositories (E-LIS and dLIST) and/or the institutional repository. There is inherent tension in the decision by librarians to support the institutional repository which they may have helped build, and to support disciplinary repositories which function across institutions and provide a 'one-stop shop' to the self-archived library literature. It will be up to authors to make choices that are most personally expedient, or in some cases, more driven by the desire to support the institutional repository. Incentive and motivation for self-archiving behaviour may be different for librarian authors than for other faculty. One wonders why there is not total support of repository archiving by LIS authors and researchers.

For readers' convenience, librarian authors will want to make sure their publications are available in a free version on the web whenever possible. Librarians, just like all other groups of scholars, are using free web search engines in great numbers. Librarians may be gathering and reading open access materials first and foremost as they search for background information on many topics. Discovery, even in library and information science, is fuelled by the existence of a large amount of free scholarship on the web. Not all academic librarians that are would-be authors are affiliated with institutions that have comprehensive collections in the interdisciplinary areas they are studying. Many turn to alternative open access resources on the web to begin or pursue a research concept and to explore current discussion on the topic. Even for those researchers not affiliated with traditional scholarly journal collections, the corpus of open access peer-reviewed research literature is increasing all the time. Librarian authors should insist on the maximum number of means of discovery for their publications so that all potential readers on the web are able to find their published articles. Many researchers and librarians also start searching for information with a Google search, and open access materials are readily discovered. Subject archives containing preprints and postprints, blogs and blog search engines, web lists, institutional repositories, listserv archives, Google, traditional abstracting/indexing services, and databases like OAIster all provide means of discovery. Librarian authors who know how to make sure their material has maximum visibility on the web are able to increase the informal impact of that material, sometimes through active marketing of their work. More readership means greater impact for individual articles and for authors as well as for the whole corpus of LIS research. Greater readership of scholarly work is one of the cornerstones of the open access movement and one that is supported by library values.

Faculty status for librarians

In the USA, both ACRL and the American Association of University Professors support faculty status for academic librarians (Hill, 2005). Of course, there are many who do not agree with faculty status for librarians found within the profession as well as among other faculty groups. In one example of a system with tenure-track faculty status for librarians, the practice of librarianship and the 'production of scholarly work' are of equal importance in evaluation for tenure. Currently, more than one half of the institutions in the USA grant librarians faculty status and most have a system analogous to that of the teaching faculty (Hill, 2005). It is true that academic librarians on a tenure track contribute more to the literature, and that librarians in public, school and special libraries publish less (Hinchliffe and Dorner, 2003). Still, there are those in LIS that feel that 'at most universities, the librarians, however well qualified, are not usually the academic equals of their faculty patrons' (Goodman, 2004). This type of rhetoric may serve to discredit to some degree the library literature in the eyes of those in the academy, or even to remove it from the discussion of the movement of important literatures to open access.

There are also different publishing patterns among academic librarians in college versus university libraries (Zemon and Bahr, 1998). These differences would not be important to moving open access initiatives forward because self-archiving, solving permissions problems, and publishing in open access journals would increase visibility of work for all librarians. College librarians author fewer articles in the library literature than librarians with similar positions at universities. Publication in the library and information science literature is a more common practice among librarians from the large university libraries. This pattern would obviously skew what topics are covered in the LIS literature. More articles would be expected to focus on the concerns of librarians and their users in this type of library. For instance from 1980 to 1991, 77.7 per cent of authors of papers accepted by *College & Research Libraries* were employed at doctorate-granting institutions. Sixty per cent of all of the articles in *Journal of Academic Librarianship* and *College & Research Libraries* are by authors in large academic libraries (Zemon and Bahr, 1998). Tenure pressure is considered to be a major motivator toward publication for academic librarians. In this same study, publishing was a requirement for tenure in the case of 80 per cent of surveyed authors. It has been reported that 89 per cent of academic institutions made funding available to librarian authors. The vast majority of college librarians state that they write to share innovations and concerns, as well as for recognition (Zemon and Bahr, 1998). Certainly, for college librarians, for reasons that are in many ways similar for librarians working in large university research settings, open access models would make published work more globally accessible via the open web. Web visibility would seem an important professional goal for all librarians regardless of type or size of institution.

Outside of promotion and tenure concerns, library administrators may play a role in encouraging or discouraging librarians from seeking publishing opportunities in open access publications. Some part of the academic library's prestige is tied to the research output of librarians. The titles of journals where the librarians publish are of importance to the reputation and status of the library and the institution. Recently, *College & Research Libraries* listed those institutions with the greatest number of accepted articles in the journal, currently labelled first in prestige by LIS deans and directors (Wiberley et al., 2006). Library administrators may reward author behaviour in some way, either by promoting the institution's librarians' publications in the academy or to the outside librarian community, or by using the librarians' publication record as proof of their stature in the field. Announcing LIS research publications by librarians in news disseminated to other departments, or integrating librarian scholarship with online mechanisms that bring all of the institutional scholarship together will advance credibility and establish a clear record of disciplinary scholarly communication behaviour. Representing librarian scholarship in institutional online webs such as those represented by Cornell's VIVO initiative, or in institutional repositories are options for showcasing librarian research. Librarians who write for publication might be better able to make the practical case for open access if they can demonstrate increased impact of their own work.

Open access publication may not be reflected in current reward systems. Library administrators must make clear whether supporting open access through librarian publication in open access journals and deposit of work in the institutional repository or disciplinary subject archives is to be encouraged or even expected. Of course, published work of faculty librarians may be covered under any university or college open access mandate. Not many institutions at present have such mandates for all faculty members. Librarians and other faculty members who are savvy about open access may choose from among a variety of open access strategies for each of their publications. Practical information may be best disseminated quickly through open access journals, and articles in expensive subscription journals not widely held in libraries may be best deposited in subject or institutional repositories. Rights to deposit would be secured early in the submission decision process. There may be many roads to open access for those librarians in a position to 'push the envelope' due to their own scholarly communication expertise and the availability of knowledgeable colleagues and library technology. Librarians can be opportunistic about further experimentation with current models of open access publication and also in pushing for more library publishing of librarian scholarship. A key question remains as to whether librarians will be willing to experiment or push agendas throughout the library workplace.

Reward systems also play a part in other ways in increasing the visibility and credibility of the open access movement. There has been at least one librarian award given for excellence in scholarly communication and open access. The Faculty of Humanities at Lund University awarded Ingegerd Robow, a senior librarian in Lund's library head office, an honorary doctorate for her work in scholarly communication and open access. She has been a leading advocate of open access within Sweden, the Nordic countries and elsewhere (Morrison, 2006; Suber, 2006a). This type of recognition helps to put open access on the map internationally, while singling out a librarian for advancing the cause of open access. This also signifies that librarians are taking prominent roles in the open access movement, and are being highly rewarded for their advocacy. Other prestigious awards, for example, the SPARC Europe Award for Outstanding Achievements in Scholarly Communications, have not previously been awarded to a librarian or library in Europe, but the opportunity exists. If libraries are the place where open access is to be fomented, then librarians will want to achieve visibility, status and recognition in these areas (SPARC Europe, 2009).

Do librarians really want to see changes in the current model?

There are many inside as well as outside the library profession who believe, and have identified ways that 'full open access transforms library policies, procedures, and services when it removes both price and permission barriers' (Bailey, 2006). Library collections work, where the model in some cases has changed from ownership to access, will include finding ways to maximise discovery of the many scholarly materials found free on the internet. Even with all of the current changes, most libraries still deal in paper books and journals, and are already operating in a hybrid environment with print and digital materials. Extending libraries' collections and services into web materials will continue to blur boundaries. Envisioning the library of the future is challenging, and librarians may be treading carefully while conducting heavy weeding of print journals, and also noticing a lack of use of traditional reference books in some areas. Best practices seem to be elusive in collections work during these transformative times. Librarians look to the literature, and to national leadership for guidance in moving forward, wanting to secure the scholarly record and take responsibility for digital preservation during a time of explosive growth of material in many formats. All efforts at open access and scholarly communications take place alongside some traditional work and practices; individual libraries are responding in different ways to the many changes. A further gulf, already challenging, may be opening up between the sciences and other library collections.

With all of the talk about the move to article-level discovery, the peer-reviewed journal in its traditional guise remains because of values such as impact factor. Impact factor and other emerging metrics continue to be a basic element of the librarian's own publishing activities, as well as collection development focus. This is especially true in the STEM disciplines. Searchers may be looking for a single article, not a journal title, and librarians may have trouble envisioning the single article economy and what it might mean for the library (Waltham, 2003). At some tipping point, there will be a change away from the journal article and a whole new vocabulary will be needed to describe digital publication objects. This vocabulary will not be predicated upon objects based on the traditional items of publication, such as journals and books. Currently, the journal is still the 'package' for the scholarship within, but that traditional model is changing. The library 'collection' is becoming more difficult to define as it extends out toward the open and deep web. Librarians may wonder how they will be building and developing the collection, still needing to vet and organise the scholarly record. If self-archiving of all but some of the most recent digital objects (if embargoed or held under copyright) becomes a reality, librarians may only be dealing with providing access to a small current listing of digital objects not freely available on the web. This changes greatly the concept of the library, and librarians will have to decide whether to marginalise much of their collecting, and instead focus on a service orientation centred on digital materials and the issues of their 'importance' to researchers and students. These questions might prevent librarians from rushing headlong into advocacy efforts without enough understanding about how open access will actually change the library irrevocably. Some of these issues might be most pronounced in research libraries.

The unbundling of content will continue apace as researchers link to content from many different starting points on the web or library website. The development of the digital object identifier (DOI), a persistent link to identify individual digital objects, is a move toward the unbundling of book and journal content (International DOI Foundation, 2009). The DOI is starting to become a requirement of some citation styles, such as that of the American Psychological Association. Mechanisms that promote seamless linking to content will be appreciated by the legions of search engine users. Librarians will need to make sure that vetted born-digital open access materials have all available library technology enabled to enhance their discovery, such as link resolvers, federated search, and linking to Google Scholar.

Academic librarians focus attention on the library as the scholarly literature portal for the institution as in-person visits to the library decline. There may be less face-to-face contact with faculty and library users, and instruction may be moving more toward online tutorials. Reference statistics may go down due to the popularity of free web search engines, and more of the peer-reviewed literature will move to the web. Vendors and publishers drive traffic to their own websites by adding value with Web 2.0 tools and effective search. There is competition for the library as provider of research resources. Librarians face struggles in trying to retain their identity as the place for information at the university. Librarians may find a lessening of power and influence in the academy. As much of librarians' public service work moves online and collections work manifests in more online content, the association of librarians with quality research services and excellent collection development could become less obvious. This could affect faculty status for librarians where it currently exists. Librarians certainly will not want to be the ones advocating for users to abandon the library and its collections. Academic librarians may harbour worry over their professional futures if open access is touted as the 'future of libraries'. Librarians will continue to discuss the future of academic libraries and the publishing activities that feed collections, and will need to find a way to incorporate the free scholarly web resources into workflows as this type of material grows exponentially. Librarians will need to be proactive in redefining their services and their indispensability to the institution even as open access continues unabated. Open access has implications for librarians and libraries, but it must be remembered that saving serial costs for libraries was never the sole purpose of the open access movement. To fully support open access (if that is what libraries intend) may require some reaffirmation of the role of the library and librarians and the value they will always add to the institution.

Implications of the aging of the current pool of academic librarians

There are many potential impediments on the road to dramatic change of any kind for librarians. One possible difficulty is the aging of the profession, well documented in the literature (Jacobson, 2002; Curran, 2003). All of the expertise that Gorman deems 'irreplaceable' is oftentimes referring to the vast stores of knowledge that traditional librarians have accumulated through years of being the 'go-to' people for anyone looking for any type of information (Gorman, 2002). Before Google, there were librarians. One had to know how and where to direct patrons to find almost anything. Librarians had built-in job security as research materials were much more difficult to find in the print past, and librarians may have enjoyed playing 'gatekeeper', a role that is now somewhat anachronistic in the age of ubiquitous access to the internet and search engines. Librarians may wish to hold on to established reputations as 'search and discover' experts in the world of scholarly literature.

With some academic libraries having no librarians in the 20–34-year-old age group, one wonders whether librarians are eager to move into the new paradigms of librarianship, especially those including open access initiatives. Librarians may be struggling to keep up with the technological knowledge necessary to truly move the library to the digital future. Continuous education for librarians is necessary to ensure that limited library budgets are used to provide collections that are truly relevant to the increasingly 'digital native' researchers and new faculty, as librarians move in age away from these groups. As for the aging of librarians, in Canada, for instance, 50 per cent of librarians in Canadian ARL libraries will be retiring over the next 15 years. Only 12 per cent of librarians are in the 25–34-year-old age group, compared with 25 per cent of that age group found in comparable professions A Concordia University study reveals that 84 per cent of the professional staff are over 40, 55 per cent are over 50, and just 3 per cent are between 20 and 30 (Lenzini, 2002; Curran, 2003). This 'graying' of the profession may have negative implications for the move toward open access and away from traditional scholarly communication paradigms for some disciplines.

The individual library's identity

Collection development librarians, administrators, and many others in an institution take pride in the stature of their library collections in comparison to peers. Statistics, such as those published by the Association of Research Libraries (ARL), have focused on ownership of materials, and competition pushes the numbers. What will the new library collection look like with all of the web materials available to everyone? Is there a resistance by librarians to moving toward 'sameness?' This concern about the stature of individual libraries plays out in contrast to the library value of 'democratisation of information'. What will academic library collections comprise, even as the subscription products move to models of access rather than ownership? Will individual libraries retain their identities? The reputation of academic libraries is important in terms of recruitment for open positions, support within an institution, and membership in the more elite rungs of librarianship. Many librarians seek out positions where they are able to work with the great collections, as it is much more satisfying for some to have access to a great depth and breadth of resources. Academic library collections may be moving toward a more 'vanilla' look, with only the unique materials and special collections retaining importance and conferring identity. Ownership, but also access will define the library's collections. New methods of assessing libraries will develop, away from numbers of items owned. Consortial collecting and the massive book digitisation projects taking place at famous institutions may further dilute each library's identity. If more materials move to open access, how will librarians and users measure, evaluate and identify the 'great' libraries? Democratisation of information is a valued goal, but individual libraries' collections may lose some stature. Libraries will promote their unique collections and the services that accompany them (Coleman and Roback, 2005). Special collections and other materials that are unique to the institution and 'owned' will become most important to the library's identity, and may become the most important focus of the repository. The repository collections and activities may confer a new excellence and identity to each library and its institution.

Librarian behaviour echoing that of their 'other' subject specialties

Librarians may not approach the LIS literature with one view of making the literature more widely available. There may not be a cohesive force bringing librarians together around this issue. Many academic librarians working as subject specialists may have extensive experience as scholars in their disciplines in addition to their contributions to librarianship and the

LIS literature. Many have masters or doctoral degrees from fields unrelated to librarianship, and bring vast knowledge of a particular subfield to their work as librarians. In their everyday work, some academic librarians focus almost exclusively on a particular subject area or broader disciplinary area. Librarians may bring attitudes about open access and other publishing models to their library research from those other, often unrelated disciplines. These librarians may be in tune with the scholarly communication norms of the disciplines with which they associate, and may view open access advocacy or debate through a narrower lens. Attitudes in library collections and advocacy discussions may reflect long and deep knowledge of disciplinary paradigms, and it will not be possible for libraries to take a broad-brushed approach to the issues of self-archiving or publishing in newer forms of digital publications. Subject-specialist librarians are of vital importance in educating those in more general positions about the stark differences that exist among subfields when it comes to author behaviour and promotion and tenure expectations. All attempts at promoting open access must be seen through a disciplinary lens.

In their own writing for publication, librarians may be moving toward open access behaviour at differing rates depending on the other subject disciplines they are working with as liaisons and collection development librarians. Depending on their disciplinary responsibilities, librarians may have more or less daily exposure to open access discussions. As open access is most developed in the STEM literature, science librarians may be much more familiar with open access in all of its forms, and be more amenable to choosing alternative models for their own work. It would be difficult to function adequately as an academic science librarian, especially in some areas like life sciences, without a working and conversational awareness of open access models. Whether in terms of the author-pays, delayed open access (making articles freely available after a short embargo), institutional membership models (BioMedCentral), the preprint culture of some subject areas (physics), or the myriad licensing and sales models they are operating with, librarians working with science collections may be well-versed in the world of open access. A science librarian, having dealt with the development of the preprint literature's importance, as in physics, for instance, may expect their own research as a librarian to be archived in a subject repository even as a preprint. However, one survey has reported that 'some academics interviewed, especially those from the science disciplines, tend to have a more limited view of repositories' (Hoorens et al., 2008). Scientists may already have well-established scholarly communication patterns that do not involve libraries. Science librarians may be called upon to try to change this perception coming out of science departments, and may be reluctant to market the institutional repository to busy faculty that may lack interest. Science librarians may find themselves in the unenviable position of recognising a lack of interest on the part of scientists, but needing to recruit material for the repository in order to be identified as a solid advocate for their library's efforts on behalf of open access. Those working with science faculty may be expected to begin to change preconceived perceptions on the part of researchers about the repository and the value of depositing material. As for promotion and tenure, and issues of research impact and web visibility, the librarian may wish to tread lightly in consulting with junior departmental faculty about these issues. Advice given by librarians in such a vital conversation as promotion and tenure might be better left to specific senior faculty advisers in individual departments. This type of consulting may be a new role for science librarians and requires current knowledge of scholarly communications, various open access journal choices for publication, new ways of ranking journals in disciplines, bibliometrics and the tools that generate impact, and the potential role of self-archiving of postprints. However, even all of this information might not be sufficiently specific for the institution and department. The learning curve is steep, and for junior departmental faculty, the stakes can be quite high. Such faculty members may not want to veer far from established norms and will look to institutional administration for guidance in choosing publication outlets for their work. Librarians cannot, through advocacy alone, change promotion and tenure norms for departments, institutions or disciplines. Librarians can provide background, start dialogues, and tie open access into promotion and tenure for disciplines served. Librarians cannot change established scholarly communication patterns for certain disciplines and risk losing credibility as knowledgeable professionals if they are too heavy-handed. Working together on scholarly communication teams or committees, populated by both librarians and departmental faculty, may provide a better roadmap forward. Further collaboration between practising librarians and LIS teaching faculty may also prove advantageous by allowing a different type of discourse and opportunity for enhanced research opportunities for both parties.

Librarians can prepare tutorials that discuss the entire publication process for junior faculty and graduate students who may want to explore ideas about open access or get more background information. Rather than only taking an advocacy position, it may be beneficial for the library to develop modular programmes that introduce concepts of open access through discussion of the entire publication process. This discussion of more general issues of publication may appeal to researchers, especially if librarians also teach new research tools and products. Librarians from the University of Colorado have created a very effective online tutorial entitled 'Publish not perish: the art and craft of publishing in scholarly journals', which fills a void left by traditional information literacy programmes targeted at graduate students and faculty (Knievel, 2008). Librarians may find a receptive audience for instruction sessions that deal with such topics and find those sessions a productive venue for discussion of open access initiatives as well as to get feedback that might lead to new opportunities for the library's advocacy initiatives.

On the other hand, some humanities librarians would not be as apt to be immersed in the world of open access initiatives, and may even be dealing with a fledgling electronic environment and an emphasis on printed books. Science librarians may well wonder why the literature of their own LIS field does not lend itself to moving toward open access, and feel a disconnect in mission with humanities librarian colleagues. Conversely, humanities librarians or those in fields where open access has not yet made inroads may become tired of advocacy efforts that do not seem to be relevant or of interest to the scholars with whom they work. A broad-brushed effort will not be effective across the library. Scholarly communication and open access discussions can serve to educate and enlighten all librarians about norms in different disciplines.

The social sciences are wide and varied in their disciplinary responses to open access. The LIS literature crosses into many other disciplines and is wide-reaching in its focus, and therefore librarian authors will follow very different behaviour patterns with their own work. It will be difficult to make generalisations about the LIS literature and associated contributions from librarians, possibly diluting the response of the library community as a whole in terms of the corpus of library literature. The LIS literature, even though classified as a social science, may evolve in very uneven ways. Library associations and institutional libraries will have to grapple with making statements or advising mandates for librarian authors that do not take into account the variety of backgrounds and motivations of readers and writers of the small, but extremely diverse world of the LIS literature.

Disciplinary differences reflect different sets of realities in the world of scholarly communication. Thus, for the library, it may be challenging to populate scholarly communications committees and other advocacy groups with librarians representing different disciplines and still reach consensus on an agenda for moving the institution and the library forward. Science librarians may feel more pressure to follow trends in open access proactively, especially following so many recent government mandates intended to open science literature to the public that has funded it. Science librarians may see open access to the scientific literature as an inevitable aspect of the library's future. Even though the discussion can take an overarching focus, the real action comes at the disciplinary or subfield level. Various groups of librarians may be less informed, and some may resist new trends, creating an impasse. Therefore, librarians from different disciplines would benefit by open discussion within the library and an education campaign focused on these disciplinary differences in scholarly communication and open access. One size does not fit all, and a science-based focus on open access may cause divisiveness among library groups, whether they are focused on public services or collection development. A singular action plan for all librarians, or for all teaching faculty may be misguided.

Promoting the institutional repository as the means to open access

The first issue that many scholarly communication committees must deal with as a cohesive group will be the institutional repository. Self-archiving, especially dealing with some of the more resistant publishers, remains a challenge for those librarians promoting this behaviour to teaching faculty. It remains to be seen whether institutional repositories will be widely utilised in institutions, and not seen by researchers and librarians as another 'silo' for information. A study of Cornell's institutional repository discussed some of the difficulties encountered in the effort to populate it with deposits of scholarly material (Davis and Connolly, 2007). Issues of the advisability of mandates and incentives for faculty remain, as well as the necessity of determining appropriate roles for all librarians, even reference librarians, in the development of the successful institutional repository. Will the amount of self-archiving ultimately determine the success of the repository, or remain just one of its many potential functions in the library and institution? If the efforts are not very successful, will librarians be 'blamed' for the lack of participation by the institution's scholars? A robust institutional repository has unlimited potential for value in the coming 'data deluge', for new roles for librarians in e-science and data curation, and for harnessing the unique scholarly output of the university, but librarians in everyday roles may be far removed from the important mission that has been ascribed to the repository. There may be parallel missions between the everyday work of front-line librarians, and the work of those trying to position the repository as a central focus of today's forward-thinking academic research library. The repository and the librarians who work with it must be integrated into the collections and services of the library so that the rest of the community will see it as a vital and dynamic part of the library itself. Otherwise, marginalisation may occur.

Priorities for funding and staffing the 'new' academic library

Library administrators may also be struggling with the task of prioritising projects as the expense of funding digital initiatives threatens to take resources from traditional collections work. Are the library's book collections going to suffer as the library takes on the role of journal publisher or repository developer? With budgets suffering in the economic downturn in many academic libraries, or in times when endowments have not met expectations, the library must focus on what is important to the institutional mission and to the individual scholars that use the library as an integral part of research. Developing electronic resource management systems, purchasing and maintaining federated search products, continuing to support the great costs of OPACs, committing to paying membership fees for publishers' open access journal programmes, 'pledging' monies to journal programmes such as SCOAP3, subsidising author fees, enlarging the mission of institutional repositories, and developing library content for course management systems are examples of initiatives that may redirect librarians from what they may have traditionally seen as their primary roles in reference, instruction or collection development. There will need to be more teamwork across technical and public services, and more cross-pollination of new groups. Adding new responsibilities, especially those that require new training and a steep learning curve in terms of the rapidly changing mores of scholarly communication may create workload issues for busy librarians. With the pervasiveness of the internet and a possible lack of foot traffic into the library to ask reference questions or to consult reference books onsite, librarians may be working in an environment where they must continue to provide traditional services virtually while expanding roles significantly.

While expanding roles into more consulting on scholarly communications matters gives librarian expertise new visibility in the institution, traditional responsibilities may be keeping academic librarians from participating more fully in open access discussions and behaviours. Librarians may be closing ranks or covering more ground than in more robust financial times, and may not be able to take on new roles as readily as expected. Staffing becomes an issue, as libraries may not be able to afford to enlarge their personnel numbers to accommodate expanded roles in the university. Librarians will need to respond to institutional priorities, even though at times this may provide an atmosphere of uncertainty about expectations in all areas of the library.

Collection development librarians and open access

The future of collections in an open access world

Some librarians may question whether the development of the open access movement will, in the end, disrupt the work of the library to such a point that libraries and librarians will become irrelevant. If all scholarly information becomes free on the web, what will library collections look like? If librarians are too eager with open access, including free open access materials (in ever-growing numbers) alongside their subscribed-to journals on their weblists, patrons may skip the library website, and hence the library, and go straight to the web. Already, the web is the first place that most people go for information, and the library and its website must compete. Academic librarians may not want to contribute to any future where library collections and services have changed to the degree that some library organisations seem to be advocating. Other librarians may be eager to contribute to a whole new world of scholarly information production and dissemination. With funding and staffing resources at a premium, libraries must decide on which collections and services priorities to focus.

A change to open access and adding free web resources to the library assumes researchers and other users will make different types of choices, based on quality as well as expediency (quick, free web access) in choosing scholarly literature for background research. With the success of Google Scholar as a search engine that is also free, researchers may eventually find sufficient free full-text peer-reviewed material from the open or deep web. With publishers under pressure from authors as well as from mandates to provide liberal self-archiving policies, to accept addenda, and to reduce embargo time periods, there are many changes afoot that may affect the business relationships between libraries and publishers. With some libraries experimenting with 'patron-driven' e-books collection strategies, and the use of usage statistics to drive decision-making becoming more commonplace, library users may have more control over what makes up the academic library collection than in the past. With quality alternatives growing in number on the free web, library patrons may skip the library altogether.

Librarians, even science librarians, may feel conflicted about the growing tide of open access materials. It is becoming more difficult for librarians to state quality and prestige with certainty, as different measures of impact, and newer models of scholarly communication become more acceptable in academia. Measures of impact will slowly change to accommodate different kinds of web publishing and the social networking that occurs around scholarly articles and books. With archived work in repositories, lengthy blog postings, and other alternative materials 'published' on the open web, some librarians may wonder what 'counts' as a publication. Clearly, librarians wish to define what constitutes scholarly work in this changing environment. This may become more difficult as there may be other measures of quality besides whether something is peer-reviewed. It seems at the moment that both librarians and researchers/authors are increasingly wedded to the idea of peer-review as the absolute determinant of quality in the scholarly system. Systems of peer review may be evolving, as exemplified by the different models being used, such as the system used by PLoS ONE, which attempts to expedite the process (*http://www.plosone.org/*). One thing that will remain constant as open access moves forward is the importance of peer review. Librarians may have a role in assuring users as to the sustainability and level of peer review utilised in all types of publications accessed from the library. Librarians also must continue to dispel the myths that surround open access journals in terms of the peer review that is inherent in any high-quality scholarly journal regardless of its business model or method of access. Quality peer review may be said to be the great leveller between subscribed and open access materials. Researchers just looking at peer-review status will find that all journal titles, both open access and subscribed, can be assessed equally for this important feature. Along with open access materials, the issue of peer review has come to the fore and has been the topic of conferences (such as the Sixth International Congress on Peer Review and Biomedical Publication, 2009), and even a whole issue of *Against the Grain* (June 2009). Topics of peer review becoming commonplace include discussion of 'open' peer review or 'community' peer review. Librarians must be very clear about peer-review status and what constitutes both traditional forms of review, as well as all of the emerging models in order to offer correct strategies and materials to various categories of library users. For their own research, librarians will have to be ready to demonstrate the level of peer review of publications chosen when being reviewed for promotion and tenure. Peer review is a linchpin of the scholarly communication chain in every discipline, and a major topic surrounding open access in libraries.

Collection development librarians at all levels must decide, for their institutions and for their individual disciplines, how to develop academic library collections in this hybrid and changing environment. What types of materials belong on web lists, pathfinders, research guides and in catalogues? Collection development or subject-specialist librarians may be in a position to make decisions to include or exclude certain types of materials. There is a sometimes overwhelming amount of information to evaluate in terms of research and collections, and librarians are expected to be able to make sense of this mountain of information. Constituents expect that librarians will be able to evaluate and present quality materials on a website, thereby putting an imprimatur on the resources. Library users seeking research materials may place a certain 'trust' in resources accessed through the library. Librarians need to be able to define the parameters of the library collection. This task is becoming more difficult as access overtakes ownership as the model for most libraries. Even with subscribed collections, librarians may now find it difficult to evaluate individual journals for quality as more and more electronic resources are tied up in packages. The open access materials still need to be vetted for quality before being added to the library collections through catalogues, weblists, subject guides and more. Some librarians rely on sources such as DOAJ or Open J-Gate (*http://openjgate.org*) for open access title availability. Others may pull titles from disciplinary indexing and abstracting services that also cover open access journals. Using the coverage lists of subject indexes assures a level of vetting that may provide assistance with separating the truly quality titles from others.

This decision-making about open access resources for collection development librarians extends from individual born-digital journals and free e-books to search engines such as Google Scholar. There can even be said to be a somewhat adversarial relationship between librarians and Google, with Google seen to be usurping libraries' and librarians' roles. For some librarians, open access may seem like the 'googlization' of research (Law, 2006). Librarians, rather than taking an adversarial role with web search entities such as Google, may wish to be part of the development team for any library-related initiatives that take advantage of either commercial or open source applications. Future plans of Google and similar companies are not shared with libraries or with the public. Preservation is a hallmark of repositories and libraries, but wide-ranging access to open access materials is under the aegis of commercial search engines. Librarians need not only to interface more with publishers and vendors, but to keep abreast of all of the corporate entities that provide the most ubiquitous access. Where libraries may have philosophies promoting openness, corporate entities may have other motives.

Google has established an online newsletter for librarians and, for a while, set up shop at library conferences in an attempt to foster collaboration. Many librarians remain suspicious of these efforts. On the other hand, some librarians see it as a 'win-win situation', knowing that library users will benefit from enhanced integration of these Google products with their libraries. Certainly, open access materials are readily discoverable through a Google or Google Scholar search and free Google Books are providing text to legions of web searchers. Recent conferences in the USA no longer seem to include a Google booth, possibly signalling a pervasiveness of, and acceptance of the search engine giant by librarians. The Microsoft Academic Live Search booth has also gone away, as that scholarly search, another good portal to open access materials, is no longer available.

Still, publishers, vendors and free search services are all together at library conferences seeking collaboration with librarians on the development of their products. In these days of escalating serials prices, many academic libraries are engaged in constant attempts at determining which subscriptions are vital to the collections, and which may end up cut in cancellations projects aimed at reducing costs. Suber has attempted to gather information about serials cancellations projects in one of his 'Lists related to the open access movement' (Suber, 2006b). Not only journal subscriptions, but indexes and abstracts may face the chopping block. As the open access situation progresses, librarians may see more cancellation of subscription-based indexing products in favour of free alternatives, and an opening up of library websites to free external web search engines such as Google. There is more competition from free indexes such as Google Scholar, even in the area of citation indexing. Budget cuts cause pressure for academic libraries to cull lesser-used subject indexing and abstracting sources in favour of free open access competitors. Morrison (2008a) argues that librarians should take authors' rights into account when analysing journal titles for cancellation, suggesting that journals with restrictive policies should be considered less favourably. With cancellations inevitable, libraries take a variety of approaches including examination of cost per use, interlibrary loan or pay-per-view availability, renegotiating pricing, or using disciplinary faculty consultation. A growing tide of open access materials may in time show some quality alternatives to subscription products, whether journals, individual articles indexes, or even books.

With changes in scholarly communication systems appearing in almost every discipline, and research impact gaining with open access models, collection development librarians and bibliographers may no longer find the old tools such as the subject core lists and traditional impact factor information as useful as in the past. Once able to rely on core lists of important journals and published bibliographies of the books most important to each discipline, librarians are now left to determine, often in a kind of vacuum, what titles must be part of strong collections. With increasingly limited funds, it is important to develop very targeted and useful serial collections. Academic librarians may be looking for best practices in each field when it comes to collection development. Publishers and vendors are also eager to know what resources librarians expect to need in building relevant collections. Many publishers and vendors are establishing librarian advisory boards to try and understand what purchases the market will bear.

Librarians may be struggling with making the best use of available usage statistics, which may still show inconsistencies. What should a collection consist of, and what should a library with a looming budget deficit continue to subscribe to? Even the traditional practice of polling teaching faculty to get their wish lists seems somehow anachronistic. Cancelling print in favour of electronic subscriptions seems to make sense, in many cases allowing small savings in disciplines where the online version is desired by researchers. In recent years, publishers have discussed charging more for the print version; this may be the catalyst that will move most libraries toward online access of their subscription products. Dropping print seems to be a common topic for both publishers and libraries, and this change in focus away from print as being the authoritative, archival version may open more minds to the credibility of born-digital publications. Unfortunately, research libraries find that large-scale print cancellations reduce ownership in favour of access, while tying up more resources in online packages and 'big-deal' type arrangements. The big-deal arrangements force libraries to subscribe to less important journals that happen to be bundled in with the big name titles. Costs become difficult to control in the transition to online, especially when it comes to publisher packages. Free open access web resources may be able to fill in some areas where subscribed collections may be weak or lagging.

Increasingly, libraries are functioning in a hybrid collection environment, with some retention of print. Access to free and subscribed resources are all part of the mix. When the online subscriptions collide with the open access offerings, the distinctions may be less important; only the quality of the publication will be the most important determining factor for addition to library collections. Open access has not yet provided the relief for library budgets that many anticipated. Open access also is not free, except to the readers that are fortunate enough to have access to the online materials that they need and want. Costs are incurred at some point by some of the players, whether to libraries that pay for the publication of open access journals, subsidising author fees, or supporting self-archiving through the institutional repository.

There have been many recent discussions about the true cost of the various open access models. As the best way forward is not yet clear, institutions will still have to provide traditional research materials in the form of books and journals from the library. Alongside subscribed materials, libraries can certainly showcase open access materials in a variety of ways. Library users in most disciplines will continue to expect to find traditional scholarly resources through the library. A tipping point has not been reached where open access materials exist at the critical mass necessary to make a significant difference. Studies have shown that there has only been a modest increase in self-archiving from 1999 to the present (Morris, 2009a). In 2006, it was estimated that only 11.3 per cent of total published articles were available as free versions somewhere on the web. This amount of archived material was felt by librarians to be 'too low to bring about feared cancellations' (Morris, 2009a). Although it is reported in some cases that 'publishers concerns are growing about the viability of the market for published journals if replicas of a significant proportion of the articles it contains were to be freely available elsewhere' (Morris, 2009a).

For now, the availability of open access publications has not provided an easy answer to the budgetary pressures of libraries when it comes to the purchase of books and serials. However, librarians have stated that they would consider the accepted version an adequate alternative if it is available without embargo (Morris, 2009a). If authors prefer the branded publisher version while librarians think that the 'accepted version' or postprint will suffice, there may be a disconnect on the one hand, or simply an information literacy shortfall on the other. If authors and librarians have different standards about which versions they will accept, the open access movement cannot be said to be successful. Clearly, the library should not develop systems or build repositories to store collections of digital materials unless researchers will find such services useful. Will more marketing, more deposits, or librarians changing their own scholarly communication behaviour make a difference and push the situation toward that important tipping point so that librarians can seriously discuss open access as a cost-saving measure? According to Cox and Cox:

> although a few academics and librarians may want to see the demise of established journals and their publishers, most do not; a clear explanation of why this could happen, if a critical mass of their value-added contents were freely available, needs to be reiterated at every opportunity. (Morris, 2009a)

This is the warning call from the publisher side, and may not reverberate within the librarian community.

The research library still has great influence in the attraction of scholars to the institution. The libraries with the great collections still are of utmost importance in the recruitment of faculty and students. Many faculty and students come to the institution with expectations of excellence in library collection support for their research. Librarians must be clear about what researchers will likely be seeking when they look for published scholarly work, and be prepared to provide access to it. Libraries seek to retain utmost relevance to constituencies by organising and providing access and discovery to the scholarly record. Provision of information services and consultation on best practices in search will remain important roles for librarians. Organisation of all of the resources, whether free open access web-based resources or expensive subscription products, can be provided from the library website. However, even the library website struggles with issues of relevance and attraction as an institutional portal for scholarly materials. The importance of the academic library within the institution, as well as in the greater chain of worldwide scholarly communications, will be determined both by the librarians and the users.

Librarians are considered the experts in collection building, and in this hybrid print/electronic (and now open access) environment, one wonders how librarians are keeping up. Are librarians driving any of the changes and being proactive in collections issues, or are they simply reacting to changes in the system and not really making a difference? Front-line collection development librarians and those working closely with faculty have a great deal of expertise to share, and hopefully will drive much of the conversation going forward. At what level in the collection development chain are librarians pushing for aggressive changes in the system toward more open access through green or gold models? Sometimes, what comes down from library organisations in terms of advocacy may seem somewhat vague in terms of the practicalities necessary to make wholesale changes in libraries and institutions.

More than ten years have passed since Harnad's 'subversive proposal' (Okerson, 1995), yet many academic libraries are still to make any large-scale changes. Academic libraries are still responding to the users' real or perceived need for *all* of the peer-reviewed scholarship: books in print, e-books in certain disciplines, traditional and 'big-deal' subscriptions, and free open access material organised from the website. Collection development work must now integrate the subscription and the free open access materials, as well as multiple versions of scholarly work. Adding free scholarly articles and indexes has not seemed to lessen dependence and desire for purchase of the materials sold by the commercial and society publishers. For now, excellent collections seem to need to hold everything deemed scholarly, even as disciplines run together and academic departments struggle with blurring of boundaries.

Ownership versus access: implications for librarians

In the past, 'ownership' allowed greater oversight of library collections by those both inside and outside the institution. The university's collection now extends to what librarians deem valuable on the free web. The activity by academic librarians of pulling relevant resources together from the web also carries responsibility in terms of evaluation of those resources. Librarians building collections can no longer rely on vetting of resources by publishers or associations, but are able to add any web materials deemed to fit the subject area profile. In some ways, this new responsibility to add materials found on the web may give librarians even more credibility in terms of their importance to the process of making the most appropriate scholarly information available to the institution through the library portal. Librarians doing collections work with free web materials will need to expand their collections policies to reflect a wider view of collection parameters. Collections librarians will need to work with webmasters, cataloguers, electronic resources experts and others to integrate open access materials adequately into the collections.

Far from marginalising librarians, the evaluation of open access materials is another valued role for collection development or subject librarians.

Through their collection development and scholarship practices, librarians in academic institutions clearly have influence in the academy. In one study, 99.7 per cent of librarians felt that they were granted the same level of academic freedom in their work as other faculty members (Cary, 2001). Open access publishing and self-archiving are examples of mechanisms to increase access to the research results that emanate from a scholarly society. Open access of the peer-reviewed literature distributes true scholarship across societies, and breaks down traditional roadblocks to learning.

Usage statistics and other assessment tools for open access resources

Usage statistics are becoming easier to produce and collect, and are being widely used to evaluate subscriptions and to determine value and even return on investment (ROI) for the individual library. In the print world, the building of collections has traditionally been more of an art than a science and it is more difficult to find quantitative ways of measuring the use of collections. Librarians with domain expertise have traditionally had the final say in what is important and necessary to the institution's collections of books and journals in a given subject area. In these days of usage statistics and their importance to both the consumer and the producer of information, web resources will be able to prove their impact (or lack thereof) to each subject area. Publishers of traditional materials will have to add value and find ways to make sure usage remains maximal for each title. Open access materials will show greater use due to greater web visibility and ease of discovery (and of course less cost), and it may become more difficult to quantitatively justify some subscription products. Librarians, especially those working with specific disciplines will need to find ways to gauge interest in, and demonstrate the relative importance of new born-digital open access titles. However, the analysis of use may require different methods and models. The subject-specialist librarian's voice will become even more important to the discussion of what to keep, what to add, and what to cancel. Librarians may be evaluated in some ways by what kinds of forward-thinking collection development strategies they are developing for the disciplines, and how they are dealing with a possible deluge of web information that may have importance to students and faculty.

Through strategic moves to showcase certain materials, librarians can to some extent drive usage. Additions to the library, such as Google Scholar on lists of indexes and databases, can also push use of subscribed and free library collections. Libraries may wish to add free resources such as Google Scholar in place of or alongside federated search products, and will be watching usage of all free and subscribed products. Some federated search products are able to provide statistics on referrals to subscribed products, and free materials will need to be evaluated as well. Comparison of use can be extended to evaluation of subscribed journal titles versus free open access titles. Statistics from Thomson Reuters' Web of Knowledge product show that citation analysis can easily be extended to open access titles. Other products such as the Scopus Journal Analyzer will also be able to show progress of open access titles in comparison to other paid titles. Open access titles would have to be covered by these products in order to be evaluated, and those included may currently be more biased towards the popular scientific author-pays titles. Major vendors will be able to provide usage statistics for journals regardless of business model. Careful consideration of the implications of collections decision-making based on assessment using usage statistics will be in order. Collection of accurate usage statistics for journal titles accessed through federated search and Google Scholar has been particularly vexing. At present, open access titles can often provide download statistics to authors and libraries if there are questions about usefulness to libraries. This will be an expanding area for electronic resources librarians and collection development specialists as institutions become aware of the possibility and the value of accountability for what is added to library collections. The development of electronic resources management systems will need to take into account all scholarly titles, not only those that are subscription-based. Librarians will need to get an idea of which open access materials, once added to the library collection through catalogues, web lists or 'A to Z' lists, are getting used by patrons. As more 'cost per use' or ROI assessment analyses by libraries include mention of quality scholarly open access titles, the visibility of free scholarly content will be enhanced.

Serials retention and preservation issues

Many years ago, there was talk of a 'serials repository' that would ostensibly hold a copy of every print journal. In many academic libraries, librarians are now struggling with the decision to reclaim precious space for other uses by discarding print serials and index backruns when purchasing backfiles. The tremendous amounts of investment put into these print runs has now run out, with many libraries (and researchers) finding no takers for their withdrawn print backruns. In 2003, SPARC proposed a cooperative programme, the Open Past Initiative, where libraries would take part in voluntarily digitising historical backfiles of print journals and make them available widely (SPARC, 2003). Librarians are now challenged with the task of digital preservation, and the tenuousness of the current state of the art may make some librarians uncomfortable with what seems a nonsecure digital record. Librarians are now well positioned to be the preservation specialists, having developed capability through institutional repositories, and are more aware than most scholars of the lack of long-term stable preservation strategies for much of the digital scholarly material. Many institutions are currently discussing the relative merits of LOCKSS (*http://www.lockss.org/*), CLOCKSS (*http://www.clockss.org*) and Portico (*http://www.portico.org/*) strategies for preservation. These initiatives do not entirely answer the question of the preservation of materials that are moving to free web models, or that are born-digital from any source that is not trustworthy in terms of curation. Academic librarian authors, concerned with preservation in their own daily work, may be more apt to consider issues of long-term stable access when submitting articles for publication. Journals published out of institutional repositories may represent a standard of preservation for authors. However, librarians may prefer to stay with more traditional publishing models for their own work, and may wonder, as other scholars often do, whether open access publications offer the sustainability and survivability that has been expected of traditionally published journals. Librarians may decide to support archiving in their institutional repository for the purpose of digital preservation of their own articles and other digital objects no matter where the original was published. Librarians have wrestled with digital preservation in their daily work, and so may be more concerned than teaching faculty with the lack of permanence of scholarly work. Some open access journals and some methods of making work available on the web do not offer the long-term guarantees of availability that have come to matter to librarians who may take the longer view. Certainly, librarians will be a voice for the need for preservation and sustainability of digital objects over time and across formats. Preservation is the province of all players: the libraries, the publishers and researchers that depend on the availability of the scholarly record. Librarians may continue to struggle with the move away from paper, which offered an archival record in most cases as well as a finite object that has been the focus of all library workflows for generations. Many library leaders continue to sound the alarm about disappearing formats and lack of migration of important scholarly materials to new formats. Librarians will be an important voice in the discussion of what should be preserved from this point on, considering how amorphous the library 'collection' has become. What should be saved, how, and by whom? All librarians have a stake in issues of digital preservation, and talk of a 'digital dark age' is always a concern. Librarians can evaluate open access materials for preservation possibilities, especially the unique institutional content.

Librarians' views on self-archiving and its effects on the traditional literature

Librarians may worry that self-archiving and other open access initiatives may damage the traditional journals. Although this would not be an openly popular stance for librarians to take, many may not want to see erosion of the traditional literature, and may not feel that open access is a panacea for the economic and other issues facing publishers and vendors. There is a certain comfort level in keeping the status quo. It has taken many years for the current system to evolve, and librarians are very experienced in dealing with traditional models of scholarly communication. Subject-specialist librarians may continue to protect and promote the publications with which they are familiar, even as the publishing world is rocked by mergers and tough economic times. Librarians may continue to support the traditional LIS literature as it now exists.

A study published by the Publishing Research Consortium entitled 'Self-archiving and journal subscriptions: co-existence or competition' provides valuable insight into collection development and the purchasing preferences of an international sampling of librarians (Beckett and Inger, 2007). Publishers have allowed self-archiving in many cases, and need to study what the implications of those decisions will be vis-à-vis the library market. For instance, results of the survey show that librarians do not favour embargos, especially the longer 12 and 24-month type, but may consider six months in some cases. Librarians do highly desire peer review; quality is seen as the most important attribute. It seems that contrary to what many publishers may state, librarians are more focused on quality of peer-review than the value of copyediting for journal articles. The study also shows that librarians do not often cancel journals based on the offerings of aggregators; they complement the publisher version for important titles. Librarians state that 'the journal is the real thing'. At the time of this study, 'librarians were willing to compromise on the article version with no difference between final published article and the author's copy of the accepted peer-reviewed article but there was rather less interest in the unreferreed original manuscript'. If librarians are not more positive about self-archived versions, then the original visions of open access allowing cancellation of 'real' journals cannot come to pass. Librarians may change their view with time and critical mass of postprint versions, but the future is not clear. Within Europe, according to the survey results, more librarians welcome the challenge to traditional publishers and consider the content on open access archives to be reliable. North American librarians were more concerned than Europeans with the future of publishers (Beckett and Inger, 2007).

Librarians working in collection development have choices in purchasing journal article content. For the same article, librarians can consider whether it is best for their researchers and budget situation to access the article via a licensed database, a journal subscription, or possibly as the critical mass grows, through an institutional or subject repository. Publishers need to know librarian preferences as far as subscription or pay-per-view products, and because there is not a critical mass in most repositories, librarians still often have a toll-based choice to make for many scholarly and commercial journal articles. The study looks at identifying the tipping point where librarians will actually change their purchasing preference (Beckett and Inger, 2007). If librarians do not prefer the versions of articles in repositories, publishers will not have to worry about this particular threat. Do librarians consider self-archived peer-reviewed 'accepted versions' or postprints as equal to the branded publisher PDFs available via subscription? Even in the case of physics, with its preprint culture, there is still no substitute for the permanent final peer-reviewed versions of work found in the journals themselves. The 2006 study showed that at that point, open access content found in repositories was not a substitute for expensive traditional journal subscriptions. Will continued advocacy and discussion among librarians make a difference in these attitudes? The answer seems to hinge more on what the researcher community wants and demands, and whether open access mandates erode the traditional literature over time.

Scholarly communication changes affecting interlibrary loan

Librarians may desire one type of content while researchers prefer another. Focus groups show that researchers prefer online access that works well, and immediate access to the current material that they use frequently (RIN/CURL, 2007). According to the study of UK researchers by RIN/CURL (2007), 80 per cent use interlibrary loan 'once in a while', 40 per cent will try to contact the author, 8 per cent use pay-per-view occasionally and charge the fee to a grant, 4 per cent use pay-per-view and charge their department or research group, and 2 per cent use pay-per-view and charge the library. Libraries will have to work to understand researcher behaviour and match those preferred work habits to funding streams. Open access may have a long way to go before making a difference and budgets need more immediate relief. Therefore, creative solutions such as subsidising pay-per-view or enhancing consortial options while studying scholarly communication networks by discipline may offer some relief in the meantime. Of course, some libraries will still be forced to cancel journals even as many publishers freeze or even drop prices.

Interlibrary loan will also see shifts in demand as more freely available materials may suffice for the researcher. In a recent study of the interlibrary loan practices of nine US colleges by the Primary Research Group, it was found that at those institutions, 'institutional repositories and open access materials have not substantially impacted interlibrary loan services' (Moses, 2009). Librarians may have to shift their attention from permissions, in the case of reserves and interlibrary loans, to organising access and promoting and suggesting the use of free alternative sources of peer-reviewed and other literature. Researchers will be able to find acceptable versions of the material they need through search services like Google Scholar and OAIster, and may bypass the interlibrary loan process. Interlibrary loan librarians may seek to save funds by suggesting other versions, possibly from repositories, that they find through their use of Google/Google Scholar. Time will tell if patrons will be accepting of substitution of postprints in repositories for the final versions that they have ordered through interlibrary loan. With more journals and indexes taking advantage of electronic publication ahead of print for various versions, resource sharing will begin to include more issues of versioning. Librarians working in resource sharing capacities may have opportunities to educate patrons about open access, although they may also worry about their changing roles if they move away from the status quo. Those working in interlibrary loan have direct access to communication with individual patrons, and can play an advocacy role in open access. The common benchmarks of 'lending' and 'borrowing' may evolve to the point where unique paper holdings or other web inaccessible special collections materials become the currency of status in interlibrary loan.

Author-pays open access and implications for the library

It is important to make a distinction between open access publishing and the type of scholarly journal publishing which requires authors to pay often large sums to publishers. The open access journals and articles published in the commercial sector are funded in different ways, but predominantly by the authors themselves. Grant funding often is used for these payments, and either entire journal issues or only certain articles may be free to readers. This type of open access differs from that of the free to publish, free to read open access journals previously discussed. There is some evidence that only a small percentage of open access journals at present employ the author-pays method of monetising the publication (Kaufman-Wills Group LLC, 2005).

In some fields and for some types of funded research results, open access journal publication has been commonly financed through a variety of author-pays models. Science librarians have unique issues to grapple with, such as the need for the library to make decisions about support for payment of author fees to various types of journals. Whereas some grant-funded research is able to support authors, in other cases, such as with the case of BioMed Central, libraries will need to support memberships in order for the institution's affiliated authors to publish. BioMed Central and the library community talk about setting up 'central funds and processes for open access publishing' (BioMed Central, 2008). Without cancellation of existing in-demand subscriptions, more money may not be easy to come by. Memberships such as these may not easily fit into established budgetary strategies, but may be of great interest to the institution's researchers. Science librarians may be put in a position of advocating for payment of memberships by libraries or institutions. Departmental faculty may expect such memberships to be readily paid.

Another of Suber's predictions is that 'libraries will pledge some portion of the savings from TA [toll access] journal cancellations to support peer-reviewed open access alternatives' (Suber, 2007c). Libraries actively advocating for open access will have to consider this type of cost. Some universities may be considering setting up a fund for researchers submitting to author-pays open access journals or publishing in those journals levying publisher fees. The University of Calgary has set up one such fund (University of Calgary Libraries and Cultural Resources, 2009). Author-pays schemes may have their own problems, even as libraries may move to redirect funds from subscriptions to assisting authors with payments or paying into membership programmes. These issues would be that, in charging authors to publish, there may be conflicts of interest in terms of publishers getting paid when an article gets published. Interestingly, Elsevier does not have any author-pays journals and does not plan any (Salisbury, 2008). Linke of ACRL also says that 'if libraries simply banded together, refusing to pay subscription fees and directing all of that money toward author fees for open access journals, traditional publishers would have no choice but to capitulate' (Salisbury, 2008). According to the Primary Research Group (2008), by 2008 some 15.56 per cent of libraries had paid a publication fee on behalf of the author. Some journals and publishers have both open access and toll articles in the same issue, such as Springer Open Choice. Authors are able to choose an option. In some ways, the situation seems more complicated than ever for librarians making collection development decisions, especially in cases where researchers are not pushing for change. According to a study of UK researchers by RIN/CURL (2007), fewer than 25 per cent support 'using library funds to help authors pay open access publication charges', while 19 per cent 'explicitly' do not. Librarians will have to respond to institution and discipline-specific requests before diverting precious library funding toward authors' publication charges or membership fees. When it comes to author-pays open access, differences among publisher practices may be confusing to the busy researcher. Still, this type of open access is not free, and libraries will have limited funds for experimentation as traditional subscription obligations remain challenging.

Collection development librarians may be used to using cancellations as a strategy to cover shortfalls during continuing times of budget cuts or rising journal costs, and may not be able to use the money saved to cover new open access programmes or initiatives. In another prominent example affecting science librarians, library support for open access initiatives may take the somewhat unusual form of the library needing to make 'pledges' of financial support. An example of this would be the Sponsoring Consortium for Open Access Publishing in Particle Physics (SCOAP3) initiative, a worldwide attempt by a community of scientists to turn an entire core set of journals in high-energy physics (seven titles) into open access publications. SCOAP3 is a funding consortium model and participants would 'redirect' funding for journal subscriptions to this new model of making literature available. There is an effort to get libraries, research institutions and consortia on a worldwide scale to support this initiative. Libraries may wish to advocate actively for open access but may have to disappoint other libraries in being unable to sign on to support such collaborative efforts. Libraries face no small amount of peer pressure to get onboard with such initiatives. While a very interesting model in a physics field already served well by a preprint culture (through arXiv), libraries may agree with the concept in principle, but may need to rework budget practices to 'pledge' money or to pool money in such a way (Anderson, 2008). In this small discipline, journals may be said to be useful only for a final certified record. Even if forward-thinking libraries would like to be part of such initiatives, there are practical matters of budget allocations to contend with, and libraries may find themselves unable to support multiple 'experiments' in open access simultaneously. Libraries will have to decide how much support for open access they can actually pay for in principle.

Another example of libraries being asked for financial support of open access comes from Creative Commons, which is also looking for donations (Creative Commons, 2009). In an example of an author-pays open access alternative, Springer has offered authors the choice of paying $3,000 to have their articles made immediately open access. Libraries must be concerned about paying subscription fees for toll content as more authors may be paying as well. In the case of the Springer Open Choice programme, the publisher will adjust the price that libraries pay for the subscription fee depending on the uptake of the author-paid open access articles (Regazzi, 2004). It is hoped that the library community will monitor such programmes carefully to make sure that subscription fees are accordingly adjusted on an annual basis. This programme will also allow collection development librarians to watch the extent of researcher interest in open access in a practical context. Author-pays open access journals are only really possible in well-funded disciplines, especially in the sciences. Other publishers are experimenting with open access publication strategies, such as Nature's open access *EMBO* journal, or *Nature Precedings*, which publishes prepublication research. Hindawi of Egypt has fully converted its 140 titles to open access (Salisbury, 2008). Librarians must watch trends carefully to fully appreciate how library funding might be affected as established journals change to full or partially open access, and new author-pays journals proliferate. These journals look no different to readers and represent another category, the commercial journals and articles that libraries do not pay for, but researchers do. Librarians may want to use open access status in some way to identify journals in collections.

Libraries may begin to focus more on assessment, especially ROI calculations. Evaluations of cost per use for subscribed journals and databases will begin to have more meaning for library and university administrators looking to justify the library budget and prove value of access to subscribed material going forward. As open access has not provided relief for budgets and costs increase, collection development librarians will need to use newly available improved usage statistics in concert with cost information (ideally in consultation with subject specialists) and find ways to justify continuing subscriptions with 'cost per use' data. With ROI strategies attracting interest, libraries (and publishers) will hope to justify the value of providing expensive subscriptions to researchers in their quests for grant funding. It will continue to be important to justify expensive subscription products with real research results and value coming back to the institution. A new level of assessment will leverage use of multiple sources of usage numbers. Currently, Tenopir is expanding previous work on ROI with electronic journals (Luther, 2008; Ripley and Boyd 2009). A debate will rage over the practice of collecting materials 'just in case', as has been the practice of research libraries, or moving to a model where items are purchased for the collection based on a specific request ('just in time'). This may be another area where patron usage trumps the 'art' of collecting by subject specialists using established norms. Subject specialists and other collections librarians may need to redefine roles to retain relevance.

Collection development, bibliographer and liaison librarian roles

Teaching faculty are often given the message that if they want information on open access, they should contact their library faculty liaison. Is the liaison sufficiently informed on open access and copyright issues in his or her particular discipline to be able to act as a credible consultant? Science librarians may be expected to pave the way. Librarians functioning in liaison roles to teaching faculty may be the best promoters of the scholarly communications agenda of the research library. Liaisons must be knowledgeable about all aspects of open access, and other faculty must be able to turn to them for guidance. Liaisons are motivated to find new ways to work with teaching faculty. Becoming a resource for self-archiving, consulting on open access decision-making, and promoting the institutional repository are other ways to partner with those doing research in the institution. Recently, academic libraries have begun to explore new ways to embed the librarian in the faculty research team by leveraging librarians' traditional expertise with data, as well as with development of classification schemes and ontologies.

Brandt of Purdue discusses the librarian's role in e-science as an integral part of research teams (Brandt, 2007).

Liaisons also working in collection development can be a great asset to teaching departments in promoting the library's collections and services, while consulting on scholarly communication matters. The subject-specialist/liaison librarian may also be part of the team advocating for the population of the institutional repository with faculty publications. The complicated business of copyrights and permissions may also be part of the new knowledgebase expected of academic librarians. There is a very steep learning curve for the academic librarian who is expected to be able to dispense advice about copyrights and permissions. Keeping up in this area is a challenge. With new digital repositories and so much scholarship migrating to the web, it is becoming difficult for authors to understand their rights. Gadd's study of self-archiving and scholarly journals found that 69 per cent of publishers surveyed asked for copyright transfer prior to refereeing the paper (Gadd et al., 2003). Even among the social sciences, Antelman (2006) illustrates many disciplinary differences with respect to author self-archiving behaviour. In another survey by ALPSP of 400 academic journal publishers in all fields, it was shown that 83 per cent require authors to transfer copyright in their articles to the publisher (Cox and Cox, 2006). Proactive scholars may attach additional addenda as they seek to retain copyright. Some libraries, such as the Boston Library Consortium have also crafted their own suggested addendum statement that authors might attach to their submitted publications (Boston Library Consortium, 2009). This added language seeks to preserve author rights, and is a visible advocacy effort by the library. Besides libraries, there are other sources for author addenda. Recently, Science Commons has introduced, with SPARC, the 'Scholar's Copyright Addendum Engine' (*http://scholars.sciencecommons.org/*). Academic librarians working in liaison roles may be called upon to promote, facilitate and craft a comprehensive source of information that is easily consulted by faculty and researchers.

According to a study by Cox and Cox (2008), 26 per cent of publishers no longer require authors to transfer copyright. Instead, there is a growing trend for publishers to offer authors a 'licence to publish' instead of a copyright transfer agreement. Librarians will need to follow such trends in the literature in order to advise researchers and to evaluate journal policies during the acquisition of new titles. Helpful charts could be created by discipline to assist authors weighing journal attributes when choosing publication as well as to highlight some of the issues that many authors are not used to considering in traditional systems.

Librarians will want to establish roles as the 'go to' professionals for issues of author rights and other publishing issues.

The convergence of factors in a bibliographer's everyday world has become challenging. Decisions about where to submit one's own scholarly work, cutting subject-based journal titles from some of the same publishers, seeking out and publicising open access alternatives for various user groups, and watching ownership being replaced with access to titles, are all part of the job. To build a collection for a major research library in this climate requires a great deal of knowledge of the many competing factors trying to influence the librarian in a time of ever-decreasing budgets. This convergence of factors is especially interesting for those bibliographers responsible for the LIS literature. These librarians, in particular, may feel compelled to try to move the LIS literature in line with current open access and copyright models. Librarians, masters at search and discovery via the internet, and consultants to others in search, will not find their LIS literature discoverable unless it moves to more open models. There is a disconnect in librarians' familiarity and expertise with online publications, and the lack of LIS publications that may be discovered online. Librarians with collections responsibilities for the institution's LIS literature who are also authors themselves may be in a unique position to study the world of open access from close up, as librarian, scholar and researcher.

Collection development or library liaison work may involve assisting faculty with depositing articles, offering to assist editors of open access journals, and developing library collections (including free and open materials) that speak to the current scholarly needs of all researchers. Personalisation and targeting information services to researchers continues to be important. The positive reputation of the collection development librarian may hinge on his or her ability to really target collections and services to faculty and students in a personalised and user-friendly manner. The librarian who tries to develop alternative, more open access collections while deciding not to continue with some of the more pricey commercial offerings may find resistance from user groups. For the nontenured faculty librarian, or for any academic librarian wishing to maintain the best possible relationships with the departments that they serve, there is a need to keep the faculty satisfied with the collections offered. Continuous education is imperative for all parties. Subject liaisons may be in a position of having to build collections that are relevant to researchers, while at the same time consulting with them on putting pressure on those same journals by self-archiving or choosing alternative publications with more open business models.

Users may still desire access to traditional subscription journals. As librarians struggle with paying for access to subscription packages, and adhering to licensing restrictions of large commercial publishers, users still desire access to toll journals. After ten years of advocacy for open access, users have still not changed behaviour. Usage statistics can still attest to the heavy use of scientific journals from the largest big-deal type publishers. Library users expect to find these sometimes high-impact titles in a research institution. Librarians in institutions that have cancelled big-deal type arrangements have had a variety of reactions, even following advocacy campaigns encouraging more open access (Suber, 2006b). Users seem to flock to many of the singular titles in the big-deal type packages, and usage statistics tell the story. Even though the prices seem exorbitant, users find the resources and the interfaces desirable. Cost per use data shows that many subscriptions are indeed cost-effective. Cancellation becomes more difficult as supplementary materials are tied up in the platforms, meaning that more invaluable research material is held under tolls. Each discipline is reacting differently, or not at all, to open access campaigns and many models are at play. The successful subject liaison will be watching changes in the subject disciplines while engaging in the conversations taking place in the wider world of the discipline served. All librarians should advocate for the LIS literature as well and join university committees looking at new ways to evaluate scholarship in the disciplines, especially for promotion and tenure.

New roles for librarians interested in open access

Institutions may look to libraries to provide leadership in scholarly communication areas, and libraries will ideally be able to leverage long experience to fill these roles. Academic librarians with great interest in open access and the continuing changes in scholarly communication may wish to investigate new career directions that may place them in leadership roles within the library, the institution, and the national and international conversation. Perusing job list services will show emerging positions for librarians in scholarly communications and related specialties. Some positions require a law degree, but others require a library science degree and various combinations of other qualifications. Scholarly communication librarians may be expected to produce blogs, websites, and other communications for faculty, students and administrators. Other responsibilities of a scholarly communication librarian, besides facilitating the open access discussion, may be to liaise with university presses or university legal personnel, provide copyright and licensing consultation, encourage dialogue throughout the university, promote the capability of the institutional repository, and contribute to curriculum development in library schools. Scholarly communication librarians may also partner with subject-specialist librarians in working with teaching faculty, participate in efforts toward e-science, repository development, library publishing initiatives, use of bibliometrics, compliance with legislated mandates, data curation, and all other emerging trends. The library may be the natural place for the office of scholarly communication within the institution, providing a 'one-stop shop' for issues of copyright, intellectual property, role of the repository, open access publishing, self-archiving, and planning of educational outreach on issues relevant to the institution. Ideally, the office of scholarly communication would be focused on collaboration and outreach in all directions within the university as well as contributing to the national and international conversation.

Many libraries may be choosing to add scholarly communications roles to existing position descriptions, for instance, adding new responsibilities to the role of repository manager, electronic resources librarian, or even to individual subject-specialist librarians. Creating new positions and titles will show a library commitment to placing the highest emphasis on advocacy and research on open access and related initiatives. One website from the Association of Research Libraries (ARL) has attempted to provide a clearinghouse for scholarly communications librarian positions, and at the time of writing, shows a variety of currently available position titles (ARL, 2009). Those librarians interested in open access will find these positions a natural fit, and a genuine opportunity for real visibility within the library and the institution. Librarians may have to be open-minded and flexible about changes to their positions as libraries continue to change. When librarians leave, decisions may be made to retool the jobs to reflect new roles, and librarians with traditional roles may find their jobs changing, or repurposed completely. The Massachusetts Institute of Technology (MIT) Library has stressed that the library is 'planning for an open access environment' and has reexamined and changed its mission and librarian positions to reflect this focus. Fourteen librarian positions, (20 per cent of its ranks) have been redefined during this transition (Duranceau, 2007). Libraries that are proactive with changing roles may find their librarians in new and exciting partnerships with IT, other faculty bodies, university presses, offices of sponsored research programmes, centres for teaching, and even university stores.

This will only strengthen the importance and relevance of the library within the university at a time when libraries may be facing a changing role within the institution.

Academic library scholarly communications committees

Scholarly communications committees are active in many academic libraries, and for libraries unable to expand their librarian ranks and have the luxury of having a librarian and an office focused on scholarly communication and issues of open access, this type of committee work will require time away from traditional roles. Librarians may use membership on these committees to become thoroughly knowledgeable about the changes facing scholarly communications, and thus may bring more of this information to their everyday work in public services and collection development. They may be more inclined to discuss issues with faculty out in the institution and can be known outside the library as a resource for changes to promotion and tenure guidelines or as consultants on new types of open access publishing. Libraries may choose either a scholarly communications librarian or a committee to spearhead the institutional effort toward open access. A many-pronged educational effort is needed to develop an appropriate outreach programme. An example of this type of communication or outreach effort would be the blog authored by Kevin Smith, the Duke University Scholarly Communications Officer (Duke University Office of News & Communications, 2007). A legal background for scholarly communications librarians may be a great asset. In a 2008 interview, Smith revealed that in the actual position, 65–70 per cent of time may be spent dealing with intellectual property questions, 10 per cent of time may be spent keeping abreast of national issues, and approximately 25 per cent of the job deals with publishing issues and author contracts. In Smith's case, there is not as much overlap with services of university counsel as some might think (Howard, 2008a). David Stern of Brown University is the Associate University Librarian for Scholarly Resources. In this capacity, Stern handles collections development as well as scholarly communications, sitting down with authors to discuss publishing choices as one part of the position. Stern watches the costs of open access, stating, 'Many libraries don't do the analysis and just pay the bill. I'm here to do the analysis' (Howard, 2008a). Each library may decide to have an office or a librarian ultimately responsible for the level of practical support for open access in budgets, personnel, and policy and advocacy statements to all members of the university. Soon, background and knowledge of open access and scholarly communications may become part of every position profile for new librarians in this new team-based library environment. Graduate library schools will have to provide coursework to prepare librarians for advocacy roles if the profession establishes this as a priority. Emphasis in LIS programmes will go a long way to promoting all aspects of scholarly communications education as a priority and responsibility of academic librarians.

Librarians on scholarly communication committees are able to advocate for scholarly communication issues that affect departmental faculty in the institution. These committees may take on the role of outreach to interested faculty. However, many do not take a role in advocacy for other librarians, even in their own institutions and in their own publishing habits. There is a disconnect, as librarians do not act as role models of archiving behaviour by depositing in institutional repositories or choosing open access journals for their own publications. Finally, some have suggested that librarians are not moving ahead with open access simply because they really do not know much about it (Salo, 2006). This may be overly simplistic, but one wonders whether academic librarians are familiar with all of the issues surrounding open access. The library's role in scholarly communications is far from clear, and will continue to evolve. This evolution will depend not on mandates, or the existence of repositories, but on librarians coming together in a common understanding and advocacy role in each academic institution. It is not clear who will fill the role to further educate librarians about open access. All of the players, including the publishers, promotion and tenure committees, administrators, funding bodies, the federal government, and others have a stake in getting their particular message out. Librarians will also have to reach out with their discussion to everyone else in the scholarly community. If librarians are going to take the lead, scholarly communications committees will probably be the groups charged with mapping out the strategy. However, there is the underlying assumption, still not proven, that most librarians believe that this is in the best interests of the library and of the researchers. Librarians' passion for the open access movement, or lack thereof, will be critical. The open access movement, which some would call mature at this stage, has still not captured the attention of all librarians. Some librarians may simply not be interested in what it may mean for the library. Scholarly communications committees may be able to provide not only education and consulting on issues, but be the group that provides a level of enthusiasm about open access within groups of librarians. Scholarly communication committees may be helpful in a research and advisory role, and will take on increasing importance in a leadership role for the library. Decision-making in these committees will reverberate in many areas of the academy, and will allow libraries to take centre stage as 'information central' in the institution. All librarians and staff will have to be pulled into discussions about these changes, otherwise marginalisation will occur and information will not be presented in a cohesive manner. It may be advantageous for the library to approach groups of faculty about disciplinary difference in scholarly communication rather than present general information at multiple settings, not targeting any one group. Symposia or conferences about open access may best focus on one discipline at a time. Changes must be coordinated and integrated quickly, and trends that affect collections anticipated. Library administration in an institution committed to the ideals and practical solutions promised by the success of the open access movement will make scholarly communication committees and scholarly communications librarians a priority even in times of lean budgets.

6

Public services work and open access

Open access and the academic librarian: its relevance for everyday

At academic library reference desks, public services librarians may begin to move away from suggesting only traditional, subscribed-to sources to both library users and would-be authors. Librarians may want to make sure that researchers understand new modes of scholarly research. A study by Swan and Brown (2004a) found that authors find open access journals to publish in most often on the recommendation of a colleague (47 per cent), followed by using the DOAJ (12 per cent); only 6 per cent of respondents identified an open access journal to publish in on the advice of a librarian. Potential authors may not be asking the advice of librarians, so librarians need to be more proactive in promoting open access titles as a publication vehicle to the liaison groups they serve, and via the reference desk. One wonders how training for those working at reference and information desks is changing to include practical information about promoting open access publications and self-archiving. In a study by RIN/CURL (2007), it was found that only 4 per cent of researchers reported being advised by a librarian to deposit work in a repository, and a mere 1 per cent said a librarian had advised them to publish in open access journals, even as 27–46 per cent of librarians have made an effort to communicate with researchers. Those working at reference desks and in virtual reference situations may not be focused on a subject area, and hence may not be as aware of open access trends and how they are affecting the disciplines. As front-line points of contact for faculty, staff, researchers, and often the public, reference librarians may be continuing to suggest only traditional subscribed peer-reviewed publications to users. This type of outreach, based on reference librarians' training from even a few years ago, further promulgates the notion that the scholarly literature comprises only the traditional resources. The conversation about scholarly communications and open access in particular may not be filtering down to many librarians who work directly with patrons in a more general sense. These academic librarians may not know quite how to introduce certain resources into their service, such as the institutional repository, self-archived postprints found in subject repositories, or open access journals found via search engines. Open access journals may be accessed through some traditional library databases such as PsycINFO. However, departmental faculty may not want librarians to deviate from traditional norms when providing assistance to students. Many library users come to librarians seeking materials that are peer-reviewed, and to many students as well as some faculty that still means subscription library resources. Some students even present with instruction from professors to use library resources, not the internet. Library instruction and reference librarians may not have reached sufficient users with information about scholarly peer-reviewed material that is open access on the web. Teaching faculty may have warned students to look specifically for information that is peer-reviewed. Sometimes, the most library-inexperienced students come to the reference librarians asking for anything that is peer-reviewed, even if they do not know what the term means. The use of such terminology in reference queries may have developed as the common language for those students seeking some certainty that material is sufficiently scholarly for use in research assignments. Faculty may have decided to use the term 'peer-reviewed', thinking that the students will be able to find this type of literature in the library. Traditionally, material found in libraries was considered to be vetted by librarians for quality. Librarians now organise and vet materials found on the free web and add them to the library's collections and services, and it seems that this is still somewhat of a gatekeeper role in a digital age. Library users may assume that all materials found using the library website as a portal have been vetted for peer-review status. Librarians must follow new types of peer review very closely, and be prepared to define in some way what types of material will be 'collected' by the library in this new era where free web and traditionally purchased materials come together to be accessed as one collection through the library website portal.

Library users and their knowledge of open access alternatives

Library users, no matter which group the academic library serves, are not concerned with costs of the materials they read. The library, as intermediary in this process between publishers and readers, pays the bills that the consumer does not see. Therefore, the library user, even the scholar, may not be aware of the costs associated with traditional journal subscriptions. Because scholars are not spending their own money, they might not feel the need to be engaged in the debates about the price of serials. It would be a rare library that published the cost of individual journals. Readers of *Tetrahedron*, priced at approximately $31,600 a year (in one library's example), may just expect the library to have the material, and not be aware of the cost to the institution or taxpayers of maintaining that subscription (Crawford, 2006). It may not matter to the researcher as they are able to get the information 'free' as a benefit of their affiliation with the university. As librarians, it may be in the best interests of change to make readers more aware of the costs to the institution, and in the case of public institutions, the taxpayers, of traditional journals. Some have even included students in discussions about the costs of library materials. Still, if the reader incurs no cost, materials on the web, whether they are accessed through the library website or the open web, may be seen to be all the same. Many readers, even when they have to authenticate themselves to use subscription-based electronic resources, see everything they find on the web as free. Younger library users, especially, may be more comfortable with the idea of getting their information and software free. One study shows that younger researchers are both more aware of open access as well as more enthusiastic about it, possibly due to the changes to the music industry or other discussions of free web culture (Cockerill, 2006). Many people are fond of saying that 'information wants to be free'. Using the library has been seen as a free benefit to attending an institution and many researchers consider use of library services such as interlibrary loan or article delivery a benefit of affiliation without consideration of costs to the university.

Along with seamless access to electronic library subscriptions, personal subscriptions to scholarly journals have declined in recent years. According to Tenopir and King, the number of personal subscriptions held by scientists has declined from 5.8 subscriptions per scientist in 1975 to 2.5 in 1995. By 2002, the number had been further reduced to 2.2

subscriptions per scientist (Tenopir and King 2000; Davis, 2003). As personal subscriptions decline, and people in all user groups get more of their information from the internet, open access journals and online repositories may begin to fill the need to keep up with personal scholarly information needs. On the other hand, some feel that individuals cancelling their own personal subscriptions are causing concomitant rises in costs to libraries (Tenopir and King 2000; Davis, 2003). Still, there are studies that show that the amount of reading from personal subscriptions has declined while reading from the library has increased (Van Dyck and McKenzie, 2004). With libraries striving to maintain relevance in their institutions, this type of behaviour exemplifies the continued desire for students and researchers to read from library-provided materials. These same patrons who are reading from library subscriptions may not desire change in the way the library provides materials, and the impetus for change may not come from the researcher community. They may continue to demand the same resources, and not see open access alternatives as a panacea for their own research needs. There have been meetings to gather information from librarians and academics about the pricing and availability of scientific publications, such as the 2004 meeting of the UK Parliament's Science and Technology Select Committee. That meeting found librarians suggesting open access to articles resulting from published research, but academics concerned about protecting traditional journals and practices (Poynder, 2004b). If academics do not want change, and libraries are used to providing services and collections to this group, then the library risks disenfranchisement with its primary customer base if it pushes too hard for a change to open access. Librarians usually respond to the desires of constituents, especially those librarians who are out on the front-lines providing reference and liaison services. If the motives of the library do not mesh with the desires of the authors and researchers, the result will be discord, which is in no one's best interest. Library liaisons will not be able to advocate too strongly for something that researchers are not necessarily receptive to.

Changes in promotion and tenure priorities and increasing institutional mandates may change the landscape, and allow libraries to begin to 'collect' open access alternatives to expensive toll literature. In the extreme, budget pressure may force libraries to cancel more subscriptions, and where libraries are unable to meet demands through interlibrary loans, they may finally be able to promote open access as the only alternative. When there is pushback from teaching faculty, the librarian has ordinarily been indoctrinated to try to appease the situation, and open access suggestions may be met with a variety of reactions. Only time will tell how far the system will go on in a hybrid manner before some tipping point is reached in the academy. Mandates such as the one at Harvard demonstrate that a strong message coming from outside the library can be the most effective as long as the repository is geared to handle larger numbers of deposits. Librarians will have to collaborate much more across the institutional culture before any change may be realised. The only constant seems that costs continue to rise, and in bad economic times, it may make sense to take advantage of loss of collection funds and quieter times at the traditional reference desk to promote new open access resources and services. Due to economic uncertainty, it may also be advantageous to experiment with some journal cancellations where a quality open access alternative exists, or where a culture of preprints archived in repositories is working as a current source of research communication.

Asking users to change behaviour

In some cases, library open access advocacy groups are appealing to authors to change certain behaviours on behalf of the library. For example, researchers may be admonished with statements such as the following: 'for the sake of the library, please consider not reading/authoring/editing expensive journals' (Davis, 2003). Still, if the reader is not paying, what is his incentive to 'help' the library? Should patrons and librarians help try to prevent the 'slow death for research libraries' (Davis, 2003)? Should researchers really be asked not to read something because it is not open access? There are no obvious consequences now for users of research libraries to reduce their use of expensive commercial journals, especially those with name recognition and high impact factors. Academic libraries are still in the business of providing the collections and services that their users need and desire.

Many academic libraries serve a variety of user groups with divergent content and services needs and may need to reassess priorities. Many public research libraries may find that their missions include serving almost everyone. This may include large numbers of research constituencies, from corporate clients, to entrepreneurs, to individuals from the public at large who may be seeking high-level information to increase knowledge during a personal family health situation. There may be undergraduate and graduate students with very different research needs. It may be that research libraries can no longer serve all of these populations at the same level. Davis (2003) discusses the role of the library as a 'public good'.

Along with strategies to contain costs for subscription journals, the library world actively advocates for open access by asking (or mandating in some cases) faculty deposit of scholarly articles into repositories as a way to the alleviate costs of STM journals. There may be a steep learning curve for some faculty and librarians when it comes to reasons and methods for using open access alternatives to traditional behaviour. Many librarians educate their patrons through dedicated web pages about open access resources, taking a strong advocacy role. Some libraries plan symposia for faculty and researchers, opening the discussion to the wider community. Still, it is the smaller decisions by librarians and other authors to self-archive their own work in subject or disciplinary archives, and publish in open access peer-reviewed journals on a large scale that will make the difference in libraries' ability to consider open access journals and self-archiving in repositories extensive enough to warrant changes to traditional collections and services. Before this system is any replacement for the current system, or even as an effective less desirable alternative, a critical mass of scholarly materials must be available through interoperable, searchable repositories. This has not come to fruition, and in many cases, libraries are expending resources on tools to enable open access (such as repositories) while continuing to struggle to pay the bills for everything else.

Using DOAJ as a source of open access materials

Reference and instruction librarians may want to take note of important sources and listings of open access journals. Many traditional indexes now include open access materials that meet their criteria, but there is one index that vets and lists only open access journals. Many librarians are familiar with the Directory of Open Access Journals (DOAJ). DOAJ is sponsored by the National Library of Sweden, the Swedish Library Association and Lund University. It has been reported that the rate of new open access journals launching has declined since peaking in 2001 (House of Commons Science and Technology Committee, 2004). At the time of writing, the DOAJ lists more than 4,000 journals published in almost 100 countries. Some feel that the DOAJ listing overestimates the number of current, actively publishing journals by 14 per cent. Some are inaccessible, some are not original journals, some are not fully open access, and 9 per cent have published no articles since 2003. Sally Morris of the Association of

Learned and Professional Society Publishers (ALPSP) suggests that the open access model seems to allow 'creation and persistence of journals which would not survive in the traditional market' (Tananbaum, 2006). DOAJ claims to conduct ongoing quality control checks on its listed titles, removing those that no longer fulfil the criteria for inclusion; for example, 94 titles were removed from the index in 2008 (Bjornshauge and Johansson, 2009). Researchers may not be aware of what constitutes a scholarly journal any more, and librarians may also be confused in trying to ascertain the quality level of open access journals. As open access is not really free, even DOAJ has proposed a 'membership' programme as its own funding sustainability has come into question (DOAJ, 2007). A 'membership' of this type, with voluntary pledging of funds, will require librarians to look closely at value, and increased scrutiny and accountability will be required if precious funds must be reallocated to these plans. Those libraries that now access these journals and call them part of their journal collections may be interested in supporting DOAJ's membership plan, but others may not. Libraries may simply not be able to spend the money. DOAJ started its membership programme in 2007 and by April 2009, the numbers of members was reported as 13 individuals, 80 libraries, universities and research centres, ten library consortia, and two aggregators. Membership in DOAJ confers benefits such as:

> acknowledgment as a DOAJ member on the DOAJ membership pages, including link to your institution's/company's homepage, access to a list of recently added titles, e-mail subscription to a newsletter, access to the list of removed titles, and the right to use the DOAJ membership in marketing activities. (Wahlgren, 2008)

This type of plea may play into librarians' concerns about sustainability about the future of such a model for a popular index, really the only comprehensive index for open access journals. Such membership opportunities are increasing in number and libraries will have to grapple with whether this is an important use of sparse academic library funds.

Hundreds of academic libraries now access the journals in the DOAJ and include them in their catalogues. DOAJ also could be included in lists of indexes and databases where library users pick and choose resources for searching for topics or journal titles, and might be featured prominently on the library website. While libraries have included Google Scholar and other sources of discovery for the world of open access materials in lists of indexes and abstracts, on weblists and in catalogues, DOAJ has now reached a level of saturation and prominence where it could be included as well. Further development of its search interface could render it more effective as a tool for conducting research, rather than just as a directory of titles. As an example of its renown, major commercial aggregators are integrating the journals from the resource as well. DOAJ reports that, as of April 2009, it is getting more than 8 million hits every month (Bjornshauge and Johansson, 2009). Library users must have access to the whole range of discovery tools as well as any resource that pulls together open access materials. Lists of indexes and databases can include quality resources regardless of whether the library pays for them. Boundaries are blurring, and it may be the case that researchers will find seamless access to the entire corpus of research literature by linking through to content. Libraries run the risk of researchers thinking that all of the journal literature they need for research is free and on the web. Librarians have a role to educate their users as to the cost to the library of the traditional journal literature, and to stimulate conversation about the budgetary implications of indexes, databases and the journals they link to. Some libraries have tried to educate students about the cost of journal literature along with teaching library research methods. Using Google Scholar and DOAJ as successful 'free' indexes may stimulate interest in open access to research. Libraries can decide how best to showcase these free indexes.

Part of the problem that reference librarians and disciplinary specialists may be having is that there is no international, comprehensive registry for new kinds of scholarship. Traditional resources exist where a user can search for a book or journal title in many sources, but outside of DOAJ, there is no tool or registry to pull together a large listing of open access materials by any subject category (Maron and Smith, 2008). New types of scholarship will have a hard time with acceptance, marketing and credibility if there is no resource that pulls them together. Subject repositories and repository aggregators do this to some extent but the situation is dispersed.

There have been concerns about the sustainability of a resource such as DOAJ, and especially about the long-term availability and preservation of open access journals not affiliated with institutional repositories. As for open access journals, DOAJ has assuaged some of the concern about the thousands of journals it works with. Lund University, in partnership with the National Library of the Netherlands, will cooperate in a programme to ensure the long-term preservation of journals indexed by DOAJ. The Swedish Library will also fund and sponsor this preservation initiative (DOAJ, 2009). Ensuring long-term preservation raises the credibility and ultimate value of these journals to libraries and prospective authors.

Open access materials available for discovery

There are many forms of new scholarship besides postprints archived in repositories and open access journals. Increasingly common scholarly materials may also include data, working papers, conference proceedings and creative works such as performances that include video and audio. Embedded video is becoming more common in some types of scholarly articles. Reference and instruction librarians will have to decide how to include such materials in their educational efforts in classes and in reference. Expanding the potential list of indexes, journals, citations and web materials offered to clientele searching for research material is a new area of knowledge for public services librarians. Librarians may wonder how best to integrate the free open access materials alongside the subscription results for each reference encounter. The reference interview will have to ascertain any limitations to the boundaries of the search. It can no longer be assumed that the best materials are the subscription materials. How will librarians handle new materials and offer them seamlessly to clientele? Do teaching faculty want limitations placed on the use of any category of scholarly open access web materials?

In 2008, Ithaka undertook a large field study to look at the bigger picture of born-digital disciplinary scholarship. Some 301 librarians at 46 institutions interviewed departmental faculty about their use of new forms of digital scholarly resources. Regardless of new form of scholarship, peer review was very important, as was the faculty desire to have access to the most current research. Traditional peer review was the value; 'modified' peer review was not as popular in this study (Maron and Smith, 2008). The field study showed differences in the types of available digital scholarship by discipline. The most common type in arts and humanities was e-only journals followed by discussion forums and blogs, while in social sciences, professional scholarly 'hubs' were common, along with e-journals. Online reviews in humanities seemed well-suited to online forms as currency adds value. Most faculty members in the social sciences mentioned the value of the Social Science Research Network (SSRN) for preprint resources. In STEM disciplines, sites where a researcher can access and publish data, e-only journals and professional and scholarly hubs were all important (Maron and Smith, 2008). Some preprint servers are extremely important to STEM disciplines. One important example is arXiv, the physics repository, where over 5,000 papers were archived in July 2008 alone (Maron and Smith, 2008). In some branches of biology, however, researchers are reluctant to post preprint work. Faculty and students in disciplines without emphasis on preprint or archiving culture will not need to be pointed to these sorts of web materials as they are not important to the discipline. This study points out once again the need to understand the different research and publication behaviour in the disciplines and structure library services to include these new types of scholarly output and interest. Subject-specialist librarians will need to provide information to generalist public services librarians so that library users will be pointed to appropriate new forms of scholarship. The subject specialist can add value to public services by educating others on important open access resources that are specific to the discipline. Libraries can also decide whether to support open access by promoting these new forms of scholarly work. All librarians can influence and transform their own LIS literature if they so desire by following trends in other social sciences disciplines closely.

Role of the reference librarian and the library website in promoting open access

Reference librarians as well as those responsible for the placement of resources on web pages are able to significantly influence usage of all types of resources in libraries. Aside from the librarians pushing resources in their reference encounters and in classes, the library website, as a portal for many library users, is the place where the library's resources can be integrated with materials from the free web, providing access to both subscribed and free scholarly content from one place. Space on the library website can be devoted to scholarly communication initiatives for all disciplines. Faculty, researchers and students will look to librarians to educate them on scholarly communications issues. For those who have not been informed about open access journals and repositories, the library website can provide education and outreach. Librarians can produce online finding aids to educate others about open access issues and make them available from the website. The degree of open access advocacy ascribed to by the institution will be obvious from the library website.

Webmasters and those librarians working with them to keep the library website relevant for all user groups will struggle against the lure of the open web as a first stop for all users. Innovative design, truly helpful interfaces, ease of use, and institution-unique features will help attract users and encourage them to start with the library when looking for scholarly research materials. The library will want to remain relevant in an open access world by making sure that web committees continue to develop policies about integrating free web and open access materials into library websites. Library users will go to the library website to search and find a scholarly subset of web materials vetted and deemed acceptable by librarians. Librarians may not all agree on what resources should be found on the library website, especially in a time of the burgeoning amount of free 'scholarly' materials. It will also be difficult to organise 'hybrid' packages and materials that are hard to fit into neat categories such as 'indexes', journals' or 'books'. Many web materials defy easy library description. A strong leadership voice from library and university administration about the future and position of the library in the institution will inform the website organisation of resources and services for prominence. Besides promoting resources in obvious ways on the library website, other ways that librarians inadvertently make some resources more visible than others is through placement on subject research guides and pathfinders. As such, librarians can greatly influence, in a proactive way, whether library users continue to use subscribed or free peer-reviewed scholarly resources, or both. Well-created subject research guides, such as the many now using 'LibGuides' (*http://www.springshare.com/libguides/*), will encourage questions through e-mail, phone or chat about new types of scholarly web resources. Through the content represented on subject research guides, librarians can promote their expertise in open access issues.

Using Google Scholar in reference work to discover open access materials

Reference librarians may need to show users new ways of searching for scholarly publications in their various versions, for instance by showing alternative scholarly search tools like Google Scholar or OAIster. Both of these search engines crawl open access material in repositories and journals. Library websites are increasingly integrating Google Scholar, the use of which makes open access journals and archives more discoverable. The placement of Google Scholar in weblists alongside subscription indexes and databases on research library websites has become more common practice, giving some librarians pause. However, Google Scholar has proven popular with library users for connecting to both subscribed and free web materials from one familiar search box (Mullen and

Hartman, 2006; Hartman and Mullen 2008). In adding Google Scholar to their websites, many libraries push the use of subscription products linked from the index while enhancing the discovery of the open access alternatives.

Google Scholar, searched from the library website, or from the open web with local libraries listed as a user's preference, can provide a portal to a wide variety of both open access and subscribed scholarly material. Users are very familiar with Google and will be happy to be shown how to use it to find scholarly publications and cited reference information, much to the chagrin of some librarians who may prefer users to search for materials using other library indexes and databases. By including Google Scholar on library websites alongside other library indexes and databases and linking it to subscribed collections, it is possible to discover a wide variety of scholarly publications. Access for affiliated patrons becomes seamless, and they will not have to focus on the business model of a publication, but instead on the discovery of relevant scholarly material. Users start their search for scholarly resources in many areas of the web, but knowing that the library is attempting to integrate and organise both open access and subscribed material together in library portals and tools will add value through using librarian expertise in the vetting process of making available quality peer-reviewed material. The library will become known as a trusted place where students and others can access the material deemed scholarly by the library and institution. This is still a 'gatekeeper' model for the library, however, and more experienced scholars will be able to use the open web effectively in accessing the necessary research materials. Students may prefer the library as one-stop shop portal, even when it is the library website that is the first stop in their search for background research materials. Librarians may still be needed to evaluate open access sources, and organise them appropriately. Vetting for quality and access can be the same regardless of format and price. Adding free quality search tools to the reference skill set is an expansion of the more traditional knowledge which is currently required of reference, instruction and other front-line librarians.

Many commercial and society publishers are participating with Google Scholar, which is especially useful for searching interdisciplinary topics. Many publishers have partnered with Google Scholar, and may see that referrals from Google Scholar to these publishers increase usage of their products. Librarians are sending information about their collections to Google so that their institutions' holdings will be highlighted when affiliated researchers search Google Scholar. Google Scholar and similar free search engines can function as a one-stop search resource for open access literature in both open access and traditional, commercially published journals. Many academic libraries feature Google Scholar and other free search engines that crawl open access repositories and disciplinary archives like E-LIS and dLIST on their websites, alongside the traditional indexes and databases. Putting resources that crawl open access repositories on library websites will increase visibility of scholarship and also show that librarians have vetted these resources in terms of quality. This type of placement of open access resources in libraries' collections via the website will reinforce the role of the library in making available publications of quality, whether paper, electronic only, CD, e-book, open access born-digital, or traditionally-published. One of the roles of the librarian will be to evaluate for quality, then to organise the resources and present a coherent collection to the researcher. This is an important role for the subject specialist in academic libraries – to organise scholarly materials into a one-stop shop or effective subject portal such as a subject research guide for the convenience of researchers. Of course, this includes vetting and listing all available and relevant open access resources as well. Customisation and personalisation may also become important to library users. The librarian will need to be able to determine what makes a work 'scholarly' beyond traditional definitions of peer review. With an overwhelming array of information presented via the web, librarians can continue to be a trusted source for determining the 'scholarliness' of information. This evolving area of expertise can be marketed as part of the emphasis on the service orientation of today's academic librarians.

Open access and other indexes and databases

In large research libraries, it is not unusual to have hundreds of indexes and databases, both subscribed and free open access, available for searching by library users. Some librarians may prefer the library's collection development efforts and reference services to be restricted to traditional subscribed and collected library materials. However, the traditional indexes and abstracts are increasingly covering open access journals, enhancing user discovery of this subset of scholarly work. Users will want to link to these journals. The library must decide which way to steer users in this complicated situation, and best practices will develop as far as which resources will take precedence when librarians are suggesting search strategies to library users. Librarians in many departments will have a major role in legitimising scholarship found outside traditional journals and books. Library users should be able to depend on the expertise of librarians when trying to choose scholarly materials for research. The practice of mixing free web materials with subscription products on the website may pose some challenges.

Librarians may now be able to use free software such as Google Analytics (*http://www.google.com/analytics/*) to determine where users are coming from, as well as analyse how researchers are getting to both subscribed and free resources. Librarians will be able to more effectively decide how to market library resources, and will need to make decisions about positioning open access materials in places where user traffic is as likely to discover these resources as often as with subscribed materials. Selectors who understand how the value of high usage statistics can confer immunity from the cancellation axe may try to give prominence to subscription journals over less expensive or free choices. This is especially true if the teaching faculty value the librarian advocating for the expensive commercial journals they may still want and need to use in their research. The librarian may feel more successful within the service orientation by advocating for continuing use of all resources that influential customers need. Free web resources do not have to be justified based on cost per use, so the marketing of open access resources may serve a different purpose, namely increasing their visibility in the hope of enticing researchers to move more in that direction. Vetting for quality should be considered independent of cost per use data, and librarians may begin to depend more on open access materials and will have to showcase them or market them effectively. It will be interesting to compare usage of free and fee products side by side. How many freely web-accessed products can make up the research library collection? Usage statistics will tell the story of user preference, and librarians may influence that usage to some degree if that is their desire.

Having access to the highest number of free scholarly web materials (including open access publications) is appealing to researchers and to the reference librarians assisting them, especially those in institutions where the library subscriptions are lacking. Researchers using the internet are used to the instant gratification afforded by the discovery of a scholarly full-text corpus of research materials collected and displayed in a single place. The simplicity of searching the web as a one-stop shop is highly desirable for busy researchers. Researchers and librarians may find that when students are given a choice of paper journals and copy machines or scanners, or even interlibrary loan, they are most happy with what is immediately accessible on the web. The shortest electronic path to full text is the most attractive situation for the researcher. Students may be happy with 'good enough' search results as long as they are able to quickly access acceptable peer-reviewed electronic content. They may not search for the highest quality or the most relevant, and the free web journals will benefit from this user behaviour. Unfortunately, the problem is that popular search engines might produce many results to articles that are difficult for unaffiliated users to access. Higher-level researchers are more apt to anticipate waiting and working harder for the materials they need, but they still prefer remote electronic access to journal literature from home or laptop. Open access speaks to this desire for instant gratification, and the librarian interested in patrons finding success with less time and effort may be apt to assist users with 'convenient' materials. Many researchers working remotely may not realise that they must authenticate themselves as a member of an institution in order to access subscription materials, and are still starting on the open web. They are most likely to find open access versions of articles when they start on the open web rather than the library's website. The library's continued relevance may hinge on the pulling together of all scholarly materials onto the website and into the collections so that researchers do not need to come and go from the library portal as they work. The only problem may be that users will have such seamless access that they believe that all materials are being accessed free on the web rather than funded through expensive library subscriptions.

Even as librarians do not want users to differentiate scholarly quality based on business model, they do risk funding declines if researchers lose touch with the expense of providing articles from commercial journals accessed through costly subscription databases. The findings of the RIN/CURL (2007) study suggest that the library needs to 'proclaim value' as researchers think the institution is bringing them scholarly resources, especially as fewer people venture from their off-campus remote journal access to visit the physical library. The study argues that 'the future library needs stronger brand identity within the institution'. Where once the library and librarian were sought out on campus, now librarians must be proactive and let others know that they can provide added value to all kinds of scholarly materials, including those found free on the web. Librarians may not be used to marketing themselves to researchers and may see a focus on open access as pushing researchers further toward the open web for scholarly work.

According to Suber (2007b), librarians want to help users find the information they need regardless of the state of their budgets. Librarians also want to help faculty increase their audience and impact, thereby helping the university raise its research profile. Reference librarians, with their thorough knowledge of all types of scholarly material, whether free web-based resources, or subscribed or owned materials, find it within their purview to offer the researcher different options. What do researchers expect from reference librarians? Library users may not expect to be referred to free web materials when they approach reference services. After all, they have come to the library to find 'library materials', not 'internet sources'. This is a common misperception in some libraries about the separation of the two entities. Reference librarians need to be able to present the most relevant and appropriate materials to patrons of all levels in all kinds of situations. Librarians may be working under time or other constraints, such as in chat rooms, and may have to maximise efficacy of responses with little time.

One wonders if librarians, even within a single institution, are on the same page as far as what they consider 'authoritative', credible scholarly information to offer in a reference session. Most would agree on the results found from traditional indexes, where there is trust in the vetting process of the producer of the index. Conversely, there may not be consensus about the scholarly value of other categories of materials found on the open web or by searching the deep web. Google Scholar, for instance, while a convenient discovery tool for open access materials, does not disclose what it covers, or how it deems materials scholarly. When assisting users, reference librarians may not consider it appropriate to offer materials found in repositories, archives and personal websites. Who decides what information should be presented by librarians at the desk, or in virtual reference encounters? How are these distinctions being taught in LIS education programmes or by reference training in the library? Training has always been of great importance, but core print materials may not need to be part of reference training in order for desk personnel to be effective with patrons. New librarians will struggle to determine whether their skill set needs to include the core reference materials that were once so essential, but may now be suffering from lack of use, or even obsolescence.

There cannot be differing definitions of 'scholarly', and librarians and teaching faculty must be in agreement in order not to confuse students. Faculty may be comfortable with anything that students present that is peer reviewed, regardless of its origin or format. Librarians and teaching faculty must not be of differing opinions about this, but instead must present a consistent approach to students when it comes to 'acceptable' types of materials to use in research papers or for other scholarly purposes. It may take some time for consensus on these issues to be reached, and 'best practices' may vary from institution to institution, and even from country to country. Teaching faculty may continue to warn students away from doing research on the web, further complicating matters for high-quality open access publications. Librarians and teaching faculty may have to collaborate and communicate more to present a united vision of what constitutes acceptable sources for discovery of, and citation of scholarly work for offering to students.

In many cases, reference librarians also have influence in suggesting use of subject and institutional repository content to patrons. At this point, indexing is still a problem, and much valuable information may be hidden from researchers. Services such as ROARMAP may simplify cross-repository searching and prevent the development of more 'silos' in the information landscape (ROARMAP, 2009). In a complicated digital search environment, library users may default to a Google search rather than taking the time to search various individual sources of content.

Will library users need to be shown all of the different search engines for each silo of information? For example, in the LIS literature, one may choose to search ROARMAP for repository content, OAIster for the deep web, DL-Harvest for the disciplinary e-prints, Google Scholar for other free open access web materials, and the traditional indexes for peer-reviewed traditional and open access journals. Adding a federated search across only some resources adds further confusion. It is hoped that next-generation federated search solutions will tackle the issue of open access materials and identify versions in repositories. Versioning will be an ongoing problem for library users. A complicated situation is apparent, and users want the simplified 'Google box' approach to getting information. An accomplished reference librarian will take care to offer the appropriate mix of resources to each individual library user based on his or her specific requirements. Considering that most users will try to find appropriate information on their own, librarians can certainly appreciate how complicated the mix of choices available on the web and from the library is at the present time.

Reference librarians may market themselves as the ones who can cut through the maze of resources to enable the researcher to separate the wheat from the chaff. The reference interview, whether it occurs in person, in a chat room or through e-mail, will be more important than ever. It will be imperative for the librarian to be able to present the most relevant information from a very wide variety of choices, including open access versions when appropriate, based on a quality reference interview. Some might say that reference librarians cling to traditional ways of doing things, and may be slow to change. Training in reference may be becoming difficult as visits to the desk and face-to-face reference interviews decline in many academic libraries, and it becomes more difficult to demonstrate enough patron encounters and types of questions to new public services librarians. With the librarian moving online for virtual reference, there is a chance to establish new librarian identities based on service, and the ability to expand the user base to new groups. Librarians can be embedded in many different ways, and be well represented on the web through their own personal websites, departmental websites, subject research guides, and places in course management systems where students will easily find assistance while taking classes.

Disciplinary differences in open access material presented to patrons

The most important factor in understanding the open access movement from a holistic perspective, whether the focus is on archiving in repositories or the publishing of journals and books, is that all of it hinges on disciplinary differences in scholarly communications. There can be no broad-brushed approach, and success will come by libraries and institutions fostering change discipline by discipline. The subject-specialist librarian could serve as a consultant to teaching faculty on archiving matters, as well as assist in recommending peer-reviewed open access journals that may be less known to the community. Senior faculty may have to take the lead when it comes to supporting newer and lesser-known ways of disseminating scholarship while supporting junior faculty research. Symposia that include practical information could be presented in a more discipline-focused way rather than the general, broad-based method often seen at conferences. Ideally, the dialogue could continue as librarians could visit faculty meetings and other venues on the turf of the teaching faculty to discuss open access options and associated fair use issues in a discipline-specific manner. It would be difficult for the librarian to present scholarly communication topics and open access initiatives to everyone in the academy in a 'one size fits all' approach, although the library website will ideally give prominent space to the discussion of the topic through web pages developed by the scholarly communication librarian or other knowledgeable librarians. There must be one credible, authoritative place where information is pulled together for faculty seeking background information. Responsibility for this 'place' could be conferred on the library if the opportunity exists in the individual institution.

Of course, each discipline has its own 'core list' of important open access resources, including search engines, subject repositories and open access journals. The culture of the various disciplines must be taken into account at all times when presenting information. Librarians must work together to present a consistent approach to teaching faculty. Too many different and disparate messages dilute the outreach effort. Not having a contact point for questions or discussion leaves the conversation very distributed and that may lead to lack of action and loss of momentum. Which groups will be responsible for training reference librarians and liaisons in all of the scholarly communications resources and services? Busy librarians may not have time or motivation to read the voluminous information that continues to emanate from many sources in the library literature and far beyond. They may not want to give incorrect information, thereby not doing the aggressive promotion and advocacy work that library organisations call for. Today's vocal advocacy efforts may be out of step with the reality of the daily work of librarians in articulating how open access can easily be promoted from the desk, the classroom or the website. Is the promotion of open access in all its iterations something that 'everyday' academic librarians really feel falls within their purview? It is unclear if librarians are motivated to carry the message out proactively when results are not clearly visible and teaching faculty are not requesting information. The critical mass may not be there among librarians to make open access a new focus in librarianship. This is especially true if the library is not realising or hearing about true change in scholarly communication coming out of years of effort. There is clearly a need for more research on the attitudes and opinions of front-line academic librarians so that the profession may understand how far open access advocacy has begun to transform the everyday roles of public services librarians and whether they are truly engaged in proactive change in reference or instruction roles.

Inclusion of open access materials in traditional and emerging indexes

Reference, instruction and subject librarians must keep up with trends in coverage by the traditional abstracting and indexing services. A generalist reference librarian may need to know what kind of material is covered by a long list of indexes. Many subscription indexes and databases have started to include open access journals in their coverage. Still, one wonders whether aggregator databases and indexes, and other traditional tools are including open access journals if they fit the coverage criteria. Open access materials are not always identifiable as such, and that distinction may not be important to readers. It may not be crucial that authors and readers know whether journals are open access, but it is absolutely essential that readers know whether they are truly peer-reviewed. It is very helpful for librarians and readers alike when peer-review status is clearly indicated in listings of journals covered, and at the article level whenever and wherever scholarly material is discovered. Librarians must be able to distinguish quality regardless of format, and assist users in finding appropriate scholarly, relevant and useful materials. Rather than focusing on business model, abstracting and indexing services may provide maximum value-added by clearly indicating which publications are peer-reviewed. For example, EBSCO uses a symbol for this purpose in its indexing of articles (EBSCO, 2009). This will greatly assist both librarians and users in choosing articles to use in writing for coursework and publication. The various versions of articles will need to indicate whether they are peer-reviewed versions. When faced with many versions of the same article, it may also be possible for librarians and researchers to see evidence that indicates whether the version accessed is really the 'final version of record', possibly through publisher branding in an initiative such as CrossMark (CrossRef, 2009). Branding by publishers indicating stewardship of a particular article version may become popular as a feature sought out by researchers interested in the trustworthiness of content used in research. This will be particularly true as authors as well as publishers contribute to the proliferation of many different versions of a single article on the web, especially as self-archiving and electronic publication ahead of print behaviour increases. Librarians will have to be able to explain both peer-review status and use and citation of various article versions of both toll and open access articles.

Searching the scholarly literature: best practices

Search itself has become a challenge for libraries. Librarians, especially in reference capacities, want to know the best way to search the corpus of available scholarly literature, sometimes exhaustively, on a specific subject. Librarians also unknowingly translate their 'favourites' to library users, hence employing bias by example. Best practices in search are subject to librarian interpretation more than ever before, and advanced training in teaching database searching is hard to come by for reference librarians. There seems no absolutely 'correct' method of searching the indexes and databases for scholarly materials these days. Methods of teaching search strategies for accessing material may vary by librarian. Time will tell how librarians and others are able to integrate and make all of the various ways of searching the literature of a discipline interoperable and efficient. At the moment, the array of search possibilities can be overwhelming for the academic library user. Users and librarians alike may tend to stay with favourite ways of searching and not venture far beyond the well known, even if other attractive options are available. Librarians may stick with learned ways of searching even as publishers and vendors change their products in attempts to provide a more basic 'Google-like' experience for the user. There is some discussion over whether users should be offered 'basic' or 'advanced' search as the default on traditional online indexes. Those starting with 'advanced' may quickly lose interest and search for a simpler interface. For those wishing to search exhaustively through a discipline's literature, the situation has become quite complicated for researcher and librarian alike. With multiple commercial and free subject indexes, bibliographic utilities such as WorldCat, the ILS, full-text packages that include a search function, disciplinary and institutional e-print archives and the services that aggregate them, and indexes that search the deep web all providing discovery of scholarly material, the librarian will be charged with matching the user to the appropriate material. Many users prefer to start their research on the open web. If they do use the library as a portal, many will seek out a single search box, such as that used in federated search engines. Users also have their own common search practices now that using the internet for information-seeking has become ubiquitous in society. It is natural to approach library searching in familiar territory or in the natural language query style that people use in searching with popular browsers.

Even for library users who prefer to, or have learned to start with the library website, the challenge for librarians will be to simplify the dizzying array of choices presented. With so many places for the user to begin on the website, whether a federated search product, Google Scholar linked to collections, long lists of indexes and databases, publishers' packages, or the catalogue, library users will develop strategies and favourites with or without intervention from a librarian. In some ways, academic libraries have measured their success by the efficacy of their library systems to use technology to empower the end user to conduct research independently and to reach scholarly literature without the librarian intermediary. The efficacy of the library website, link resolver, authentication services for remote access and other technology, has made search more seamless and in some ways less associated with the library. Reaching library users to offer advice requires a many-pronged approach. Whether a resource is open access or not may not be important in the future to the academic librarian suggesting resources to the researcher.

The question will be whether librarians have reasons to advise patrons in ways that favour subscription-style abstracting and indexing services over free methods of search. When budgets are tight, will librarians in science and medical libraries still feel that subscription Medline is necessary when PubMed is available free? As mandates are requiring medical research to be open access within a reasonable embargo, PubMed may be sufficient and instantly recognisable as an index for biomedical researchers. As disciplinary boundaries blur, Google Scholar may suffice for searching across literatures. Users are linking to research articles from all kinds of web locations that librarians may not have considered. Librarians have seen that many students, although forbidden by faculty from citing Wikipedia as a scholarly source, admit to using it as an index to link to articles through the hyperlinked references. With high use of Wikipedia as an open access encyclopaedia that can link to scholarly sources, especially at universities where subscription content is readily available, it is obvious that students are discovering new methods of linking to material for papers. Librarians must keep abreast of the many ways that library users access content and also be prepared to offer expert opinion on a variety of researcher choices.

Federated search and open source solutions

Developers of federated search products and implementers in libraries will have to grapple with what to federate in terms of indexes and databases, knowing that including a particular resource will drive usage. Libraries can add free web materials to link resolvers and federated search products, but may feel that this would be confusing to the researcher. Librarians will still be seen as gatekeepers, as even with open access materials free on the web, librarians will be the arbiters of quality, and will have a role in separating the wheat from the chaff. Producers of federated search products will have to offer connection files for the free open indexes as well as the subscribed. Google Scholar cannot presently be used with federated search, and this can be seen as an incomplete realisation of federated search by many librarians and library users. Google Scholar may be one of the most heavily used databases at some institutions, and is being left out of federated search. Librarians may wish to federate all of the library's offerings along with free open access web materials into one large resource which includes all scholarly resources useful to students, no matter what their business model. Free e-books from all sources as well as peer-reviewed open access materials should be targets of federated search. The gold standard of federated search would be that solution that delivers all of the relevant scholarly content to the researcher, regardless of business model, format or source. Open access materials will only reach maximum credibility and acceptance when they are not considered as a different digital object when peer-review status is on par with other types of resources. It is hoped that a product such as Summon by Serials Solutions, or a similar open source product, could make linking users to all subscription as well as vetted open access content from a single search a reality (SerialsSolutions, 2009). Librarians will grapple with the known value of native database searching, and have to decide how to manage the various approaches to subject search against the enticement of the one-stop shop type of searching that will appeal to library users.

Various article versions causing confusion in public services

Indexes, abstracts and journal websites will include citations to various versions of the same article. This is going to be a challenging new situation for researchers and for librarians. The concept of versioning has been vexing librarians as collections move toward including more iterations of scholarly material. There has been a struggle for the community of researchers and even librarians to come to grips with the terminology describing various iterations of the same article. The terms 'postprint' and 'accepted version' may be interchangeable, but are they? If the peer-reviewed copy of the article has been shown to be popular, how is it described? The popularity of preprint cultures, in physics for example, may lead some to believe that preprints are acceptable in all fields as citable research works. Preprints may become mixed up with 'epub ahead of print', where the most current articles are made available online before being completely copyedited and formally published and branded.

In partnership with ALPSP, the National Information Standards Association has published guidelines that will provide clarity in nomenclature for all different versions of an article through its lifecycle. Various librarians and library groups may want to quickly adopt preferred and accepted nomenclature so that further confusion can be avoided. These recommendations only deal with the high-level wording, especially focusing on five terms: author's original, submitted manuscript under review, proof, corrected version of record, and enhanced version of record (Morgan 2008; National Information Standards Association, 2008). It remains to be seen how these terms will permeate the open access or journal publication conversation. Not only useful in communication with library users, simplifying terms will also help librarians who work with the repository engage in more meaningful conversations with public services librarians. In libraries with a designated scholarly communication librarian, it would make sense for that office to continue to provide the latest information so that all interested parties will refer to articles in similar ways. Public services librarians need clear and consistent information to pass along to patrons in reference and instruction sessions when teaching library users the various forms, in terms of versions, that an article may now take. Even popular indexes will be including many versions of an article before 'final' publication. It is hoped that initiatives like CrossMark will be able to certify a final version.

Those researchers using search engines such as Google Scholar will likely see different versions of the same work presented together in search results. A single published article may show up as preprint, postprint and publisher PDF. Searchers may ask reference librarians for clarification and help in distinguishing the most authoritative version of a work. Citing electronic works in various versions and formats has become a challenge for researchers and librarians alike. Conventional style manuals, some still only available in print, have had difficulty remaining current, especially in establishing standards for all types of electronic materials. Recently, the American Psychological Association has published its new electronic style guidelines, moving toward using the DOI as a persistent identifier for each article (International DOI Foundation, 2009). Librarians will start to move toward use of the DOI to describe any digital object. Librarians may need to keep up with style changes that employ new terminology and methods to describe the products of a shift toward open access. Reference training will need to include information about DOIs, citing of acceptable versions, and information about open access materials.

Bibliographic management software has had the daunting task of formatting new types of citations according to established norms that may not be up to date. Library users may wonder whether they can cite a refereed postprint or whether only a branded publisher PDF is acceptable in a paper based on scholarly sources. Students and faculty continue to ask for the branded PDF as the authoritative copy. This branded publisher version will continue to be held behind tolls, and with budget cuts may be less available. Online article versions may link to open access or subscribed supplementary data out on the web or on a proprietary platform, making the PDF or paper copy less desirable or even useless to the researcher. If the platform includes the data, the library will need to subscribe to that platform in order to deliver the article plus the data. Open access materials can link to open data and researchers will need to cite their sources for open data. Conventions may be lagging behind. Librarians working in public services will have to wrestle with these issues and present consistent information to user groups even as the landscape is rapidly changing. It would be assumed that librarians would be able to answer questions about which versions of scholarly articles are acceptable to be cited in scholarly work or student papers. There may be widespread confusion on this in the library world and among teaching faculty. With open access citation managers such as the popular Zotero proliferating, librarians will also struggle to exhibit expertise with different citation management software, both subscribed and open access.

Citation managers incorporating open access materials

Academic libraries have made products like RefWorks and EndNote available through site licences in some cases, and users have come to expect availability of value-added software products that facilitate managing digital objects in the research process. Producers of bibliographic management software, in their quest to provide as many import filters as possible, will have to make sure that open access and free web tools can be easily used with these products. Searchers will want the ability to add citations found in open access web materials to their bibliographies as easily as the current protocols available for direct export from many subscription databases. The ability for library product developers to extend functionality to open access materials will be important to the success of researchers looking for a way to integrate all sources in research papers, no matter how they are published, or where. Users will need to cite materials from institutional repositories and subject archives, especially as preservation advances make materials found in such places more enduring and as standards for versioning continue to develop. All of the peer-reviewed literature will need to be cited by researchers, whether free or subscribed.

Other products used with library resources, such as federated search products and link resolvers, will have to include born-digital open access materials. In an interesting example of competition for these products, Zotero, LaTek and other free citation managers have been making inroads into academic libraries. In a twist, librarians will have to respond to this open access challenge by watching development in these products, and making sure the subscribed library materials can be added to these products. Enterprising librarians in many institutions have turned to YouTube to disseminate tutorials on using Zotero and other resources. Rather than reinvent the wheel, librarians can link to video instruction, giving attribution to creators. In time, there may be great numbers of online videos assisting researchers with use of a variety of products. Effective instruction and reference librarians will be able to compare and contrast for patrons the pros and cons of all types of bibliographic management software, whether subscribed or free and open source. If librarians ignore trends from open source products originating outside the library world, it will be a missed opportunity to share expertise as well as to keep the library relevant for users who have moved to free solutions in their own work. Librarians may be conflicted about teaching open source tools as alternatives to the common subscription products EndNote and RefWorks. Patrons will want to choose a method of managing citations and may come to the librarian for consultation. In 2008, the producers of Zotero were sued by Thomson Reuters (the producers of EndNote) for use of a piece of proprietary software utilised in the EndNote program (Beja, 2009). Even though the lawsuit was eventually dismissed, library users may have been concerned about sustainability in using products like Zotero for valuable bibliographies. Such legal challenges may prove challenging at times. However, open source products are certainly making inroads into libraries as acceptable alternatives, providing budget relief and shared development opportunities. Libraries can enhance their reputations as experimenters and innovators while saving valuable funds to put toward other priorities including staffing for new initiatives.

Information literacy with open access

Practices are also changing in areas of library instruction. Traditional methods of teaching library skills need to include new scholarly communications models, at least in presentations to more advanced groups. At this point in time, those involved in information literacy find themselves with challenges in terms of what to include in library instruction courses for students. Open access has forced instructors of library research skills to decide whether to step outside the boundaries of library-subscribed paid resources to consider alternatives when presenting scholarly materials to students and faculty. Even the teaching of federated search as a complement to the subscribed databases has not proven to be the panacea for complicated search offerings (Cox, 2006). Some libraries teach the use of free tools such as Google Scholar while others do not. Even within a single institution, librarians may have different teaching philosophies about free web materials, and students and faculty may be the recipients of these divergent opinions. Instruction librarians can push referrals to free scholarly materials, or choose to stick with recommending traditional library resources only.

The responsibility to teach students and researchers the 'right way' to conduct searches for scholarly information will undoubtedly become more confusing as more types of versions of individual articles are displayed, and the idea of the article itself evolves. Many a librarian involved with bibliographic instruction has brought a copy of a scholarly, peer-reviewed paper-bound journal volume along to class to illustrate to students what it is they are looking at on the web when looking at a PDF article. Many students have never looked up paper-based articles and do not realise that the paper analogue to the electronic peer-reviewed journal may still exist on the shelf of the library. While born-digital journals increasingly have no paper counterpart, they still use the term 'article' to describe the digital object that is presented. They are called 'journals' to offer a recognisable term for the package even as the article-level economy is developing. As more digital information is presented on the web, library users may begin to have difficulty with traditional library terms, such as journal, monograph, index, catalogue, or even 'book'. The digital format does not evoke the traditional look of the paper, and the tipping point where researchers have not had experience with the print journal may still be years away. The traditional print package will no longer define the digital objects that students and faculty will use in the future.

In time, all library users may truly understand that there is no discernible difference between peer-reviewed quality scholarship, no matter how it is published for reading. Open access materials must be made available in the everyday teaching that reference librarians do at the desk and in bibliographic instruction. This 'grassroots' way of moving forward the open access agenda may be very effective. Whether librarians will resist moving away from traditional instruction strategies and materials, even as newer information literacy methods migrate to online formats, such as easily updated tutorials or videos, remains to be seen. Of course, the successful librarian will need to work in concert with teaching faculty and others to develop information literacy programmes that maximise the ability of all students to evaluate information no matter what its source may be. These issues may give the librarian easy entry into discussions about 'open education research' or some of the other open access topics that others in higher education are grappling with. Evaluation of online scholarly resources, whether from the library or the open web, will remain an important part of the academic librarian's teaching skill set.

Open educational resources

An outgrowth of the open access conversation that is affecting public services librarians is the growth of open educational resources practices and products. Open educational resources were the focus of an American Library Association midwinter meeting in 2008 (SPARC, 2008). This forum sought to advance discussion of the integration of all kinds of library and course materials in all formats into classrooms. Librarians who teach classes and wish to be embedded in courseware as well as those librarians who actively assist course instructors with pulling together appropriate materials for teaching will want to be cognisant of latest best practices in the area of open educational resources.

The role of the digital library will evolve toward more integration in the classroom through association with open learning management systems such as Sakai (*http://sakaiproject.org/*). The climate is ripe for innovation and collaboration in online learning across the institution, and across the world. Librarians will need to organise and aggregate all of this content in all of these formats and collaborate in a more symbiotic way with others in the academy, especially teaching faculty. Librarians will be 'embedded' in the online classroom, and may have opportunities to work more closely with teaching faculty in bringing resource materials to courses. Another objective of the movement known as 'open education' is the ability to create open courses and textbooks. Librarians must be able to engage with open education discussions in order to understand changes to the academy as well as to effectively utilise new methods of creating and reusing materials from the library. Librarians can strive to create effective online library instruction materials that will really engage students in library research and new ways to look at information. A start to the wider discussion involved an international effort culminating in the release of the 'Cape Town Open Education Declaration', an example of an initiative which can guide future discussion and action (Wales and Baraniuk, 2008). Library schools might also be expected to experiment with open courseware or open textbook initiatives if librarians are to display support for open access to library-related information. The textbook issues will eventually involve the college stores in many cases. Stores may also end up partnering with libraries as the cost of textbooks drives collaborations to solve this pressing problem for students. Library collaboration can be seen stretching in many directions.

Open access programmes planned for students

Librarians must be cognisant of incentive and awards programmes that may potentially involve the students of the institution. If libraries want to foster open access literacy among the next generation of researchers, there should be an open access presence in the library to attract the attention of students of all levels toward thinking about trends in scholarly communication, and essentially the future of publishing. If the library's practices are significantly affected by the open access movement, librarians can build awareness through websites, handouts, blogs, and other information targeted at library visitors and students. SPARC and the Public Library of Science (PLoS) have produced a video series that may appeal to librarians for use with students. This video series, entitled 'Voices of Open Access' was produced in connection with the first Open Access Day, which was organised by SPARC and PLoS along with Students for Free Culture (McLennan, 2008b). Libraries many wish to celebrate Open Access Day with programmes and other events. The first Open Access Day involved interested campuses in many countries, including Canada, Chile, India, Italy, Japan, Moldova and many others

(McLennan, 2008a). This type of worldwide effort gives international librarianship a chance to discuss open access as a truly global concern and movement. Campuses are enriched by becoming connected through mutual interests, and librarians may see this as a focus of globalisation efforts for the library. Extending the concept of an international day devoted to the movement, Open Access Week, celebrated for the first time in 2009, allowed for a full week for activities that enabled libraries to plan programmes or initiatives (McLennan, 2009b). Libraries may not know what types of programmes would both appeal to students as well as advance agendas past general conversation and activities.

An example of an open access advocacy effort targeting students through a contest is the SPARKY awards, given to short videos that 'offer a glimpse of student views on the importance of access to information'. If libraries indeed want to focus on open access, they would be the place (both literally and figuratively) on campus to promote this sort of public relations contest. Students may be very open to the conversation because many of them are familiar with movements such as those related to free culture and expanded social networking and sharing of information. Another SPARC initiative targeting students is called The Right to Research and pulls together comprehensive information in a website and brochure that librarians may disseminate to engage students, especially those that will become the scholars and researchers of the future (McLennan, 2008c). Students may appreciate a library that speaks to their interests in free culture, with the library establishing a role as a place on campus that can host meet-ups or even play open access videos on prominent screens in the lobby. Librarians, especially those who have been in the profession for a while, may want to listen very carefully to various groups of students and refrain from making sweeping judgments about how they use and seek information. Baker (2007) describes various examples of student activism activities on college campuses as well as students' involvement and stake in many areas of scholarly communication in the academy. Librarians can provide support for these initiatives through the library by using the library to promote student-led open access activities. A strong student voice can be a powerful ally while bringing new energy to the open access movement. Involving and working with students is also an important way to keep the library's mission and advocacy efforts fresh and new for that prominent group of stakeholders in the information chain. Keeping the library relevant for students is a priority.

There are other ways that reference librarians can promote open access. Many academic libraries offer information on open access publishing and copyright issues on their websites, and certainly appear to be strong advocates that everyone in the institution should move toward open access behaviour. Create Change is a prominent example of a librarian advocacy initiative. Sponsored by ARL, ACRL and SPARC, librarians have been expected to sign up to this initiative. Librarians at reference desks, and in advocacy positions in the scholarly community, can certainly give out Create Change brochures at desks while promoting an agenda to move open access forward from their websites. Posters are available for download from SPARC and other advocacy groups, and they can be displayed prominently in the library. For instance, SPARC has a poster describing its 'Author's Addendum', which can assist authors in retaining rights when dealing with publishers (SPARC, 2009). Librarians can share this information widely. Are many librarians exhibiting this advocacy role while at work in the library and do they seem eager to display posters or other materials? Are LIS publishers seeing much use of the 'Author's Addendum' with librarians submitting papers? Further study is needed to determine whether academic librarians are really working as advocates for open access, or whether there is informed apathy. It may also be that the work of library open access advocacy groups has not trickled down to the front-lines. Front-line librarians are often most deeply affected by the requests for information, complaints, or change in trends exhibited by users. The perpetuation of the status quo may also be driven by user behaviour. Change in reference and instruction due to open access may come more slowly, as a reaction to cancellations or other changes in availability of traditional books and journals which will result in corresponding user dissatisfaction and search for alternative sources to satisfy research needs. When cancellations mesh with a critical mass of self-archived material on the web, users and librarians may find some degree of satisfaction with repository content for research. When librarians and users still have access to satisfactory traditional subscription material, they may not wish to seek scholarly information out on the open web. Library leadership will set the tone for each individual institution.

LIS education and open access

Library schools are educating new academic librarians who will go out into the universities and promote open access if that is the philosophy they have seen promoted in LIS programmes. Are the library schools teaching open access even as many have even given up on the teaching of science and technology reference courses? Even as the STEM disciplines have been the breeding ground for open access, the number of library school courses with a science focus has been declining. Library school faculty must provide a well-rounded background to assist new librarians with responsibilities for open access advocacy in the library. This, of course, assumes that LIS faculty teaching library school courses, as well as the future academic librarians they instruct, have studied the situation thoroughly and are really uniformly on board with strong support for the movement. This is an assumption that may not have been studied. The library school faculty groups may or may not be self-archiving, taking on new roles as editors of library-published open access journals, or teaching open access in courses. All of this uncertainty among librarians and LIS faculty plays out against a backdrop of saturation of open access concepts by library organisations such as ACRL and ARL. Librarians and LIS faculty may not all agree with the advocacy positions put forth by these groups, and may be continuing to teach traditional methods of collection development, instruction and reference service. In addition, there may not be adequate cross-pollination of LIS groups and expertise for discussion of open access behaviour, or a common agenda for the profession. As with all transformative topics, scholarly communication may be an area that is not sufficiently discussed in venues that bring together library administrators, practising academic librarians, interns, those seeking library positions, and those in LIS education. Alongside these discussions, librarians will need to interface with the publishing world and well as repository developers and others to craft a singular agenda that includes action plans.

Library organisations and many academic libraries have instituted formal mentoring programmes for shepherding junior faculty through the promotion and tenure process, or for the purpose of sharing professional expertise. It would be assumed that many of these faculty mentors are giving advice on where and how to publish, and the training of mentors would now need to include the particular institution's policy for librarians when it comes to expected behaviour in terms of publishing scholarly work in open access archives and journals. Both new librarian authors and veterans may need advice on open access publishing in LIS. This also represents an expanded role for the librarian mentor, and advice about publication choices carries great weight when it comes to the nontenured mentee. The nontenured librarian must not make decisions that jeopardise promotion and tenure by publishing outside the boundaries of what is expected in the institution. There must be a clear message from those on library promotion and tenure committees as regards what is expected or desirable for librarian publishing when it comes to promotion and tenure. If senior library faculty and library administrators do not give a clear message, librarians will behave as other junior faculty and stay with the 'safe' route and publish in traditional LIS venues. Junior faculty mentored to stay with traditional publication strategies may likely transfer a similar sentiment to the other faculty they provide library consulting to as part of everyday work as a library liaison/subject specialist. Without university mandates or policies about deposition in the institutional repository of all work before promotion and tenure actions, librarians will continue to make individual decisions for each of their publications rather than adopt self-archiving for their total scholarly output. Individual libraries will have to set expectations for self-archiving, whether the archiving itself is the goal, or specifically archiving in the institutional repository. Stevan Harnad often restates the importance of self-archiving of all scholarly articles (the green road) as the way to success for the open access movement (see, for example, *www.eprints.org/openaccess/*).

7

Open access and technical services

Effects of open access on the work of technical services librarians

Online public access catalogues (OPACs), link resolvers and federated search products are seeing changes regarding the use of open source solutions for collection support and access. Link resolvers ideally need to connect library users to all types of material. Open access resources will not be discovered unless the technology can link researchers to materials in subject or institutional repositories as seamlessly as it does for subscription products (Sugita et al., 2007). One successful type of library technology, the link resolver, has proven very desirable to users, and may be driving researchers back to the library website as a starting place. Inger and Gardner (2008) studied publisher website issues by focusing on how readers navigate to scholarly content. Sixty per cent of respondents to their survey recognised that it was link resolver technology that mediated their path to electronic journals. If libraries can provide a one-stop shop for patrons to navigate from the library website directly to full text, whether free or subscribed, the user experience will be seamless and the library will point to quality resources regardless of business model. Librarians may decide to point users to peer-reviewed material regardless of whether the material comes through an open access portal or through library subscriptions and link resolvers.

Librarians must insist that available open access materials are included in plans for library technology initiatives. If librarians are apathetic about exposing whole categories of materials to users through library technology products, then these materials may continue to be hidden or not thought to be part of the library's accessible material. As libraries are providing access as well as ownership to electronic materials already, there may be no impediment to ensuring that all library products such as link resolvers work for open access materials. Libraries developing open access journals, or working in any capacity with such a journal will need to make sure the content is exposed to Google crawling, that article-level linking uses common algorithms such as OpenURL, and even that such journals are able to be tracked in electronic resource management systems (ERMS). Open access journals could consider participating with CrossRef, which will establish article-based digital object identifiers (DOIs) (Machovec et al., 2006). Technical services librarians may be value-added members of open access journal or monograph publishing teams when the library is publisher. Librarians know the value of positioning a journal for ultimate discoverability and usability, as well as the benefits of making sure a journal fits in easily with commercial and society journals in the subject area in terms of technical capabilities. Technical services and electronic resources librarians can bring their perspectives to any publishing effort as they know the implications for enhancement of effective technology in terms of linking, usage statistics, serials management, management of licences, 'A to Z' lists, ERMS implementation, and cataloguing/metadata development.

In technical services areas, librarians are dealing with many issues regarding the cataloguing of open access materials and the inclusion of them in workflows (Koehler, 2006). The library catalogue, once containing only the physical holdings of the library, now extends to free materials out on the web, and the boundaries are blurring. The catalogue may lose its relevance, as what is owned is replaced by what can be accessed. It is now possible for patrons to find books in the catalogue through services such as OCLC WorldCat, Google and Google Scholar. Open access to digitised books through services such as Google Book Search and Project Gutenberg will put many monographic materials on researchers' desktops as well. Cataloguers will wrestle with cataloguing and creating metadata for open access materials found in ever-increasing numbers on the internet. There are many new opportunities for librarians in metadata creation for institutional repositories, for instance, and those engaged in cataloguing and other traditional areas are seeing transformation of roles. As budget pressures remain, there may be pressure from other groups to study the use of free resources in relation to subscribed, and harvesting and analysing usage statistics will become a more commonplace method of justifying collections expenditures. Still, ten years after Harnad's subversive proposal (Okerson, 1995), libraries are still building collections with books and journals in all manner of fee-based formats, and one wonders how fast and how dramatic the change in workflows to accommodate open access materials will be for librarians working in cataloguing, serials acquisitions and technical services. Open access has not yet transformed the scholarly journal literature, and librarians are wrestling with ERMs and standardisation of many functions such as usage statistics and versioning. The stress on workflows may be continuing with traditional work while working on integrating the internet into the collections and services of the library.

Librarians will continue to gravitate toward more open source solutions to move the library's mission forward, and they will be able to develop customised solutions and quicker enhancements in-house. Although discussion of the wide range of open source products perfectly suited to libraries is beyond the scope of this book, such products are worth a brief mention as they take the open access self-archiving and gold journal discussion one step further by developing a culture of experimentation, collaboration and community expertise in the development of products that will be most useful to an institution's particular customer base. The successful libraries will be those that value innovation and locally-grown solutions to problems. Academic libraries can collaborate and share expertise to come up with common solutions. In public services and collection development, the content must be delivered to the library user through effective, state-of-the-art products, and many who work in libraries have expertise in the areas needed for development. Libraries are well suited to using open source products in many ways, and product development just extends a conversation about free and open access to information.

Also beyond the scope of this book is another important piece of the system – the use of open standards. Examples of open standards now commonly used in the library world are the Metadata Object Description Schema (MODS) and Metadata Encoding & Transmission Schema (METS), as well as the now common DOI and OpenURL systems. Each of these initiatives, as well as many others, directly impacts the processes of getting information effectively from digital sources to library users. The content is one piece of the puzzle; the technology behind seamless access is just as necessary for users to have a successful library experience. Users will come back to the library that organises and facilitates easy access to scholarly literature through effective library technology.

OPACs are in a time of transformation. Libraries already looking at new models of scholarly communication will want to look for alternatives to costly subscription products, such as developing alternatives to integrated library systems (ILSs), like Georgia Public Library's Evergreen (*http://www.open-ils.org/*). Koha is an open source ILS with a worldwide development team and user base. Another type of ILS alternative is represented by the Open Library Environment (*http://oleproject.org/*). The

Open Library Environment is an example of an international collective of academic libraries working collaboratively on next-generation open source systems to transform the future of library technology. The past few years have seen an explosion of social networking tools associated with catalogues and other library tools. For example, *Open Source Integrated Library Systems* by Marshall Breeding (2008) provides detailed information on open source software for ILSs. In the federated search arena, an open source alternative, LibraryFind, has been developed by Oregon State University (*http://libraryfind.org/*).

Creative, technically-savvy librarians will take the lead in this area, leverage similar technical expertise, and save their libraries money while enhancing the organisation and discovery of scholarly materials for various user groups. The institutional goal of lowering costs while still providing discovery and access to a well-organised suite of resources and services has not been met, but one hopes will be attainable. For now, free solutions work in concert with subscription products, and costs are still outstripping budgets. The future of libraries will depend on the dedication of the stakeholders to work together toward common goals in building open source solutions while showcasing library talent for developing such solutions. Libraries will be able to provide access to a wide variety of research materials in many formats using library-produced solutions. Libraries producing the technology products for unique situations is a way of taking control of in-house issues with open source solutions and available staffing. Libraries anticipating this trend may want to ensure that they have the personnel on board who can innovate and find creative technical solutions in a collaborative atmosphere.

Institutional repositories, open access and academic librarians

No discussion of technical services aspects of open access in libraries could fail to take into account the increasingly common presence or the utmost importance of the institutional repository. Librarians who work with repository development, both in terms of policy and infrastructure, may be the ones closest to the realisation of open access strategies for institutions and for libraries. It may then just be assumed that all librarians in the institution will be involved in encouraging content depositions or fielding requests from affiliates for open access publishing or other initiatives. There may have been a feeling that 'if you build it, they will come'. This may not be a realistic notion. Some have suggested that without institutional mandates, or at least a strong suggestion from high-level university/college leadership, library-developed digital repositories will not reach their potential to increase the visibility of their institution's refereed scholarly output or help to change existing modes of scholarly communication. The repository may not develop as an integral part of the library, and may not be supported in any consistent fashion by other librarians. Institutional or departmental mandates like the ones in place at private institutions like MIT or Harvard, or at public universities like the University of Kansas put high-level emphasis on open access and may assist librarians in local efforts at populating the repository with scholarly output. These mandates and policies elevate the open access discourse to high-level institutional bodies. Kansas has a waiver for its 'policy' (Suber, 2009). The discussion around scholars' choice to 'opt out' of such policies or mandates is that offering researchers this option may take some of the teeth out of the most ambitious plans. In an example of a successful implementation, the University of Liege's institutional repository, ORBi, boasts full-text access to 9,000 publications only six months after launching (*http://orbi.ulg.ac.be/*). It will be instructive to follow the successful implementers where self-archiving is a goal of the repository. Deposits from science researchers may follow well-publicised legislation to provide global access to taxpayer-funded work, but the case may be harder to make for other disciplines, especially those without a history of funding, or in subject areas where it is not so vital for the public to have access. For these disciplines, archiving in the repository might revert to realisation of the 'value' of providing global access to scholarly works of all kinds. It may be interesting to study which types of literature librarians are motivated to make available through open access, and whether only science is felt to be a priority. Researchers in all disciplines may be interested in archiving results of older research only previously available on paper, or data that has not been digitised but might still be important for research purposes. Further study may be needed to analyse librarian opinions about their roles in promoting the repository in other aspects of public services work. The repository may be forgotten in reference encounters or in library information literacy sessions. As some technical services librarians transition into new roles in working with repositories, it is important to have public services or collection development librarians present on implementation teams, or a disconnect will develop in terms of relating the service to actual patron discovery. Many reference and instruction librarians may not consider the repository at all when dealing with library users in any situation.

Many universities are attempting to fully integrate the repository into the workings of the institution. According to a Rand Europe report by Hoorens et al. (2008), higher education institutions 'currently lack a coherent vision of how digital repositories can assist those organizations in accomplishing their vision'. The SHERPA LEAP Consortium includes the London School of Economics and University College London. Hoorens et al. state that 'in order to reap their full potential, the consortium argues, the repositories need to become better embedded in the institutional strategic planning'. The institution as a whole must have a plan for the repository's role in the organisation and be able to envision a scaling up of the service. A Council on Library and Information Resources (CLIR) survey of library administrators in the USA has also demonstrated that 'there is no consensus of what institutional repositories are for' (Markey et al. 2007; Lercher, 2008). Librarians advocating for open access partly through population of the institutional repository will need strong support and comprehensive information if they will be doing marketing and public relations for the repository. Without strong support, library liaisons may not want to place emphasis on the marketing effort when the particular discipline may not be well served by the repository. Liaisons know the stark disciplinary differences between the scholarly communication behaviours of researchers.

If university or library administrators also feel that there must be changes in promotion and tenure practices in the disciplines in order for author self-archiving in the repository to become a priority, librarians will need clear direction in order to see any potential role in working with departmental faculty researchers. Researchers may not be pushing for change in traditional practice. Librarians and LIS faculty may be included in groups not pushing for change in their own disciplinary scholarly communication practices. In a California Digital Library study of 1,118 respondents from the University of California faculty at 13 campuses, labs and branches, 'scientists were significantly more inclined to say that no changes are needed' (as compared with other groups) (Lercher, 2008). Outside of mandates motivating authors to look at open access issues, there may not be an identification with the library as a source for author negotiations with publishers. A demand for services from the researcher side would engage librarians to become more involved with repository efforts, and also ratchet up the scholarly communication conversation within various groups within the library. Librarians working in reference, liaison or collection development roles may find themselves asked to advocate for something that researchers are not demanding, but administrators and repository managers have labelled a priority for the library. Salisbury frames the situation thus: 'While many library associations are staunch supporters of open access, individual libraries cannot forget that their mandate is to provide their researchers with access to the scientific literature', and, ACRL's Linke adds, 'it's a balancing act' (Salisbury, 2008). Librarians want to provide the services that researchers want. Some want to redirect money for subscriptions to author fees while developing robust repositories (at least for the science materials tied to funder mandates). Researchers want access to top-tier journals, and libraries know this. Libraries may not be able to pay for subscriptions, memberships to assist authors, and the costs of repository development as well. After all of the rhetoric, it seems the repository may not develop as a top priority for all librarians, and while it has an important role, it may not be the central place in the wholesale move toward open access as was once envisioned.

The Rand report also mentions the 'quality' issues with repository content (Hoorens et al., 2008). If the repository cannot be a trusted source of scholarly materials, standing for levels of expected peer review, students and other researchers may be wary of the mixed bag of content. Confidence in using materials vetted by repository managers or others may be an issue for students and researchers who have been previously steered toward material in scholarly published journals and books. If the repository contains other materials, such as PowerPoint presentations or classroom materials, alongside postprints of articles subsequently published, the scholarly value of the material may be unclear to readers. As publishers have moved to some types of 'branding' initiatives such as CrossMark to deal with issues of versioning, repositories may have to brand deposits for peer-review status or final version. Researchers may want to be sure of certification before citing and disseminating versions accessed through the repository. Librarians in public services capacities may be reluctant to show repository materials to patrons due to concerns about the scholarly value of some of the contents. It will be up to institutions to decide whether the repository will be primarily a source of institution-specific special collections-type material, or a service that pushes the scholarly output of the institution to the wider world. This requires exposure to search engines, public service behind discovery, and integration with the library's other holdings.

The repository will also be important as a tool for digital preservation of institutional output. Librarians who are writing for publication may be expected to be early adopters of deposition behaviour in the library-hosted institutional repository. It is hoped that when talking with faculty in their liaison roles, librarians will be able to point to their own submissions to the institutional repository. This may require a change in behaviour for librarians who may have begun to self-archive with LIS subject repositories such as E-LIS and dLIST. Librarians may want to participate at the disciplinary level, or may have chosen a LIS repository for enhanced web visibility. Librarians may wonder whether they need to extend self-archiving behaviour further in supporting the institutional repository by depositing their work, and may question whether it is worth depositing work in more than one repository. There may be concerns about having versions other than the branded publisher PDF available on the web. LIS authors may not see the need to deposit material as urgently as the need to deal with scientific research output in the repository plan.

Digital librarians and those working in reference roles may also be called upon to assist authors with help in doing 'proxy' self-archiving on behalf of authors (eprints, 2006). Of course, one would assume that the authors among these librarians are self-archiving their own work in either disciplinary or institutional repositories. Further study is needed to determine the extent of librarian authors' self-archiving in institutional repositories. LIS curricula may not be covering institutional repository issues well enough from either side – the public services implications or even in the educating of future librarians for roles with the repository as an integral part of every academic library. LIS education programmes may be also unsure how to deal with this topic outside of coursework on informatics, metadata development, e-science or other similar issues.

It may be a challenging role for any subject specialist or other librarian charged with making sure the institutional repository continues to see rising numbers of deposits. Writing in 2007, Suber predicted that 'spontaneous author self-archiving will only increase slowly in 2008' and that 'self-archiving will start to rise significantly when the volume of open access literature on deposit in repositories reaches a critical mass'. (Suber, 2007c) also predicts that the more researchers use repositories as readers, the more they will think of them as authors. This suggests that if a library is advocating for self-archiving, it will want to push readers toward repository content in reference encounters through visibility on the library website, and through instruction sessions and class handouts. At this point it will be still be difficult to say to constituencies that the library can save money on costly journal subscriptions due to open access, meaning that advocacy will have to focus on free and open availability of scholarly information as a library value. Outside of federal funding mandates, it may be difficult to entice researchers in many fields to support repository efforts.

According to Suber, 'we're entering the post-panic period of the open access revolution'. Publishers may be inclined to experiment with certain open access materials as part of their suite of offerings, or offer options to authors wanting open access without necessarily fearing great loss to established business practices. Libraries are still waiting to see how open access will set them free from runaway costs in times of tough economic downturns, and may for now have to promote open access based on other library principles while watching the academy for changes in scholarly communication practices, especially in terms of promotion and tenure in a discipline-by-discipline manner.

Disciplinary differences in scholarly communications behaviour will require the library to tailor its services and message to departmental faculty. A broad-brushed appeal for voluntary deposits might not produce results. Librarians with a good knowledge of individual disciplines will know what the tenure and promotion practices entail and should have an idea of which aspects of the repository will appeal. This may mean 'selling' the idea that open access increases research impact to teaching faculty, graduate students and other researchers. Junior faculty may respond better to a conversation about web visibility and the potential for increased research impact resulting from use of the repository, while other groups may need other incentives. Challenges also include persuading faculty to change from other established behaviours such as archiving in subject repositories or posting articles on personal or departmental websites. Posting branded publisher PDFs in violation of journal policies may be common practice among many faculty members. Without 'take-down' orders and with scholars readily sharing electronic copies, as they did with former reprint services, sharing is still commonplace.

Copyright issues and all librarians

Open access issues affecting librarians revolve to some extent around an understanding of copyright, licensing, and other issues such as 'fair use'. Librarians have not traditionally been required to be conversant in the more detailed issues of copyright and licensing. Researchers may also be very unclear about their rights as authors, and may not have the time or inclination to investigate all options. Librarians may want to showcase copyright information very prominently on the library website. Even though this is a complicated matter, some library organisations, such as the Association for Research Libraries (ARL) have mass-produced materials intended to focus on basic tenets of copyright. The brochure *Know Your Copy Rights* is an example of something librarians can easily disseminate or utilise to start an important conversation with authors of scholarly materials (ARL, 2007). Another useful guide for librarians as well as researchers that explains the basics in an easily readable format is a publication entitled *Authors' Rights, Tout de Suite* (Bailey, 2008). In addition, the Canadian Association of University Teachers (CAUT) has produced a useful brochure entitled *Retaining Copyright in Journal Articles* which uses straightforward language to explain new issues with retention of author rights (CAUT, 2008). It may be helpful for librarians to have relevant handouts such as these available for meetings with faculty and researchers, or for disseminating from service desks. Videos can be produced that may be appealing to time-pressed researchers. Effective conversations about author rights, university publishing efforts involving the repository, electronic theses and dissertations, and new forms of scholarship such as use of video in web materials all can involve the library and represent another example of a value-added service for researchers working in a complicated information landscape. Many libraries have a designated scholarly communication or copyright librarian, but in other cases at least the first point of contact about author rights might come to reference or liaison librarians. All academic librarians might be expected to have a basic understanding of the current copyright and licensing issues confronting researchers.

Other repository services

Faculty may respond to conversations that include the ability for the library to help in data curation or other services that the repository staff may provide, or they may need more information or incentive to use the repository. Most helpful would be a central source of information and marketing so faculty are not receiving mixed messages about the services provided and the potential benefits of self-archiving. A time-consuming task besides the usual issues of author permissions, versioning, and all of the technical side would be the development of a comprehensive collection development policy for the repository. This policy will give the repository a clear identity and mission by positioning it prominently within the existing library structure. Librarians may not see how the repository fits with the collection strategies of the rest of the library, and a diluted or less than strong message may marginalise the effort. Some may see the repository as simply collating 'digital special collections', although its potential is so much greater. Jantz and Wilson (2008) advocate changing the term 'institutional repository' to something that evokes scholarship and research, while analysing specifically the role of the academic library in the 'reform of current practice of scholarly communication'. Again, the role may not be clear, focused or spelled out for librarians in most institutions, and rather assumed and integrated without discussion or debate.

Jantz and Wilson examined the library websites of the ARL libraries to determine whether the inclusion of specific web pages devoted to scholarly communication had any bearing on the development of institutional repositories at each institution. This study went on to report that in the summer of 2006, 56 per cent of ARL libraries had some sort of institutional repository, but that 'the findings of this and earlier studies indicate that individual faculty participation is either low or nonexistent in one-third of current university institutional repositories at ARL libraries'. Further, institutional repository deposits differ greatly by disciplinary area, with humanities faculty depositing the least number of their works (Jantz and Wilson, 2008). Clearly, although institutional repositories are only one important part of the library's 'commitment' to open access, teams including a variety of librarians and stakeholders will need to examine the best uses for repositories outside already successful initiatives such as electronic theses and dissertations. Regarding the lack of correlation between scholarly communication web pages and the development of repositories, Jantz and Wilson state that 'our research here suggests that libraries are ambivalent about their relationship to institutional repositories as evidenced by the variety of navigation paths and, in some cases, the total absence of any reference to institutional repositories' (Jantz and Wilson, 2008). A Cornell study also points to the lack of deposits in the institutional repository (Davis and Connolly, 2007).

Librarians will have to reassert their backing for any integral role for the repository in daily library work or risk creating another silo outside library workflows and priorities. Any service operating outside of the one unified understanding of library collections or services will not be discovered, accessed or used by library patrons. If the library is using a sophisticated federated search, the repository must be included. With library budgets already stressed, repositories may not be considered cost-effective if not populated. Some have suggested that 'digital repositories can help to reduce the vulnerability of libraries to changes in subscription fees' (Hoorens et al., 2008). This assumes a reaching of critical mass of available scholarship in repositories, and that in order to do the necessary marketing, some success must be shown. In terms of the institutional repository, librarians must be the community who define what 'success' is and whether it can be entirely quantifiable. Everything in the library, including the institutional repository, is subject to assessment and continuous scrutiny over costs. Grant funding may be fuelling some areas of repository development but sustainability may eventually be an issue. Reiterating the seriousness of library serials budgets and the pressing hope that open access will provide relief for academic libraries, it has been reported that between 1996/97 and 2000/01, the 'information resources budget of UK university libraries decreased by 29 per cent in real terms, while the average journal price over the same period increased by 41 per cent' (Hoorens et al., 2008). Various studies have reported on the costs of repositories to their institutions and to libraries. Without tangible reports of return on investment in the repository, librarians may see the lack of sustained funding from external grants as damaging to the library. Developing methods to assess usage in a consistent manner will be important to researchers and also to librarians working on making the repository visible (Xia and Sun, 2006). No area of the library is immune from stringent assessment in times of tight budgets and all librarians investing in the success of the repository effort will have a place in reiterating its mission as well as providing clear evidence of how it benefits the institution and the wider scholarly community.

At the 2005 meeting of the International Federation of Library Associations (IFLA), there was a full-day session on open access where David Prosser of SPARC Europe emphasised 'the strategic link between institutional repositories and open access journals' (Oliver and Swain, 2006). Following the IFLA meeting in 2006, the IFLA Health and BioSciences section investigated the directories of institutional repositories and identified 23 existing directories. The University of Nottingham's OpenDOAR stood out as a leader in this area. As Oliver and Swain (2006) have asked, can the material identified through searches of these directories of institutional repositories function as a barometer of global innovation? One wonders whether academic librarians working with the disciplines have considered the total deposits in worldwide institutional repositories as fodder for assessment of scholarly work and markers for new research interests in various disciplines. As more data moves into repositories, this may be considered a cumulative source of information, even though it is not necessarily crawled by Google or other popular search engines. Librarians can publicise global repository content as another access point for scholarly work as long as there is understanding by library users that the versions available are authoritative, and the repository is a credible source where research results are reported in peer-reviewed articles.

A prominent function of institutional repositories is the enabling of the publication of new open access peer-reviewed journals, and even digital publishing of monographs. Working closely with librarians responsible for repository development, librarians in the institution can reach out to departments and disciplinary faculty to encourage the suggestion for new high-level born-digital publications. Librarians with disciplinary expertise can first be part of the vetting process as new journals or projects are being considered and once accepted, be part of the publication team. This teamwork provides a mechanism for the integration of the institutional repository with the work of the collection development and subject-specialist librarians. Failure to work across traditional boundaries may be detrimental to the full development of the repository as an integral part of library collections and services. Developing new journal publications gives the library a vital role in the information chain and is another opportunity for librarians to work together across traditional roles.

The commercial sector has had interest in the work of institutional repositories. In an interesting move, Thomson ISI (now Thomson Reuters) developed a commercial institutional aggregation product as part of its Web of Knowledge which is described thus: 'Web Citation Index creates a global listing of institutional repositories and open access articles' (Chillingworth, 2005). Web Citation Index purportedly 'brings consistent resource for preprints are difficult to find [sic] and brings them into professional research' and 'the open access and institutional repository community need a serious index and search tool to make their content more discoverable' (Chillingworth, 2005). Librarians may be curious about the implications of commercial tools that charge libraries specifically to assist in the discovery of open access materials. The value-added features may be worth the money for some librarians, but this may be an example of a 'mixed message' for the library community as open access materials in repositories are often used as an example of a corpus of material that is free to readers. Even though a commercial product can provide another avenue of discovery, the library community must ensure that open access materials found in repositories can be easily discovered without toll-based indexes. Many librarians may not be suggesting repository content to researchers while engaging in reference work either. Of course, many repository materials can be found using Google. Given that libraries' relationships with Google continue to grow, it is possible that the two may be becoming more interdependent over time.

One area that may speak to both librarians and faculty about the repository is its role in exposing grey literature on the web. Even if they struggle with the need to archive their postprints, faculty and students may seek greater web visibility for their conference proceedings, PowerPoint presentations, poster sessions, and other academic content that may be of interest to other scholars. Usage statistics provided by the repository can highlight the importance of previously unexposed grey literature. It has been suggested that librarians could develop their knowledge regarding the role of grey literature in different disciplines, and focus the repository effort on those disciplines in which grey literature has traditionally been important (Bell et al., 2005). While Bell et al. note that 'faculty members do not speak the same language as librarians', those working with repositories and other tools and vehicles used to promote open access must also remember that many academic librarians may not have had much experience with the tenets or terminology of the whole open access movement. It is important to provide training at all levels for librarians, and not to assume knowledge of a movement that may be seen as a 'non-library' issue for some.

An example of a university focused on providing institutional repository training for librarians is that of the University of Rochester, using its DSpace installation (Bell et al., 2005). Because the impetus for development of the repository came from the provost and the benefits were clearly felt to be institutional, it was natural for the training to involve all librarians. The training covered the actual deposit process – information to give all librarians a solid understanding of the repository. Training library personnel across the spectrum of position descriptions may help generate buy-in for the work of the repository. Many librarians may not have daily contact with the repository and may see it as redirecting funds and staff from other stretched library programmes. Some studies have focused on self-archiving across disciplines, and on who is actually physically performing the article deposition. In the study of open access self-archiving by Swan and Brown (2005), it was shown that in a cross-disciplinary group of 1,296 respondents, 80 per cent of self-archivers deposited their work themselves, 19 per cent had the library do the actual archiving for them, and in 10 per cent of cases, depositing was done by students or assistants. Only 4 per cent of the scholars who did the depositing themselves found the task difficult. Still, librarians may need to add this function to their ever-expanding skill set, or may feel that it is a clerical function best left to others.

Lynch and Lippincott (2005) provide a survey of institutional repository activity in the USA and suggest that deployment of such repositories has been limited outside of major research libraries. However, the authors state that it is the research libraries that have taken on the leadership roles in both policy formation and implementation within the larger research institutions. This leadership role means that librarians, through their involvement with the deployment of the repository, can expect enhanced collaboration and connection with their institutions. This collaboration between librarians, teaching faculty and researchers can spur discussion on other aspects of scholarly communication initiatives, and display a new type of expertise for librarians in the academy, further raising the profile of the library within the institution. Lynch and Lippincott's study dovetails with an analysis of the institutional repository development of 13 nations (van Westrienen and Lynch, 2005). At the time of these studies, it was difficult to state with certainty the number of objects in repositories, and the studies discuss impediments to deposit by faculty. Internationally, different types of repositories operating out of libraries show a great deal of diversity in institutional and even national deployment. An example of a repository operating on a national scale was Cream of Science in the Netherlands (van Westrienen and Lynch, 2005). To lend visibility, this initiative showcased the work of senior scholars, making the point that repositories and open access in general commonly suffer from a perception that they include lower-quality scholarship (van Westrienen and Lynch, 2005). By including work of important scholars in all repositories and making discovery by popular search engines a given, necessary status will be conferred.

It is possible for smaller libraries to establish institutional repositories with a somewhat more limited mission while still keeping the open access discussion at the forefront of the institutional culture. Using a team approach and available software such as DSpace, smaller libraries and institutions may be able to start on a smaller scale using available staff and facilities. An example would be the Humboldt Digital Scholar repository, which has been operated with minimal budget and existing library staff (Wrenn et al., 2009). Researchers may need services for complying with ever-increasing open access mandates, such as from the NIH or Wellcome Trust, no matter what type of institution they are affiliated with. Even for smaller academic libraries, this type of service raises the profile of the library.

An area of concern shared by Lynch and Lippincott is that of moving forward with efforts to make content in institutional repositories more discoverable to researchers outside of the home institution. Most institutional repositories employ the Open Archives Initiative Protocol for Metadata Harvesting (OAI-PMH), allowing content from those repositories to be harvested by services such as OAIster, and crawled by other search engines such as Google. The appeal to the researcher of depositing work online, where it will be crawled by Google, is irresistible for the author who desires impact and web visibility. Still, it appears uncertain which groups or organisations would be responsible for moving these initiatives forward in terms of federating institutional repositories and making them interoperable. Institutional repositories will also appeal to researchers and faculty who are working in multi or interdisciplinary areas that do not fit neatly into existing and well-defined subject or disciplinary archives. Interdisciplinary attraction will only be possible if there is maximum possible discovery of the repository's content and collections.

There are many specialty conferences devoted to the institutional repository, such as Open Repositories 2009: The Premier Venue for Implementers and Managers of Repository Infrastructure and Services. Although conferences may provide an opportunity for developers and managers to gather, it will be crucial to generate interest among librarians involved more directly with library users. Public services or collections librarians may want to consider presenting research from the user or instruction side at one of these conferences (Hahn, 2008). Collaboration might lead to better marketing and ultimate success of the library effort. Public services, collection development, and subject-specialist librarians could all add value to the institutional role by contributing viewpoints that would lead to better visibility and usefulness within the institution as well as by outside searchers.

A promising role for the repository may centre on issues of research data. Librarians' expanding role in data curation and e-science is of utmost importance. Ultimately, those aspects of the repository that are focused on data may prove to be a crucially important niche for a library's suite of offerings. Librarians will have to grapple with many issues in populating the institutional repository with data from many disciplines while ensuring that it can be curated, repurposed, reused and discovered by library users. There are many roles to fill for those entering fields of librarianship as well as those librarians looking for new roles focused on data curation in general or the data of a specific discipline. The institutional repository can fill this niche but needs a visionary plan to do so.

E-science and open access to data: the role of libraries

Where open access to scholarly publications and its effect on the work of librarians has been widely discussed, the movement toward open data practices is still in its infancy. An important issue on the periphery of the open access movement that will concern academic librarians in the sciences and social sciences relates to the management of the lifecycle of data. Data is being created by researchers in many different settings within each institution. With the capability of the institutional repository to handle data sets, this role of acquiring and preserving data across its lifecycle is new and exciting for academic librarians. Subject specialists may be called upon to lend expertise to metadata development, and new positions for bioinformatics librarians and data curation specialists will become available. This may be one area of incredible growth and opportunity for academic libraries, especially research libraries. It can be an area of intense interest for those LIS educators looking for new areas to entice future librarians to the field. To move into the future, library administrators, subject librarians, and technical services and repository developers will need to coordinate a response to the coming 'data deluge', and the library must forge a place at the table within the institution and the greater scientific community. High-level librarian expertise and a natural enhancement of roles can raise the reputation of academic libraries and those librarians who are well poised to take a leadership role in e-science, e-research and data curation. It is an opportunity to realise the often-mentioned goal of 'embedding' librarians in relevant teams across the library and the institution, further raising the profile of the research library in the chain of scholarly communications. Administrators involved in institutional research activities at higher levels may not expect the library to take a lead role in e-science, and it will be necessary to be proactive. Librarians may find a coordination and consulting role in virtual teams and organisations made up of collaborations of scientists and others involved in the management and discovery of data behind scholarly work.

Use of the term 'e-science' is reportedly more common in the UK and Europe, whereas the term 'cyberinfrastructure' may be in more common use in the USA. Where both terms have similar connotations, cyberinfrastructure is more of an umbrella term, encompassing other fields outside of those in the sciences. E-research is another term that has broader scope in terms of disciplines. All terms refer to 'use of networked computing technologies to enhance collaboration and innovative methods in research' (Jones, 2008). Articles examining e-science can be found in journals from a variety of fields, such as a recent compilation of articles in *Nature* (Frankel and Reid, 2008). Tony Hey and Jessie Hey described and defined e-science in their 2006 paper (Hey and Hey, 2006), and in October 2008, ARL distributed a short list of talking points that may be used to help fuel library discussion (Jones, 2008). In recent years, library organisations such as ARL and the Coalition for Networked Information (CNI) have begun to provide a venue for discussion of new roles dealing with data for librarians. Some libraries, such as the MIT libraries, have produced web pages that showcase science data services available from the library, and even examples of faculty success in gaining exposure by sharing data (MIT Libraries, 2008). A role for librarians will be to consult and be a point of contact for researchers, and there will be a marketing role for the library in showcasing assistance and expertise available from librarians. Librarians will want to extend their service orientation to this new e-science area, providing a proactive and approachable one-stop shop for information in this and other scholarly communication areas. Practically speaking, librarians currently working in academic libraries may not fit these roles well without extensive training. However, library education programmes can promote career tracks in e-science and provide opportunities for librarians in existing roles to consider the expansion of skill sets to include new roles with data.

With their expertise in repository development, knowledge of scholarly communication differences by discipline, and the use of metrics to demonstrate both personal and institutional research impact, librarians can become valued members of the scholarly communications discussion in the various disciplines. Alongside the changing of publication paradigms to more open models, data associated with those publications will need to be curated and made available for discovery and reuse by other researchers. Librarians have always assisted researchers in finding relevant and appropriate books, articles and other publications. In the near future, it seems certain that librarians will also have to develop expertise in many areas involving data, including assisting researchers in the discovery of useful and relevant data sets. Moving data out of the office and laboratory and into the mainstream as part of the open data movement will be a great boon for researchers, and one hopes they will be looking to librarians for reference assistance. Libraries and other institutional stakeholders worldwide will have to grapple with the challenges of management and preservation of data, and priorities will have to be set in terms of decision-making about which data sets will have enduring value to the institution, the author and to society.

Integral parts of the future of e-science, the well developed fields of scientometrics and informetrics, as well as other associated areas of information science, will also become increasingly more valuable to the daily work of librarians consulting in new roles in e-science. There is great potential for collaboration with graduate LIS programmes, and LIS researchers in institutional consulting roles. Positions such as 'scholarly communications librarian', now cropping up at many institutions, may take on a coordination role, bringing stakeholders together in new teams devoted to harnessing the disparate sources of data generated by the institution's researchers and their collaborators. The institutional repository development must prepare for this potential new role with science data, and may be in a position to develop policies before competing opportunities from the commercial sector present themselves. Libraries need to establish this territory if they want to incorporate the data piece, or services may move to various areas of the 'cloud' (Katz, 2008). Commercial publishers are also moving to integrate data into journal platforms. This is clearly a growth area for academic libraries and the institutional repository, and a prime opportunity for embedding subject-specialist librarians in the research process.

Some in libraries wonder whether the new e-science roles will be added to current subject-specialist position responsibilities, or whether jobs will have to be repurposed or added. Knowing that science data management and preservation will have to be addressed in the near future, personnel issues need to be addressed and planned for. University librarians and others may struggle to find appropriate members for e-science teams, needing to re-examine degree and experience requirements for positions. Teams of librarians and others who have not worked closely together in the institution will be most effective, but they will need to learn to speak a 'common language'. Public services librarians will need to work closely with repository developers and other technical services librarians, which may require new library organisational and functional groupings. Will 'librarian' need to be part of titles, or will libraries need to move away from traditional terms in position descriptions? Will there be a dilution of the librarian identity with the move away from the requirement of the library degree for all positions? Success and efficacy may require recruiting individuals for e-science, bioinformatics and data curation library positions that are able to present with a variety of highly relevant education and experience for new types of library roles. A vital emergent role for the institutional repository with respect to data is at stake.

Even though academic libraries have been discussing e-science, or e-research as it is sometimes known, for the past few years, there has so far been limited wholesale library engagement with the movement. At this time, the 'data deluge' certainly seems imminent. With many conferences and publications in LIS and other fields discussing e-science, the conversation has remained largely focused on planning and theory rather than the practical applications currently in use by libraries. At this point, more work is being done in Canada, the UK and Australia (Jones, 2008). A prominent example of bringing collaborators together has been the development of the VIVO project at Cornell, and the Distributed Data Curation Center at Purdue (Brandt, 2007). One hopes that the coming years will see the resolution of many issues, including development of funding strategies that will allow libraries to take on new long-term roles. As other departments in the institution are working with data using a variety of strategies, the library world must come out as a strong contender for a role that may pass the library by. This role may also bring new revenue streams in terms of large grants for data curation into libraries, benefiting other areas of repository development.

As always, librarians have been part of the discussion of promotion and tenure at the institution, and they may have a place in demonstrating the impact of sharing data. Studies have shown that the sharing of data can increase research impact by up to 70 per cent (Pinowar et al., 2007). With the increasing popularity of new groups of researchers involved in 'open science', where data is posted on the web, librarians will also have to watch trends in this more 'community-based' open system of peer review (Johnson, 2008). Along with the accrual of research impact due to open access publishing of scholarly journal literature, the next frontier will involve associated data, currently linked by commercial publishers as 'supplementary materials'. Publishers have realised the value of this type of linked data, and researchers will now need to access a journal platform, not simply a PDF, to access the entire article and data. Once again, commercial publishers will sell access to the value-added, in this case, data, back to the institutions where the data may have been created in the first place. Journal publishers may begin to mandate direct deposit of data into appropriate databases along with the article text (Frankel and Reid, 2008). The journal 'package' will evolve into a digital document with important associated linked data and other supplementary materials. Interlibrary loan of such materials will be impossible, as the value-added nature of the data will be in demand. When publishers merge, discontinue or sell journal titles, or go out of business, one wonders about the sustainability of the data piece. Existing preservation initiatives used by publishers and libraries in case of 'trigger events' may not be up to the challenge of protecting and preserving data in the collective sense. Clifford Lynch (2008) discusses the challenges faced by disciplines, institutions and librarians in data stewardship. An Office of Cyberinfrastructure programme named 'DataNet' will invest $100 million over five years to build 'data stewardship' capabilities. Librarians will undoubtedly seek grant funding at first to develop infrastructure. Lynch also remarks that 'community standards are lacking'. Preservation of data is best not left in the hands of publishers, and libraries may employ a more 'trusted' route to preservation.

Open access, whether for self-archived material, or through open journal publishing, will need to deal with the lifecycle of data, and librarians will need to be there at the beginning of the process. The development of institutional repositories will make available the capability for data curation, and this is indeed an exciting yet somewhat overwhelming task for academic libraries. Adding any type of new service has budgetary considerations, and e-science may be an obvious choice for library support due to the infrastructure already in place, and the important place that the data holds in terms of institutional priorities. The library is seeing an enticing opportunity to play a vital role in the curation and discoverability of data associated with the formal publication process in sciences and some social sciences. However, data issues are extremely discipline-specific, thwarting efforts at any general solution.

The 'open data' mandates coming along will only put further pressure on libraries to extend their advocacy of open access to managing the data that is created at all stages of the research process, finally culminating in a version that is to be shared with the public. One study has shown that 85 per cent of scientists doing original research retain data themselves, while 28 per cent have their data stored in their departments or institutes (Kuula and Borg, 2008). Long-term solutions for curation and preservation are clearly needed so that raw data can be reused in improving future research endeavours while improving access to important science. The roles for librarians at research institutions are becoming increasingly clear. Science Commons is a series of initiatives extending the mission of Creative Commons licensing further into areas of scientific research, and is currently developing the Open Data Protocol (Poynder, 2008). In 2004, the OECD countries adopted the Declaration on Access to Research Data from Public Funding. Ministers asked the OECD to develop a set of guidelines for open access to data emanating from public funding, and the charge was taken up by the OECD Committee for Scientific and Technological Policy (Kuula and Borg, 2008). In 2006, the Ministry of Education in Finland charged the Finnish Social Science Data Archive with surveying the social and behavioural sciences faculty in Finnish universities about data practices. The Finnish study showed that researchers often take their data with them when they change positions. The need to steward data through the process, and the institutional place for this process becomes clear when looking at the current data practices of scientists working outside disciplines that have well-developed consortial data archives. From the autumn of 2008, the Academy of Finland has started requiring a 'long-term data management plan' to be submitted alongside any funding application (Kuula and Borg, 2008).

Australia has a national mandate for sharing data resulting from research using state funding (Jones, 2008). Currently, at many institutions worldwide, it may be difficult to comply with such mandates, and more funding agencies will likely develop such policies to promote sharing and reuse of data that evolves from taxpayer monies. With recent open access mandates and policies coming out of universities, most notably Harvard, there will also be institutional mandates to comply with going forward. University administrators considering open access mandates regarding the output of their university's scholars will have to grapple with data in the sciences and some social sciences.

In the USA, following the recent NIH mandates for open access to publicly-funded scholarly research, data mandates will certainly follow. Once again, librarians doing quantitative research studies destined for either open access LIS journals, or for some of the commercial or scholarly LIS journals, may be considering the issues around the data that they have used in studies of library and information science topics. Certainly, there is data being stewarded or even discarded by librarians completing research studies destined for publication. One wonders if there has been any discussion in the library science areas regarding the curation of LIS data. This will be especially important as researchers in the areas of the profession that rely on quantative studies, for example areas of scientometrics, will also need to discover and reuse available data. With libraries developing open access journal publishing services, the library will need to develop policies around data associated with those publications. This may become an integral planning discussion around talk of any library-published journal. Libraries may evolve to a state where any 'publication' is only considered complete when the associated data is available to readers and researchers. This may an unfamiliar area for many librarians.

Once these mandates appear, it is incumbent upon institutions, and potentially libraries, to be able to provide a structured plan for the management of the data throughout its lifecycle. Librarians and institutional stakeholders such as IT and high-level research administrators must be ready to play a role. There is a distinction between the situation of smaller researchers, and those contributing to large multi-institutional archives such as the Protein Data Bank. There are also real disciplinary differences at play – not just between social sciences and sciences. In the Finnish study, for example, one in four respondents regarded 'the loss of competitive advantage' as a significant barrier to open access to research. Some disciplines cannot easily move to a culture of data sharing. This is where the subject-specialist librarian would be able to work with repository developers and other members of the team to develop policies and plans that speak to individual researchers' concerns about access to data. The learning curve for subject-specialist library liaisons may be steep, and may require advanced degrees or recent research experience in the subject field, or at the very least, close contact with researchers doing work using current protocols. Opportunities such as this will push the subject specialists closer to the faculty and researchers, and raise the profile and value of librarians across the institution.

In collection development, librarians will need to be cognisant about the forces in the publishing world that harness the enduring value of scientific data, as well as the issues involved with reuse and preservation of the institution's valuable data sets. Aside from preservation, collection development librarians as well as those in public services may find increasing desire for access to tools of discovery and reuse of data associated with the more traditional publications. With a move toward open access, librarians will have to see the output of the research process as not only culminating in the certified publication, but also the associated data. Along the spectrum of the data lifecycle, librarians may be involved from the beginning, and various versions may be preserved in the repository. Subject librarians or other specialist librarians may be involved in the documentation process, lending expertise to the development of metadata in a discipline-specific fashion, and being involved in the dissemination, reuse and discovery tools to provide other researchers with maximum access to the data. Along with this will come the necessary policy development regarding a host of other issues including intellectual property, resistance of researchers to expose data, rights management, and privacy concerns. Policies will be important in the development of criteria that will enable libraries and scientists to work together to prioritise and put a value on data that need to be preserved in perpetuity. Some data will have enduring value; some will only need temporary stewardship. Many also worry about a 'digital dark age', where much data will inadvertently be lost due to 'ever-shifting platforms and file formats that will render so much data being produced today inaccessible' (Ciciora, 2008). This clearly is a traditional role and value in librarianship – to steward and preserve valuable research materials otherwise in danger of being permanently lost to science and society.

Interested librarians may find new roles, but all librarians in both social sciences and sciences fields will need to understand the potential of data sharing to affect the discipline's research process, and make sure clientele have access to the fruits of previous research initiatives. This will include working with researchers to expose older data sets that may be sitting in offices in paper or other inaccessible formats, and may need to be handled and made available through the institutional repository. With declines in some other service areas due to movement toward the digital library, many librarians will welcome new challenges. Librarians will be important in the movement of data to open access, and in knowing which disciplines will find their structures amenable to this type of transformation. It will be up to individual libraries and the various consortia and library organisations to decide which roles each will play in this very new aspect of librarianship.

The global importance of open access

Open access is truly a global phenomenon with implications for breaking down barriers and benefiting scholars without access to toll literature. Librarians have always had a global view of scholarship, and the internet has considerably extended that reach. Open access initiatives are bringing librarians together in discussion of the journal literature and of associated data. Libraries may or may not be changing traditional practices in collection development or reference, but there is certainly much advocacy and activism by librarians all over the world. One would expect librarians, as a group, to want their own research to have a global reach. IFLA, in its statement on open access, strongly supports global open access initiatives (IFLA, 2004). Some would say that free access to information is a vital role for libraries. Librarians would be expected to support such a move, on account of their general propensity toward equal (free) access for all.

Collection development librarians are also involved with weeding print collections, as well as with issues surrounding the sharing of resources with others, especially in developing countries. By moving deaccessioned books through services like Better World Books (Better World Books, 2007) or local initiatives such as the Global Literacy Project in New Jersey (*http://www.glpinc.org/*), librarians work toward their common mission to share scholarly information with others that may not be able to afford it. Publishers, working with the World Health Organization, participate through the Health InterNetwork Access to Research Initiative (HINARI; *http://www.who.int/hinari/en/*) and its sister project, Access to Global Online Research in Agriculture (AGORA; *http://www.aginternetwork.org/en/*), to bring traditional journal content to the developing world free of charge. Online Access to

Research in the Environment (OARE) is another philanthropic initiative that publishers are employing to enhance global accessibility to STEM researchers in developing countries (*http://www.oaresciences.org/en/*). Elsevier states 'we work with the library community internationally to help train researchers, physicians and educators on how to use HINARI, AGORA and OARE as well as similar programs to which they have access' (Elsevier, 2008). Librarians can certainly appreciate the impact of such initiatives while finding difficulty bringing these high-cost subscriptions to researchers in their own institutions. Still, such efforts at bringing high-impact journal subscriptions to developing nations level the playing field for scientists worldwide. The open access movement would share those values – providing opportunities to make all research articles free on the web through self-archiving or free open access journals. The democratisation of information is only realised when all readers have access to scholarly material, especially that which has been funded by taxpayers. Which of these methods appeal most to libraries in their efforts to advocate and support such values in promoting dissemination of important scholarship? Beyond a budgetary or public relations role in supporting the outreach programmes of commercial publishers, librarians may in fact have no role to play. One recent study shows the increasing importance of the availability of open access scientific research output in the developing world. Findings show that 'the influence of open access was more than twice as strong in the developing world' and that the availability of this corpus of research material has the ability to 'widen the global circle of those who can participate in science and benefit from it' (Evans and Reimer, 2009). Assisting the developing world, at least that which has electronic access, is part of librarianship's long history and value system. Will this reason encourage more librarians to participate with their own work and with the open access movement? Librarians may take interest in seeing their own publications disseminated via the web to all corners of the world when they choose open access venues such as self-archiving in repositories or the truly free (to authors and readers) open access journals. It goes without saying that librarians would like to see the LIS literature included in any effort to reach a worldwide audience with the intent of advancing LIS scholarship around the world. Open access to the LIS literature would level the playing field, and make the profession more visible for would-be librarians worldwide. All librarians should be concerned with the publication, organisation, and accessibility of information in LIS areas worldwide.

8

Conclusion

While the concept of open access to the scholarly literature is not new, realisation of it is a moving target. Libraries have taken a very strong advocacy position as regards the open access movement, even though it is something that may produce changes in the traditional relationships that libraries have had with publishers, the workflows of everyone involved in the library, and the types of materials commonly recommended to students by traditional reference and instruction programmes. Librarians advocate actively while sometimes not exhibiting changes to their own publication behaviour. The library and information science (LIS) literature, while expected by some to be the first to change to open models, in fact has not. The tenets of the open access movement may be most beneficial to researchers needing access to scientific literature. Most social sciences and humanities scholars may not have the same interests in open access outside of the promise of increased research impact or greater web visibility. Librarians who are not pressed by researchers for information about self-archiving or open access publications may turn their attention to the more pressing issues in the library. Most of all, the 'serials crisis' that provided impetus for much of the response by library groups has evolved, and it has been shown that researchers are still interested in the established journals of their fields, and want access to them. Libraries continue to pay publishers if they can. The library may risk irrelevance and marginalisation if librarians push researchers toward the open web and away from what have been traditionally-provided library books and journals. Many librarians may be comfortable with the status quo, both with their current responsibilities and with trying to provide the collections and services that researchers continue to demand. The open access movement may have developed as a parallel or peripheral situation to the everyday work of the academic library. Librarians may not have motivation or strong interest in getting involved at a level that would push the situation toward the tipping point where there is enough peer-reviewed scholarly material in repositories to render library subscriptions less necessary. At that time in the future where copies of all research articles have been archived in repositories, usage statistics of subscribed products will show less demand and journals can be cancelled, thus saving the library precious money. This remains a vision, even though self-archiving and new open access publications continue to rise in number.

Librarians may not see great advantages to open access behaviour with their own publications, and therefore may be missing an opportunity to understand the ramifications of participation in new forms of library scholarship. Even though newer or younger librarians may be more likely to look for open source or open access solutions, this depends on emphasis in library schools. There is no real evidence that changes in scholarly communication patterns, or an emphasis on teaching open access issues are being pushed to the forefront of priorities in graduate library programmes. Those who work with repository development of library-published open access materials may not be interfacing effectively with public services librarians. People may be misunderstanding the different roles of various open access journals, such as author-pays versus free for authors and readers. Most of all, the conversation gets steered to the established journals' experimentation with open access business models, while important advocates like Harnad continue to stress the importance of self-archiving-the deposit of every scholarly article in an open access repository. There are too many colours of open access beyond 'green' and 'gold' and so much daily information coming through lists and blogs and advocacy efforts, that the terms and the concepts might be reaching a saturation point. Librarians may send information to constituencies and may not be hearing demand for information. This fact may boil down to the vast array of disciplinary differences evident with open access behaviour seen even among different science fields.

Some have taken a broad-based approach, a one-size-fits-all kind of activism that may not have resonated with those in disciplines where self-archiving in disciplinary archives or publishing in born-digital open access journals has not meshed with expectations of promotion and tenure committees or become part of the culture of the field. Some disciplines lend themselves to preprints and others are focused in other directions and may not be interested in making changes to the traditional literature of the field. Disciplines vary widely, and the subject specialist has an opportunity to become an expert on open access journal options as well as repositories available to researchers in the discipline. Librarians would also be expected to understand the state of scholarly communication and open access in their own profession. LIS, whether for teaching faculty or practising faculty librarians, has its own specific journal hierarchy, publishing norms for promotion and tenure by institution, and other scholarly communication traditions. As is the case with many other disciplines, the library and information sciences literature is at a time of great change. Librarians, acting as advocates for change in the models for other disciplines, must also concentrate on their own literature. It is time to take stock and decide what is best for the academy and for librarians on a global scale. Librarians can publish their own journals, change the path of their own membership organisations, collaborate with university presses, IT and scholarly publishers, and archive their own work in institutional repositories or specialised subject archives. Librarians in all types of libraries, whether academic, public, or corporate, must remain up to date on open access and other changes. Users seeking information deserve to be kept abreast of changes in the information landscape. At the desk, in the chat room, in the scholarly communications committee, and as liaisons, the everyday work of the academic librarian is being affected by the current shift toward open access. Librarians must decide as a profession what the everyday 'best practices' will be for public services, collection development and the LIS literature as new models evolve. Certainly, more than ten years after Harnad's proposal (Okerson, 1995), librarianship as a profession (speaking holistically) should have more of a handle on the movement. The disconnect between advocates and those practising in the profession may be real. Certainly, librarians need to take a more active position in the open access movement, and join what would seem to be the few staunch and vocal advocates who work tirelessly to promote change both in libraries and the academy. Most importantly, in matters of open access, librarians must be on the vanguard, not behind the curve.

Some feel that the debate has become too loud; that supporters run the risk of becoming their own worst enemies and that 'the most vocal open access proponents can come off as zealots; their proselytizing of a new approach just a bit too strident for most people's comfort' (Salisbury, 2008). In all of their activities surrounding open access, it might behoove librarians to remain in open dialogue with all stakeholder groups including the publishers, but especially with each other so that the conversation is a real learning opportunity about library service to the research community, and an important opportunity to fully integrate the library into the lifeblood of the institution as a forward-thinking intellectually-driven enterprise. Librarians can be easily marginalised by pushing an agenda that does not appeal to researchers, faculty and students. Librarians cannot sit back and wait, but must take action in a variety of ways to showcase academic libraries as a continuing voice for the support of research in their own institutions as well as in the wider society. LIS research must focus more on librarian attitudes and behaviours toward open access, both in the promulgation of the practices to their own constituencies, but also to understand where the LIS literature stands. Rather than taking a stand for librarian advocacy, the focus of this volume has been to inform librarians and others about the open access movement and how it has, or has not been effectively incorporated in relevant areas of the academic library. Academic librarians, especially those with close access to researchers and classrooms have every chance to effect change with the everyday information they share, and the example they set with their own publishing behaviour. Time will tell what the eventual outcome will be, and whether libraries and librarians will indeed 'get on board' with a movement that can certainly change the worlds of libraries and publishers, yet promises to open up the world's scholarly literature to all of the citizens of the world.

Bibliography

ACRL (2007) 'Scholarly communication toolkit', available at: *http://www .acrl.ala.org/scholcomm/* (accessed 1 September 2009).

Adkins, D. and Budd, J. (2006) 'Scholarly productivity of US LIS faculty', *Library & Information Science Research* 28(3): 374–89.

ALA (2006) 'Open access to research', available at: *http://www.ala.org/ ala/aboutala/offices/wo/woissues/copyrightb/openaccesstoresearch/ accessresearch.cfm* (accessed 23 July 2009).

Anderson, I. (2008) 'The audacity of SCOAP3', *ARL* 257, available at: *http://www.arl.org/bm~doc/arl-br-257-scoap3.pdf* (accessed 19 July 2009).

Antelman, K. (2006) 'Self-archiving practice and the influence of publisher policies in the social sciences', *Learned Publishing* 19(2): 85–95.

APA (2007) 'Open access journal coverage in PsycINFO', *PsycINFO News* 26(4): 4–5, available at: *http://www.apa.org/databases/pin/07fal.pdf* (accessed 25 July 2009).

Arch, X. (2007) 'Electronic Resources & Libraries, 2nd Annual Conference 2007: Another Perspective', *Library Hi Tech News* 24(9): 17–18.

Ashmore, B. and Grogg, J. E. (2008) 'The race to the shelf continues', *Information Today* 16(1), available at: *http://www.infotoday.com/ searcher/jan08/Ashmore_Grogg.shtml* (accessed 6 July 2009).

Association of Research Libraries (ARL) (2007) 'Know your copy rights: using copyrighted works in academic settings', available at: *http://www.knowyourcopyrights.org/* (accessed 27 July 2009).

Association of Research Libraries (ARL) (2009a) 'Developing a scholarly communication program in your library', available at: *http://www .arl.org/sc/institute/fair/scprog/* (accessed 29 July 2009).

Association of Research Libraries (ARL) (2009b) 'Position descriptions collection', available at: *http://www.arl.org/sc/institute/fair/position-descriptions .shtml* (accessed 29 November 2007).

Atkinson, R. (2006) 'A new world of scholarly communication', *The Chronicle Review* 50(11): B16.

Bailey, C. W. (2005) 'Open access bibliography: liberating scholarly literature with e-prints and open access journals', available at: *http://www .escholarlypub.com/oab/oab.pdf* (accessed 20 April 2007).

Bailey, C. W. (2006) 'Open access and libraries', available at: *http://www .digital-scholarship.com/cwb/OALibraries2.pdf* (accessed 27 July 2009).

Bailey, C. W. (2008) 'Authors' rights, tout de suite', available at: *http://www .digital-scholarship.org/ts/authorrights.pdf* (accessed 16 July 2009)

Baker, G. (2007) 'Student activism; how students use the scholarly communication system', *College & Research Libraries News* 68(10): 636–8, 643.

Barbera, M. and DiDonato, F. (2006) 'Weaving the web of science: HyperJournal and the impact of semantic web on scientific publishing', available at: *http://elpub.scix.net/data/works/att/204_elpub2006.content .pdf* (accessed 26 April 2009).

Bazerman, C., Blakesley, D., Palmquist, M. and Russell, D. (2008) 'Open access book publishing in writing studies: A case study', *First Monday* 13(1), available at: *http://firstmonday.org/htbin/cgiwrap/bin/ojs/index .php/fm/article/view/2088/1920* (accessed 6 July 2009).

BBC (2008) 'European online library launches', available at: *http://news .bbc.co.uk/2/hi/europe/7738318.stm* (accessed 18 July 2009).

Beckett, C. and Inger, S. (2007) 'Self-archiving and journal subscriptions: co-existence or competition: an international survey of librarians' preferences', available at: *http://www.publishingresearch.net/documents/ Self-archiving_report.pdf* (accessed 19 July 2009).

Beja, M. (2009) 'Judge dismisses software-licensing case against George Mason University', *Chronicle of Higher Education*, available at: *http://chronicle.com/blogPost/Judge-Dismisses/7199* (accessed 27 July 2009).

Bell, S., Foster, N. F. and Gibbons, S. (2005) 'Reference librarians and the success of institutional repositories', *Reference Services Review* 33(5): 283–90.

Better World Books (2007) 'Library discards & donations', available at: *http://www.betterworldbooks.com/Programs/Library.aspx* (accessed 10 June 2007).

BioMed Central (2008) 'Setting up a central open access fund', available at: *http://www.biomedcentral.com/info/about/openaccessfund* (accessed 10 April 2008).

Bjork, B.-C. (2004) 'Open access to scientific publications-an analysis of barriers to change', *Information Research* 9(2), available at: *http://informationr.net/ir/9-2/paper170.html* (accessed 12 May 2007).

Bjork, B.-C., Roos, A. and Lauri, M. (2009) 'Scientific journal publishing', *Information Research* 14(1), available at: *http://informationr.net/ir/14-1/ paper391.html* (accessed 10 March 2009).

Bjornshauge, L. and Johansson, A.-L. (2009) 'Now there are 4000 journals in DOAJ', available at: *http://www.doaj.org/doaj?func=load Templ&templ=090401b* (accessed 27 July 2009).

Boston Library Consortium (2009) 'Authors' rights and publishing', available at: *http://www.blc.org/authorsrights.html* (accessed 27 July 2009).

Boyle, J. (2008) *The Public Domain: Enclosing the Commons of the Mind*, New Haven, CT: Yale University Press.

Brandt, D. S. (2007) 'Librarians as partners in e-research', *College & Research Libraries News* 68(6): 365–7, 396.

Branin, J. and Lowry, C. B. (2008) 'LIS editors launch effort to develop best practices for LIS journals', *D-Lib Magazine* 14(3/4), available at: *http://www.dlib.org/dlib/march08/03inbrief.html* (accessed 19 July 2009).

Breeding, M. (2008) 'Open source integrated library systems', *Library Technology Reports* 44(8): 4–32.

Brown, L., Griffiths, R. and Rascoff, M. (2007) 'University publishing in a digital age', available at: *http://www.ithaka.org/saved-pages/strategic-services/ Ithaka%20University%20Publishing%20Report.pdf* (accessed 10 July 2009).

Buckholtz, A. (2002) 'New international scholarly communications alliance', posting to SPARC-Europe@arl.org, 6 February, available at *https://mx2.arl.org/Lists/SPARC-EUROPE/Message/14.html* (accessed 17 July 2009).

Budapest Open Access Initiative (BOAI) (2001) 'Budapest Open Access Initiative', available at: *http://www.soros.org/openaccess/* (accessed 12 May 2007).

Budapest Open Access Initiative (BOAI) (2006) 'What you can do to help', available at: *http://www.soros.org/openaccess/help.shtml* (accessed 30 April 2006).

Campbell, R. (2004) 'Libraries: do they have a future in academia – or only a past?', *Serials* 17(1): 9–13.

Canadian Association of University Teachers (CAUT) (2008) 'Retaining copyright in journal articles', *CAUT Intellectual Property Advisory*, available at: *http://www.caut.ca/uploads/IP-Advisory1-en.pdf* (accessed 17 July 2009).

Carlson, S. (2002) 'Scholarly publishers aim to woo librarians away from self-published research', *Chronicle of Higher Education*; *Information Technology* 49(13): A53.

Carr, L. (2006) 'Use of navigational tools in a repository', posting to American Scientist Open Access Forum, 9 March, available at: *http://users.ecs .soton.ac.uk/harnad/Hypermail/Amsci/5169.html* (accessed 24 July 2009).

Carr, L. and Harnad, S. (2005) *Keystroke Economy: A Study of the Time and Effort Involved in Self-Archiving*, Southampton: University of Southampton.

Cary, S. (2001) 'Faculty rank, status, and tenure for librarians', *C&RL News* 62(5), available at: *http://www.ala.org/ala/mgrps/divs/acrl/publications/crlnews/2001/may/facultyrank.cfm* (accessed 27 July 2009).

Chillingworth, M. (2005) 'Thomson herds open access into single index', *Information World Review*, available at: *http://www.iwr.co.uk/information-world-review/news/2146510/thomson-corals-open-access* (accessed 15 July 2009).

Ciciora, P. (2008) '"Digital dark age" may doom some data', available at: *http://news.illinois.edu/news/08/1027data.html* (accessed 29 October 2008).

CLIR (2007) 'Mellon Foundation awards CLIR $2.19 million operating grant', available at: *http://www.clir.org/news/pressrelease/07mellonpr.html* (accessed 20 March 2007).

Cockerill, M. (2006) 'Business models in open access publishing', in N. Jacobs (ed.) *Open Access: Key Strategic, Technical and Economic Aspects*, Oxford: Chandos Publishing, pp. 89–95, available at: *http://demo.openrepository.com/demo/bitstream/2384/2367/4/businessmodelsinoa.pdf* (accessed 20 July 2009).

Coleman, A. (2007) 'Self-archiving and the copyright transfer agreements of ISI-Ranked library and information science journals', *Journal of the American Society for Information Science and Technology* 58(2): 286–96.

Coleman, A. and Roback, J. (2005) 'Open Access Federation for library and information science: dLIST and DL-Harvest', *D-Lib Magazine* 11(12), available at: *http://www.dlib.org/dlib/december05/coleman/12coleman.html* (accessed 29 July 2009).

Cornell (2009) 'VIVO: research and scholarship', available at: *http://vivo.cornell.edu/about* (accessed 24 July 2009).

Cox, C. (2006) 'Analysis of the impact of federated search products on library instruction using the ACRL standards', *portal: Libraries and the Academy* 6(3): 253–67.

Cox, J. and Cox, L. (2006) *Scholarly Publishing Practice: Academic Journal Publishers' Policies and Practices in Online Publishing, Second Survey 2005*, West Sussex: Association of Learned and Professional Society Publishers.

Cox, J. and Cox, L. (2008) *Scholarly Publishing Practice 3: Academic Journal Publishers' Policies and Practices in Online Publishing*, 3rd edn, Cambridgeshire, Association of Learned and Society Publishers.

Crawford, W. (2006) 'Library access to scholarship', *Cites & Insights: Crawford at Large* 6(7): 12–21, available at: *http://www.citesandinsights .info/v6i7e.htm* (accessed 13 June 2007)

Creative Commons (2009) 'Support the commons', available at: *https://support.creativecommons.org/* (accessed 16 July 2009).

CrossRef (2009) 'CrossMark', available at: *http://www.crossref.org/ crossmark.html* (accessed 27 July 2009).

Crow, R. (2002) *The Case for Institutional Repositories: A SPARC Position Paper*, Washington, DC: The Scholarly Publishing & Academic Resources Coalition, available at: *http://www.arl.org/sparc/ bm~doc/ir_final_release_102.pdf* (accessed 26 July 2009).

Crow, R. (2009) *Campus-Based Publishing Partnerships: A Guide to Critical Issues*, Washington, DC: The Scholarly Publishing & Academic Resources Coalition, available at: *http://www.arl.org/ sparc/bm~doc/pub_partnerships_v1.pdf* (accessed 10 July 2009).

Curran, W. M. (2003) 'Succession: the next ones at bat', *College & Research Libraries* 64(2): 134–40.

D-Lib Magazine (2007) 'D-Lib alliance participants', available at: *http://www.dlib.org/dlib/alliance-participants.html* (accessed 26 July 2009).

Davis, P. (2003) 'Tragedy of the commons revisited: librarians, publishers, faculty, and the demise of a public resource', *portal: Libraries and the Academy* 3(4): 547–62.

Davis, P., Ehrling, T., Habicht, O., How, S., Saylor, J. M. and Walker, K. (2004) *Report of the CUL Task Force on Open Access Publishing*, Ithaca, NY: Cornell University Library, available at: *http://ecommons .library.cornell.edu/bitstream/1813/193/3/OATF_Report_8-9.pdf* (accessed 27 July 2009)

Davis, P. M. and Connolly, M. J. L. (2007) 'Institutional repositories: evaluating the reasons for non-use of Cornell University's installation of DSpace' *D-Lib Magazine* 13(3/4), available at: *http://www.dlib .org/dlib/march07/davis/03davis.html* (accessed 29 July 2009).

De Robbio, A. and Katzmayr, M. (2009) 'The management of an international open access repository: The case of E-LIS', *GMS Medizin-Bibliothek-Information* 9(1): 1–8, available at: *http://www.egms .de/pdf/journals/mbi/2009-9/mbi000137.pdf* (accessed 29 July 2009).

Dill, E. and Palmer, K. L. (2007) 'Survey of librarian attitudes about open access', available at: *http://www.slideshare.net/desy/survey-of-librarian-attitudes-about-open-access* (accessed 1 September 2009).

Directory of Open Access Journals (DOAJ) (2007) 'Membership program and option for supporting contributions', available at: *http://www .doaj.org/doaj?func=membership* (accessed 27 July 2009).

Directory of Open Access Journals (DOAJ) (2009) 'Long-term preservation of open access journals secured', available at: *http://www .doaj.org/doaj?func=loadTempl&templ=090401* (accessed 29 July 2009).

Drake, M. A. (2007) 'Scholarly communication in turmoil', available at: *http://www.infotoday.com/it/feb07/Drake.shtml* (accessed 17 June 2007).

Duke University Office of News & Communications (2007) 'Everything you want to know about scholarly communications', available at: *http://news .duke.edu/2007/07/scholarship.html* (accessed 29 November 2007).

Duranceau, E. F. (2007) 'The role of the librarian in an open access world', available at: *blogs.openaccesscentral.com/.../Ellen%20Finnie %20Duranceau%20presentation.ppt* (accessed 16 July 2009).

EBSCO (2009) 'About peer review policy', available at: *http://www .ebscohost.com/thisTopic.php?topicID=396&marketID=* (accessed 27 July 2009).

Elsevier (2008) 'Information philanthropy initiatives: a guide to helping libraries & researchers worldwide', *Library Connect Pamphet #11*, San Diego, CA: Elsevier, available at: *http://libraryconnect.elsevier.com/ lcp/1101/lcp1101.pdf* (accessed 19 July 2009)

eprints (2006) 'Self-archiving FAQ for the Budapest Open Access Initiative (BOAI)', available at: *http://www.eprints.org/openaccess/self-faq/* (accessed 4 July 2006).

eprints (2007) 'EPrints for digital repositories: open access', available at: *http://www.eprints.org/openaccess/* (accessed 20 April 2007).

Evans, J. A. and Reimer, J. (2009) 'Open access and global participation in science', *Science* 323: 1025.

Facebook (2009) 'Librarians who support open access', available at: *http://www.facebook.com/group.php?gid=2243293184* (accessed 29 July 2009).

Foster, A. L. (2008) 'Readers not wanted: student writers fight to keep their work off the web', *Chronicle of Higher Education* 54(36): A14.

Frank, M. (2007) 'Nonprofit publishers oppose government mandates for scientific publishing', available at: *http://www.dcprinciples.org/ press/2.htm* (accessed 19 June 2007).

Frankel, F. and Reid, R. (2008) 'Big data: distilling meaning from data', *Nature* 455 (7209): 30.

Frankish, H. (2004) 'Publishing wars', *Lancet* 364(9443): 1391–2.

Furlough, M. J. (2008) 'Purposeful collaboration for research libraries and university presses', *Against the Grain* 20(6), available at: *http://www.against-the-grain.com/TOCFiles/v20-6_Furlough.pdf* (accessed 26 July 2009).

Gadd, E., Oppenheim, C. and Probets, S. (2003) 'RoMEO Studies 4: An analysis of journal publishers' copyright agreements', *Learned Publishing* 16(4): 293–308.

Gedye, R. (2004) 'Open access is only part of the story', *Serials Review* 30(4): 271–4.

Goodman, D. (2004) 'The criteria for open access', *Serials Review* 30(4): 258–70.

Goodman, D., Dowson, S. and Yaremchuk, J. (2007) 'Open access and accuracy: a comparison of authors' self-archived manuscripts and published articles', *Learned Publishing* 20(33): 203–15.

Google (2009) 'gpeerreview: A tool that enables peers to review and sign each others' works', available at: *http://code.google.com/p/gpeerreview/* (accessed 16 July 2009).

Gorman, M. (2002) 'The value and values of libraries', available at: *http://mg.csufresno.edu/papers/Value_and_Values_of_Libraries.pdf* (accessed 27 July 2009).

Greco, A. N., Wharton, R. M., Estelami, H. and Jones, R. F. (2006) 'The state of scholarly journal publishing: 1981–2000', available at: *http://utpjournals.metapress.com/content/f22161203v86711l/fulltext.pdf* (accessed 27 July 2009).

Grillot, B. (2008) 'PubMed central deposit and author rights: agreements between 12 publishers and the authors subject to the NIH public access policy', available at: *http://www.arl.org/bm~doc/grillot-pubmed.pdf* (accessed 16 July 2009).

Guedon, J.-C. (2001) 'In Oldenburg's long shadow: librarians, research scientists, publishers, and the control of scientific publishing', paper presented at the 138th ARL Membership Meeting, 23–25 May, Toronto, available at: *http://www.arl.org/resources/pubs/mmproceedings/138guedon.shtml* (accessed 20 April 2007).

Guernsey, L. (2008) 'Bringing tenure into the digital age', *Chronicle of Higher Education* 55(16): A8.

Hagedorn, K. and Santelli, J. (2008) 'Google still not indexing hidden web URLs', *D-Lib Magazine* (7/8), available at: *http://www.dlib.org/dlib/july08/hagedorn/07hagedorn.html* (accessed 1 September 2009).

Hahn, K. (2008) *Research Library Publishing Services: New Options for University Publishing*, Washington, DC: Association of Research Libraries, available at: *http://www.arl.org/bm~doc/research-library-publishing-services.pdf* (accessed 10 July 2009).

Hardesty, S. and Sugarman, T. (2007) 'Academic librarians, professional literature, and new technologies: a survey', *Journal of Academic Librarianship* 33(2): 196–205.

Harnad, S. (2008) 'Open access book-impact and "demotic" metrics', *Open Access Archivangelism*, available at: *http://openaccess.eprints .org/index.php?/archives/467-guid.html* (accessed 27 July 2009).

Harper, G. (2009) 'OA, IRs and IP: Open access, digital copyright and marketplace competition', available at: *http://wikis.ala.org/midwinter 2009/images/5/5e/Harper_G_MW09handout.pdf* (accessed 29 July 2008).

Hartman, K. A. and Mullen, L. B. (2008) 'Google Scholar and academic libraries: an update', *New Library World* 109(5–6): 211–22.

Haschak, P. G. (2007) 'The "platinum route" to open access: a case study of *E-JASL: The Electronic Journal of Academic and Special Librarianship*', *Information Research* 12(4), available at: *http://informationr.net/ir/12-4/paper321.html* (accessed 26 July 2009).

HathiTrust (2009) 'HathiTrust: a shared digital repository', available at: *http://www.hathitrust.org/press* (accessed 26 July 2009).

Hey, T. and Hey, J. (2006) 'E-Science and its implications for the library community', *Library HiTech* 24(4): 515–28.

Hill, J. S. (2005) 'Constant vigilance, Babelfish, and foot surgery: perspectives on faculty status and tenure for academic librarians', *portal: Libraries and the Academy* 5(1): 7–22.

Hinchliffe, L. J. and Dorner, J. (eds) (2003) 'How to get published in LIS journals: a practical guide', available at: *http://www.elsevier.com/ framework_librarians/LibraryConnect/lcpamphlet2.pdf* (accessed 29 July 2009).

Hood, A. K. (2007) *Open Access Resources*, SPEC Kit 300, Washington, DC: Association of Research Libraries.

Hoorens, S., Dijk, L. V. v. and Stolk, C. v. (2008) *Embracing the Future: Embedding Digital Repositories in the University of London*, Santa Monica, CA: Rand Corporation, available at: *http://www.rand.org/pubs/ technical_reports/2008/RAND_TR625.pdf* (accessed 15 July 2009).

House of Commons Science and Technology Committee (2004) 'Responses to the Committee's Tenth Report, Session 2003–04, Scientific Publications: Free for All?', available at: *http://www.publications .parliament.uk/pa/cm200304/cmselect/cmsctech/1200/1200.pdf* (accessed 30 July 2009).

Howard, J. (2007) 'Online network is established for scholars in humanities', *Chronicle of Higher Education* 54(10): A1.

Howard, J. (2008a) 'For advice on publishing in the digital world, scholars turn to campus libraries', *The Chronicle of Higher Education* 55(13): A8.

Howard, J. (2008b) 'A new field study identifies eight major types of digital scholarship. *Chronicle of Higher Education* 55(13): A11.

IFLA (2004) 'Statement on open access to scholarly literature and research documentation', available at: *http://archive.ifla.org/V/cdoc/open-access04.html* (accessed 15 July, 2006).

IFLA/IPA (2009) 'Enhancing the debate on open access', available at: *http://www.ifla.org/files/hq/documents/enhancing-the-debate-on-open-access_final-20090505.pdf* (accessed 23 July 2009).

Infonortics (2009) 'Search engine meeting', available at: *http://www.infonortics.com/searchengines/* (accessed 24 July 2009).

Inger, S. and Gardner, T. (2008) *How Readers Navigate to Scholarly Content*, Abingdon: Simon Inger Consulting and Tracy Gardner Marketing, available at: *http://www.sic.ox14.com/howreadersnavigatetoscholarlycontent.pdf* (accessed 19 July 2009).

Internet Archive (2009) 'Internet Archive: universal access to human knowledge', available at: *http://www.archive.org/about/about.php#future* (accessed 26 July 2009).

Jacobson, J. (2002) 'A shortage of academic librarians', *Chronicle of Higher Education*, 14 August.

Jantz, R. C. and Wilson, M. C. (2008) 'Institutional repositories: faculty deposits, marketing, and the reform of scholarly communication', *Journal of Academic Librarianship* 34(3): 186–95.

Johnson, C. Y. (2008) 'Out in the open: some scientists sharing results', available at: *http://www.boston.com/news/local/massachusetts/articles/2008/08/21/out_in_the_open_some_scientists_sharing_results/* (accessed 9 July 2009).

Johnson, M. and Roderer, N. K. (2008) 'ASIS&T scholarly communication survey', *Inside ASIS&T: Bulletin of the American Society for Information Science and Technology* 34: 510–13.

Jones, E. (2008) *E-science talking points for ARL Deans and Directors*, Washington, DC: Association of Research Libraries, available at: *http://www.arl.org/bm~doc/e-science-talking-points.pdf* (accessed 7 July 2009).

Kaiser, J. (2008) 'Scholarly publishing: house weighs proposal to block mandatory "open access"', *Science* 321(5896): 1621.

Kaser, D. and Ojala, M. (2005) 'Open access forum', *Online* 29(1): 14–19.

Katz, R. N. (ed.) (2008) *The Tower and the Cloud*, available at: *http://www.educause.edu/thetowerandthecloud* (accessed 26 August 2009).

Kaufman-Wills Group LLC (2005) 'The facts about open access: a study of the financial and non-financial effects of alternative business models for scholarly journals', available at: *http://www.alpsp.org/ngen_public/article.asp?id=200&did=47&aid=270&st=&oaid=-1* (accessed 27 July 2009).

Keller, M. A., Reich, V. and Herkovic, A. C. (2003) 'What is a library anymore, anyway?' *First Monday* 8(5), available at: *http://131.193 .153.231/www/issues/issue8_5/keller/index.html* (accessed 9 July 2006).

Kleinman, M. (2008) 'The beauty of "some rights reserved": introducing creative commons to librarians, faculty, and students', *College & Research Libraries News* 69(10): 594–7.

Knievel, J. E. (2008) 'Instruction to faculty and graduate students: a tutorial to teach publication strategies', *portal: Libraries and the Academy* 8(2): 175–86.

Koehler, A. E. C. (2006) 'Some thoughts on the meaning of open access for university library technical services', *Serials Review* 32(1): 17–21.

Kohl, D. F. and Davis, C. H. (1985) 'Ratings of journals by ARL library directors and deans of library and information science schools', *College & Research Libraries* 46(1): 40–7.

Kuula, A. and Borg, S. (2008) *Open Access to and Reuse of Research Data – The State of the Art in Finland*, Tampere: University of Tampere, available at: *http://www.fsd.uta.fi/julkaisut/julkaisusarja/ FSDjs07_OECD_en.pdf* (accessed 6 July 2009).

Lankester, A. (2006) 'The value of publishers', *Library Connect Newsletter* 4(2): 4–5, available at: *http://libraryconnect.elsevier.com/ lcn/0402/lcn0402.pdf* (accessed 27 July 2009).

Lannom, L. (2007) 'Current and future status of *D-Lib Magazine*', *D-Lib Magazine* 13(1/2), available at: *http://www.dlib.org/dlib/january07/ 01editorial.html* (accessed 3 June 2007).

Law, D. (2006) 'Delivering open access: from promise to practice', *Ariadne*, No. 46, available at: *http://www.ariadne.ac.uk/issue46/law/ intro.html* (accessed 27 July 2009).

Lenzini, R. T. (2002) 'The graying of the library profession: a survey of our professional association and their responses', *Searcher* 10(7), available at: *http://www.infotoday.com/searcher/jul02/lenzini.htm* (accessed 27 July 2009).

Lercher, A. (2008) 'A survey of attitudes about digital repositories among faculty at Louisiana State University at Baton Rouge', *The Journal of Academic Librarianship* 34(5): 408–15.

Liblicense: Licensing Digital Information (2007) 'A resource for librarians', available at: *http://www.library.yale.edu/~llicense/index .shtml* (accessed 1 May 2007).

Lowry, C. B. (2008) 'The small market professional journal: how idiosyncrasy informs the future and why it matters', *portal: Libraries and the Academy* 8(3): 223–31.

Luther, J. (2008) *University Investment in the Library: What's the Return? A Case Study at the University of Illinois at Urbana-Champaign*, San Diego, CA: Elsevier, available at: *http://libraryconnect.elsevier.com/whitepapers/0108/lcwp0101.pdf* (accessed 9 July 2009).

Lynch, C. (2008) 'Big data: how do your data grow?', *Nature* 455: 28–9.

Lynch, C. A. and Lippincott, J. (2005) 'Institutional repository deployment in the United States as of early 2005', *D-Lib Magazine* 11(9), available at: *http://www.dlib.org/dlib/september05/lynch/09lynch.html* (accessed 9 July 2006).

Machovec, G., Whitehead, H. and Morrison, H. (2006) 'Open access in practice', available at: *http://eprints.rclis.org/7718/1/oainpractice.pdf* (accessed 19 July 2009).

Malenfant, K. J. (2009) 'ACRL legislative agenda 2009', available at: *http://www.ala.org/ala/newspresscenter/news/pressreleases2009/april2009/acrllegagenda.cfm* (accessed 16 July 2009).

Malone, C. K. and Coleman, A. S. (2005) 'The impact of open access on library and information science (a research project)', available at: *http://dlist.sir.arizona.edu/967/* (accessed 25 July 2009).

Markey, K., Rieh, S. Y., Jean, B. S., Kim, J. and Yakel, E. (2007) *Census of Institutional Repositories in the United States: Miracle Project Research Findings*, Washington, DC: Council on Library and Information Resources, available at: *http://www.clir.org/pubs/reports/pub140/pub140.pdf* (accessed 27 July 2009).

Maron, N. L. and Smith, K. K. (2008) *Current Models of Digital Scholarly Communication*, Washington, DC: Association of Research Libraries, available at: *http://www.arl.org/bm~doc/current-models-report.pdf* (accessed 19 July 2009).

Mayor, S. (2006) 'Search engines increase online journal use more than open access', *BMJ* 332(7554): 1353.

McLennan, J. (2008a) 'First open access day is to be held October 14, 2008', available at: *http://www.arl.org/sparc/media/08-0828.shtml* (accessed 14 October 2008).

McLennan, J. (2008b) 'PLOS and SPARC release new "Voices of Open Access" video series', SPARC-OpenData listserv announcement, 15 October, available at: *https://mx2.arl.org/Lists/SPARC-OpenData/Message/222.html* (accessed 29 July 2009).

McLennan, J. (2008c) 'SPARC releases new campaign for student engagement', available at: *http://www.arl.org/sparc/media/08-0128.shtml* (accessed 16 July 2009).

McLennan, J. (2009a) 'First US public access policy made permanent', available at: *https://mx2.arl.org/Lists/SPARC-OAForum/Message/4849.html* (accessed 6 May 2009).

McLennan, J. (2009b) 'Open access week declared for 2009', available at: *http://www.arl.org/sparc/media/09-0305.shtml* (accessed 10 March 2009).

Medical Library Association (2003) 'MLA statement on open access', available at: *http://www.mlanet.org/government/info_access/open access_statement* (accessed 29 June 2006).

Meho, L. I. and Yang, K. (2007) 'Impact of data sources on citation counts and rankings of LIS faculty: Web of Science vs. Scopus and Google Scholar', *Journal of the American Society for Information Science and Technology* 58(13): 2105–25.

MIT Libraries (2008) 'Help yourself: subject guides: data management and publishing', available at: *http://libraries.mit.edu/guides/subjects/data-management/why.html* (accessed 25 September 2008).

Modern Language Association (2002) *The Future of Scholarly Publishing*, New York: Modern Language Association, available at: *http://www.mla.org/pdf/schlrlypblshng.pdf* (accessed 24 July 2009).

Modern Language Association (2007) *Report of the MLA Task Force on Evaluating Scholarship for Tenure and Promotion*, New York: Modern Language Association, available at: *http://www.mla.org/pdf/taskforcereport0608.pdf* (accessed 19 July 2009).

Montanelli, D. S. and Stenstrom, P. F. (1986) 'Benefits of research for academic librarians and the institutions they serve', *College & Research Libraries* 47: 482–5.

Morgan, C. (2008) 'Journal article version nomenclature: The NISO/ALPSP recommendations', *Learned Publishing* 21(4): 273–7.

Morris, S. (2009a) *Journal Authors' Rights: Perception and Reality*, London: Publishing Research Consortium, available at: *http://www.publishingresearch.net/documents/JournalAuthorsRights.pdf* (accessed 19 July 2009).

Morris, S. (2009b) 'RE: Darnton on the Google Settlement', posting to Liblicense-l@lists.yale.edu, 5 February, available at: *http://www.library.yale.edu/~llicense/ListArchives/0902/msg00033.html* (accessed 27 July 2009).

Morrison, H. (2004) 'Professional library and information associations should rise to the challenge of promoting open access and lead by example', *Library Hi Tech News* 21(4): 8–10.

Morrison, H. (2006) 'Ingegerd Rabow: OA librarian receives honorary doctorate', available at: *http://oalibrarian.blogspot.com/2006_01_01_oalibrarian_archive.html* (accessed 29 July 2009).

Morrison, H. (2008a) 'Authors' rights as evaluation criteria', posting to Liblicense-l@lists.yale.edu, 11 March, available at: *http://www.library .yale.edu/~llicense/ListArchives/0803/msg00044.html* (accessed 11 March 2008).

Morrison, H. (2008b) 'Open access: a role for the aggregators', posting to Liblicense-l@lists.yale.edu, 19 March, available at: *http://www .library.yale.edu/~llicense/ListArchives/0803/msg00087.html* (accessed 19 March 2008).

Morrison, H. and Waller, A. (2008) 'Open access and evolving scholarly communication', *College & Research Libraries News* 69(9): 486–90, available at: *http://acrl.ala.org/crlnews/september08/openaccess.pdf* (accessed 19 July 2009).

Moses, J. (2009) 'New publication: profiles of best practices in academic library interlibrary loan', posting to STS-L@ala.org, available at: *http://lists.ala.org/wws/arc/sts-l/2009-05/msg00029.html* (accessed 11 May 2009).

Mullen, L. B. (2008) 'Increasing impact of scholarly journal articles: practical strategies librarians can share', *Electronic Journal of Academic and Special Librarianship (E-JASL)* 9(1), available at: *http://southernlibrarianship.icaap.org/content/v09n01/mullen_l01.html* (accessed 27 July 2009).

Mullen, L. B. and Hartman, K. A. (2006) 'Google Scholar and the library web site: the early response of ARL libraries', *College & Research Libraries* 67(2): 106–22.

Mark Ware Consulting Ltd. (2007) *Peer Review in Scholarly Journals: Perspective of the Scholarly Community – An International Study*, London: Publishing Research Consortium, available at: *http://www .publishingresearch.net/documents/PeerReviewFullPRCReport-final .pdf* (accessed 24 July 2009).

nature.com (2009) 'Peer to peer: for peer-reviewers and about the peer-review process', available at: *http://blogs.nature.com/peer-to-peer/* (accessed 16 July 2009).

Newman, K. A., Blecic, D. D. and Armstrong, K. L. (2007) *Scholarly Communication Education Initiatives*, SPEC Kit 299, Washington, DC: Association of Research Libraries.

Nguyen, T. (2008) *Open Doors and Open Minds: What Faculty Authors can do to Ensure Open Access to their Work through their Institution*, Cambridge, MA: SPARC/Science Commons, available at: *http://www .arl.org/sparc/bm~doc/opendoors_v1.pdf* (accessed 15 July 2009).

NISO (2008) *Journal Article Versions (JAV): Recommendations from the NISO/ALPSP JAV Technical Working Group* (No. NISO-RP-8-2008),

Baltimore, MD: NISO, available at: *http://www.niso.org/publications/ rp/RP-8-2008.pdf* (accessed 1 September 2009)

Nisonger, T. E. and Davis, C. H. (2005) 'The perception of library and information science journals by LIS education deans and ARL library directors: a replication of the Kohl-Davis Study', *College & Research Libraries* 66(4): 341–77.

OASIS (2009) 'Open Access Scholarly Information sourcebook/publish your book in open access', available at: *http://www.openoasis .org/index.php?option=com_content&view=article&id=566&Itemid=395* (accessed 26 July 2009).

OECD (2007) 'OECD principles and guidelines for access to research data from public funding', available at *http://www.oecd.org/ dataoecd/9/61/38500813.pdf* (accessed 24 August 2008).

Okerson, A. S. and O'Donnell, J. J. (ed.) (1995) *Scholarly Journals at the Crossroads: A Subversive Proposal for Electronic Publishing*, Washington, DC: Association of Research Libraries, Office of Scientific and Academic Publishing, available at: *http://www.arl.org/ bm~doc/subversive.pdf* (accessed 20 April 2007).

Oliver, K. and Swain, R. (2006) *Directories of Institutional Repositories: Research Results & Recommendations*, The Hague: IFLA, available at: *http://archive.ifla.org/IV/ifla72/papers/151-Oliver_Swain-en.pdf* (accessed 15 July 2009).

Open Citation Project (2009) 'Reference linking and citation analysis for open archives', available at: *http://opcit.eprints.org/oacitation-biblio.html* (accessed 27 July 2009).

Orphan, S., Petrowski, M. J., Rockwood, I. and Thompson, H. (2004) *Open Access and the ACRL Serial Publishing Program*, White Paper No. ACRL AC04Doc 1.0, Chicago, IL: Association of College and Research Libraries, available at: *http://www.ala.org/ala/mgrps/divs/ acrl/publications/whitepapers/OA_Final.pdf* (accessed 1 September 2009).

Palmer, K. L., Dill, E. and Christie, C. (2009) 'Where there's a will there's a way? Survey of academic librarian attitudes about open access, *College & Research Libraries* 70(4): 315–55.

Peek, R. (2004) 'Elsevier allows open access self-archiving', *Information Today NewsBreaks/Weekly News Digest*, 7 June, available at: *http://newsbreaks.infotoday.com/nbreader.asp?ArticleID=16436* (accessed 25 July 2009).

Peterson, E. (2006) 'Librarian publishing preferences and open-access electronic journals', *Electronic Journal of Academic and Special Librarianship (E-JASL)* 7(2), available at: *http://southernlibrarianship .icaap.org/content/v07n02/peterson_e01.htm* (accessed 23 March 2007).

Pfanner, E. (2008) 'Google signs a deal to e-publish out-of-print books', *The New York Times*, 10 November, p. B8.

Pinowar, H. A., Day, R. S. and Fridsma, D. B. (2007) 'Sharing detailed research data is associated with increased citation rate', *PLoS ONE* 2(3): e308, available at: *http://www.plosone.org/article/fetchArticle .action?articleURI=info:doi/10.1371/journal.pone.0000308* (accessed 30 July 2009).

Pope, B. K. and Kannan, P. K. (2003) *An Evaluation Study of the National Academies Press's E-Publishing Initiatives*, final report of the National Academy Press, available at: *http://aaupnet.org/resources/ mellon/nap/final_public.pdf* (accessed 27 July 2009).

Poynder, R. (2004a) 'Ten years after', *Information Today* 21(9): 23, available at: *http://www.infotoday.com/it/oct04/poynder.shtml* (accessed 20 April 2007).

Poynder, R. (2004b) 'UK academics and librarians disagree over open access', Information Today, Newsbreaks, 3 May, available at: *http://newsbreaks.infotoday.com/nbreader.asp?ArticleID=16459* (accessed 3 November 2008).

Poynder, R. (2008) 'The open access interviews: Peter Murray-Rust', available at: *http://poynder.blogspot.com/2008/01/open-access- interviews-peter-murray.html* (accessed 23 January 2008).

Primary Research Group (2008) 'The survey of academic & research library purchasing practices [abstract and excerpt]', available at: *http://www.researchandmarkets.com/reports/661631/the_survey_of_ academic_and_research_library* (accessed 27 July 2009).

Quint, B. (2004) 'The end of the "big deal" era'. *Information Today* 21(1): 7.

Regazzi, J. (2004) 'The shifting sands of open access publishing, a publisher's view', *Serials Review* 30: 275–80.

RIN/CURL (2007) 'Researchers' use of academic libraries and their services', available at: *http://www.rin.ac.uk/files/libraries-report-2007.pdf* (accessed 19 July 2009).

Ripley, E. and Boyd, M. (2009) '24th Annual Conference (2009): PPC Update-Carol Tenopir to Present 2009 Vision Session', NASIG Newsletter, 4 February, available at: *http://nasignews.wordpress.com/ 2009/02/04/241-200903-tenopir/* (accessed 27 July 2009).

ROARMAP (2009) 'ROARMAP (Registry of Open Access Repository Material Archiving Policies)', available at: *http://www.eprints.org/ openaccess/policysignup/* (accessed 19 July 2009).

Roosendaal, H. E., Guerts, P. A. T. M (1998) 'Forces and functions in scientific communication: an analysis of their interplay', *CRISP 97 Cooperative Research Information Systems in Physics*, available at:

http://www.physik.uni-oldenburg.de/conferences/crisp97/roosendaal.pdf (accessed 25 July 2009).

Rutgers University Libraries (2007) 'Editorial policies', available at: *http://pcsp.libraries.rutgers.edu/index.php/pcsp/about/editorialPolicies #openAccessPolicy* (accessed 7 May 2007).

Salisbury, M. W. (2008) 'Ready or not, here comes open access', *Genome Technology* 41 (November), available at: *http://www.genomeweb.com/ ready-or-not-here-comes-open-access-0* (accessed 19 July 2009).

Salo, D. (2006) 'Libraries and open access', available at: *http:// cavlec.yarinareth.net/archives/2006/09/06/libraries-and-open-access/* (accessed 27 July 2009).

Schmidle, D. J. and Via, B. J. (2004) 'Physician heal thyself: the library and information science serials crisis', *portal: Libraries and the Academy* 4(2): 167–203.

SerialsSolutions (2009) 'Summon: Web Scale Discovery', available at: *http://www.serialssolutions.com/summon/* (accessed 27 July 2009).

SHERPA/RoMEO (2006–2008) 'SHERPA/RoMEO: Publisher copyright policies & self-archiving', available at: *http://www.sherpa.ac.uk/romeo/* (accessed 24 July 2009).

SHERPA/RoMEO (2009) 'SHERPA/RoMEO/American Library Association', available at: *http://www.sherpa.ac.uk/romeo.php?type= publisher& search=American%20Library%20Association* (accessed 25 July 2009).

SPARC (2003) 'The open past initiative: a discussion paper', available at: *http://eprints.rclis.org/7465/1/Open_Past.pdf* (accessed 27 July 2009).

SPARC (2008) 'The transformative potential of open educational resources (OER)', available at: *http://www.arl.org/sparc/meetings/ala09mw/ index.shtml* (accessed 16 July 2009).

SPARC (2009a) 'Author rights: using the SPARC author addendum to secure your rights as the author of a journal article', available at: *http://www.arl.org/sparc/author/addendum.html* (accessed 29 July 2009).

SPARC (2009b) 'What is SPARC', available at: *http://www.arl.org/ sparc/about/index.shtml* (accessed 23 July 2009).

SPARC Europe (2009) 'SPARC Europe announces call-for-nominations for the fourth award for outstanding achievements in scholarly communications', available at: *http://www.sparceurope.org/news/ sparc-europe-announces-call-for-nominations-for-the-fourth-award- for-outstanding-achievements-in-scholarly-communications/* (accessed 15 July 2009).

Suber, P. (2003) 'Removing barriers to research; an introduction to open access for librarians', *C&RL News* 64(2), available at:

http://www.ala.org/ala/mgrps/divs/acrl/publications/crlnews/2003/feb/ removingbarriers.cfm (accessed 2 November 2005).

Suber, P. (2006a) 'Honorary doctorate to Ingegerd Rabow for her OA work', available at: *http://www.earlham.edu/~peters/fos/2006_01_22_ fosblogarchive.html#113836818639899881* (accessed 27 July 2009).

Suber, P. (2006b) 'Lists related to the open access movement', available at: *http://www.earlham.edu/~peters/fos/lists.htm#incomplete* (accessed 27 July 2009).

Suber, P. (2006c) 'What you can do to promote open access', available at: *http://www.earlham.edu/~peters/fos/do.htm* (accessed 23 February 2007).

Suber, P. (2007a) 'Open access news: news from the open access movement', available at: *http://www.earlham.edu/~peters/fos/fosblog.html* (accessed 1 May 2007).

Suber, P. (2007b) 'Open access overview: focusing on open access to peer-reviewed research articles and their preprints', available at: *http://www.earlham.edu/~peters/fos/overview.htm* (accessed 9 June 2007).

Suber, P. (2007c) 'Predictions for 2008', *The SPARC Open Access Newsletter*, No. 116, available at: *http://www.earlham.edu/~peters/ fos/newsletter/12-02-07.htm#nih* (accessed 2 December 2007).

Suber, P. (2008a) 'ACRL's mixed messages on preprint access', available at: *http://www.earlham.edu/~peters/fos/2008/03/acrl-mixed-messages-on-preprint-access.html* (accessed 27 February 2009).

Suber, P. (2008b) 'Brisbane Declaration on OA', *Open Access News* October 8, 2008, available at: *http://www.earlham.edu/~peters/fos/ 2008/10/brisbane-declaration-on-oa.html* (accessed 24 July 2009).

Suber, P. (2009) 'U. Kansas adopts an OA policy', available at: *http:// www.earlham.edu/~peters/fos/2009/06/u-kansas-adopts-oa-policy .html* (accessed 27 July 2009).

Sugita, S., Horikoshi, K., Suzuki, M., Kataoka, S., Hellman, E. S. and Suzuki, K. (2007) 'Linking service to open access repositories', *D-Lib Magazine* 13(3/4), available at: *http://www.dlib.org/dlib/march07/sugita/ 03sugita.html* (accessed 16 July 2009).

Sutton, C. (2008) 'Announcing the launch of the Open Access Scholarly Publishers Association', available at: *http://www.eurekalert.org/ pub_releases/2008-10/spu-atl101408.php* (accessed 14 October 2008).

Swan, A. and Brown, S. (2004a) 'Authors and open access publishing', *Learned Publishing* 17(3): 219–24, available at: *http://eprints.ecs .soton.ac.uk/11003/1/Authors_and_open_access_publishing.pdf* (accessed 16 August 2006).

Swan, A. and Brown, S. (2004b) *JISC/OSI Journal Authors Survey*, Truro: Key Perspectives, Ltd.

Swan, A. and Brown, S. (2005) *Open Access Self-archiving: An Author Study*, Truro: Key Perspectives Limited, available at: *http://www.jisc .ac.uk/uploaded_documents/JISCOAreport1.pdf* (accessed 26 July 2009).

Tagler, J. (2005) 'Alternative scholarly publishing: a commercial publisher's perspective', *Serials Librarian* 48(1/2): 85–99.

Tananbaum, G. (2005) 'I hear the train a comin': an interview with Heather Joseph', *Against the Grain* 17(5): 1, 85.

Tananbaum, G. (2006) 'I hear the train a comin': an interview with Sally Morris', *Against the Grain* 18(3): 81–3.

Tenopir, C. and King, D. W. (2000) *Towards Electronic Journals: Realities for Scientists, Librarians, and Publishers*, Washington, DC: Special Libraries Association.

Thomas, K. (2005) 'Academic authors favour peer review over open access', available at: *http://www.iwr.co.uk/information-world-review/ news/2147408/academic-authors-favour-peer* (accessed 16 July 2009).

Thomson Reuters (2007) 'Journal Citation Reports', available at: *http://scientific.thomson.com/products/jcr/* (accessed 17 May 2007).

Tsakonas, G. and Papatheodorou, C. (2008) 'Exploring usefulness and usability in the evaluation of open access digital libraries', *Information Processing and Management* 44: 1234–50.

UMI Dissertation Publishing (2008) 'Open access publishing: an overview for graduate schools and libraries', available at: *http://www .proquest.com/assets/downloads/products/open_access_overview.pdf* (accessed 19 July 2009).

University of Calgary Libraries and Cultural Resources (2009) 'Open access authors fund', available at: *http://library.ucalgary.ca/services/ for-faculty/open-access-authors-fund-0* (accessed 27 July 2009).

Van Dyck, C. and McKenzie, C. (2004) 'The evolving relationships between libraries and scholarly publishers: metrics and models', *Advances in Librarianship* 28: 95–119.

Van Westrienen, G. and Lynch, C. (2005) 'Academic institutional repositories: deployment status in 13 nations as of mid 2005', *D-Lib Magazine* 11(9), available at: *http://www.dlib.org/dlib/september05/ westrienen/09westrienen.html* (accessed 10 July 2009).

Velterop, J. (2003) 'Should scholarly societies embrace open access (or is it the kiss of death)', *Learned Publishing* 16(3): 167–69.

Velterop, J. (2008) 'Open access and publishing', in *The E-Resources Management Handbook*, Newbury: UK Serials Group, pp. 117–21, available at: *http://uksg.metapress.com/media/dltehjxvwg4xq3yyrqau/contributions/d/p/l/a/dplay0kyn6nkvk7u.pdf* (accessed 21 July 2009).

Wales, J. and Baraniuk, R. (2008) 'Bringing open resources to textbooks and teaching', available at: *http://www.sfgate.com/cgi-bin/article.cgi?f=/c/a/2008/01/22/EDRTUJ346.DTL* (accessed 19 July 2009).

Wahlgren, I. (2008) 'DOAJ offer to new members', posting to Liblicense-l@lists.yale.edu, 27 September, available at: *http://www.library.yale.edu/~llicense/ListArchives/0809/msg00094.html* (accessed 27 September 2008).

Waltham, M. (2003) 'Challenges to the role of publisher', *Learned Publishing* 16(1): 7–14.

Waters, D. J. (2006) 'Managing digital assets in higher education: an overview of strategic issues. *ARL: A Bimonthly Report on Research Library Issues and Actions from ARL, CNI, and SPARC*, No. 244: 1–9, available at: *http://old.arl.org/newsltr/244/ARLBR244.pdf* (accessed 24 July 2009).

Wiberley, S. E., Jr., Hurd, J. M. and Weller, A. C. (2006) 'Publication patterns of US academic librarians from 1998 to 2002', *College & Research Libraries* 67(3): 205–16.

Wilson, M. C. (2005) 'Journal publishing in the library and information science (LIS) field: librarians' "moral and professional"[101] dilemma in leading reforms in scholarly communication' in *Wissenschaftskommunikation im Netzwek der Bibliotheken/Scholary Communication in Libraries Networking*, Berlin: BibSpider, pp. 129–40.

Wrenn, G., Mueller, C. and Shellhase, J. (2009) 'Institutional repository on a shoestring', *D-Lib Magazine* 15(1/2): available at: *http://www.dlib.org/dlib/january09/wrenn/01wrenn.html* (accessed 15 July 2009).

Xia, J. and Sun, L. (2006) 'Factors to assess self-archiving in institutional repositories', *Serials Review* 33(2): 73–80.

Young, J. R. (2008) 'In case Google bails out on its library project, universities create a backup', *Chronicle of Higher Education* 55(9): A10.

Zemon, M. and Bahr, A. H. (1998) 'An analysis of articles by college librarians', *College & Research Libraries* 59(5): 422–32.

Index

CPSIA information can be obtained
at www.ICGtesting.com
Printed in the USA
FFOW01n1137180315
11954FF